Reader's Digest
WildBritain

WILD FLOWERS

PUBLISHED BY
THE READER'S DIGEST ASSOCIATION LIMITED
LONDON ■ NEW YORK ■ SYDNEY ■ MONTREAL

CONTENTS

HOW TO USE THIS BOOK

A rich tapestry of wild flowers is woven into the landscape of the British Isles, about 1700 species in all. More than 500 of these are illustrated and described in this book, including many of the species you are most likely to encounter.

To aid identification the flowers are divided into six chapters by flower colour. Within each chapter, the flowers are subdivided according to whether their petals are all the same size and shape (regular) or different sizes and shapes (irregular). Species are then grouped by their apparent number of petals – including sepals, ray florets and bracts, where these look like petals (see The parts of a flower, page 8). For example, marsh marigold (page 165) has five sepals which look like petals and so for easy identification it has been placed in the 'five to seven petals' section.

By observing the colour, counting the petals and looking at the shape of the flower that you are trying to identify, you can narrow down your search to a small number of pages. Within each section, flowers of similar appearance are placed side by side for comparison, with labels pinpointing the tell-tale differences. These may include the shape, or 'habit' of the growing plant, the shape of the leaves and how they are arranged, the shape of the seed-bearing part of the plant (known as a fruit, whether or not it is edible) and of the seeds themselves, and the way the flowers are arranged. The illustrations also show the plants as they grow wild with common companions.

Wild flowers are living things, and a species found in the field may vary in colour or shape from the specimen illustrated in this book. Colour is also extremely subjective – for example, what some people consider to be blue, others might call purple – so check other sections of a similar colour if you are having problems finding a particular species.

THE PARTS OF A FLOWER

Petals These may be all the same size and shape (regular) or different shapes and sizes (irregular). In some flowers, such as daisies, the parts which look like petals are complete flowers in themselves, called florets. Sometimes what appear to be petals are actually sepals.

Sepals Most petalled flowers have green sepals outside the petals. These are a protection for the flower-bud. Sometimes the sepals are the same colour as the petals.

Stamens These are the flower's pollen-bearing male organs, and grow inside the flower.

Stigma This part of the flower's female organs receives pollen from the stamens.

Flower These grow in many different ways – with stalks or without them, at the end of the stem or scattered along it, singly or in clusters.

Leaves Some leaves are simple, others are lobed, toothed or divided into separate leaflets. They may be spread about the stem, grow in pairs or clusters from points on the stem, or all grow from the bottom of the stem.

Single flowers at the ends of stems

Yellow flowers with many equal petals

Leaves all at the base of the stem, or scattered along it

Lesser celandine

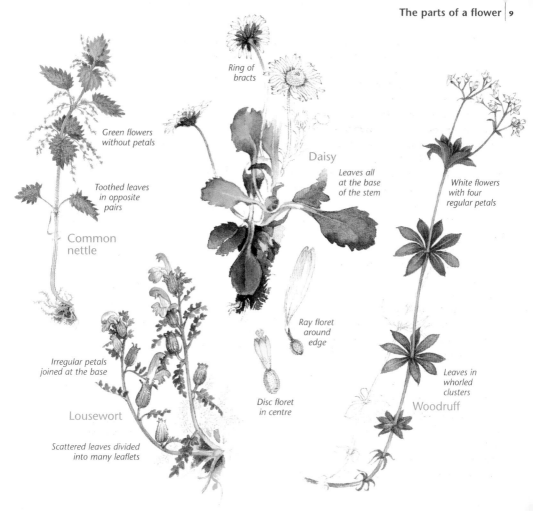

Ring of bracts

Green flowers without petals

Daisy

Leaves all at the base of the stem

Toothed leaves in opposite pairs

White flowers with four regular petals

Common nettle

Ray floret around edge

Irregular petals joined at the base

Leaves in whorled clusters

Lousewort

Woodruff

Disc floret in centre

Scattered leaves divided into many leaflets

THE NAMING OF FLOWERS

The common names by which many plants are known seem to echo in their lyrical language some of the natural beauty of the flowers themselves. Shepherd's purse, fat hen, field penny-cress – even common, so-called weeds often have names which trip off the tongue like ancient charms. Sometimes the original meaning of the name is lost in antiquity. The name may describe a quality of the plant, or the use to which man once put it. Woundwort was used to dress wounds, for example, while fleabane got rid of fleas and soap was made from soapwort.

However, the common names of plants are frequently misleading. They vary from place to place, and sometimes the same name is applied to different plants in different places. Ground elder is known by many names, including goutweed, bishop's weed and pope's weed. A bluebell in Scotland is not the same flower as a bluebell in England, where the Scottish flower is usually called a harebell. Only the scientific names of flowers are always the same – in all parts of Britain and throughout the world, the bluebell remains *Hyacinthoides non-scripta* and ground elder is *Aegopodium podagraria*.

The scientific system of naming plants was devised by the 18th-century Swedish naturalist Linnaeus, in order to clarify this confusion about names and to simplify the study of nature in all its forms. The first part of the scientific name defines the genus to which the plant belongs – the group of similar plants such as *Viola* (violets) or *Primula* (primroses). The second part of the name describes the species – a group of virtually identical, usually interbreeding plants. Thus the sweet violet is called *Viola odorata*, Latin for 'scented violet', and the hairy violet is *Viola hirta*, a literal translation into Latin of the common name.

Most scientific names are based on Latin or Greek as international languages, and often, as in the case of *Viola odorata*, the specific name describes some particular attribute of the plant. For instance, the plant may be upright, *erecta*, creeping, *repens*, or drooping, *pendula*; the colour of its petals may be white, *alba*, yellow, *lutea*, red, *rubra*, purple, *purpurea*, or blue, *caerulea*. The name may describe where the plant usually grows – in a meadow, *pratensis*, an arable field, *arvensis*, a wood, *sylvatica*, by the sea, *maritima*, on sand, *arenaria*, on a mountain, *montana*, on a wall, *muralis*, in a marsh, *palustris*, in water, *aquatilis*, or both on land and in water, *amphibia*. Many other names record the practical value of the plant. It may be edible, *edulis*, a crop plant, *sativa*, used by apothecaries, *officinalis*, valuable for healing wounds, *vulneraria*, for treating dysentery, *dysenterica*, or used as a dye plant, *tinctoria*.

Where one genus of plants closely resembles another, or several others, they are grouped together in a family. Daisies, dandelions and thistles all have flower-heads composed of many separate florets. They all belong to the daisy family, Compositae, one of the largest of all families of flowering plants.

Two species of a genus sometimes cross-fertilise to produce a hybrid. The hybrid shows characteristics of both parent species, and is often more vigorous than both. An x placed before the species name indicates that the flower is a hybrid. Russian comfrey, *Symphytum* x *uplandicum*, for instance, is a hybrid between common comfrey and rough comfrey. More rarely, plants of a different genera are cross-pollinated to produce what are known as inter-generic hybrids.

MAJOR FLOWER FAMILIES

Buttercups

These vary widely in size and habit of growth but have similar flowers usually with five white or yellow petals or petal-like sepals and more than ten stamens. The flowers are bisexual, with both stigmas and stamens.

SEE PAGES: *35, 67, 101, 165-169, 183 and 397.*

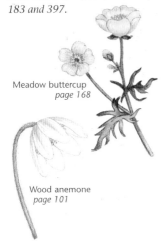

Meadow buttercup
page 168

Wood anemone
page 101

Cabbages

Because of their four-petalled, cross-shaped flowers, plants of the cabbage family are known as crucifers. Their seed-pods are divided by a thin wall down the centre. The flowers have four sepals.

SEE PAGES: *24-34, 125-133 and 243-244.*

Shepherd's purse
page 33

Charlock
page 128

Pinks

This family includes pinks, campions, catchflies, stitchworts and sandworts. The flowers usually have five pink or white petals. The leaves are undivided and often narrow.

SEE PAGES: *40-48, 51 and 315-320.*

Field mouse-ear
page 42

Three-nerved sandwort
page 46

Peas

Members of the pea family have flowers with a wide upper petal, two side petals and two lower petals joined to form a keel. The leaves may be undivided, or composed of few or many leaflets, and each leaf may end in a point, a leaflet or a tendril.

SEE PAGES: *102-104, 174-182, 267-273, 346-349 and 401.*

Parsleys

Most members of the parsley family are easily recognisable by their umbrella-like heads of tiny, stalked flowers. Their leaves are usually divided into several distinct leaflets.

SEE PAGES: *76-94, 155-159, 223, 345 and 398.*

Forget-me-nots

Members of the forget-me-not family have undivided leaves and curved sprays of flowers with five petals. In some the flowers open pink, only becoming blue with age. The fruit is a cluster of four dark nutlets enclosed by sepals.

SEE PAGES: *63, 224-229, 255 and 337.*

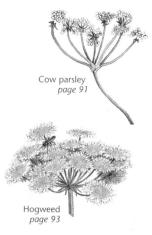

Cow parsley
page 91

Hogweed
page 93

Common
bird's-foot trefoil
page 176

Lucerne
page 268

Bugloss
page 225

Tufted forget-me-not
page 227

MAJOR FLOWER FAMILIES

Mints

Square stems, opposite leaves and tubular flowers that often have two lips distinguish the mint or dead-nettle family from any other.

SEE PAGES: *23, 38, 136, 217-220, 239-241, 247, 249, 253, 292, 304-310 and 376.*

Daisies

In this large flower family, many members are superficially alike. The flowers have dense flower-heads made up of many ray and disc florets. A ring of small, green leaf-like bracts surrounds the flower-head.

SEE PAGES: *96, 109-115, 184-207, 235, 277-285, 357-359 and 404-406.*

Roses

A very diverse family, including trees, shrubs and herbaceous plants. The flowers usually have five petals, five sepals and numerous stamens.

SEE PAGES: *68-72, 74-75, 108, 134, 152-154, 341, 344 and 372-374.*

White dead-nettle
page 38

Marsh woundwort
page 308

Smooth hawk's-beard
page 200

Daisy
page 109

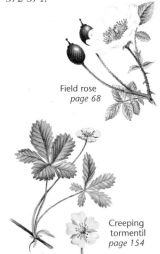

Field rose
page 68

Creeping tormentil
page 154

WILD FLOWERS AND THE LAW

The search for wild flowers is a rewarding trail that can begin outside your own front door but can lead through our wildest and most beautiful countryside. The real nature lover takes pride in helping to preserve that beauty while observing and learning about it. In 1981 the Wildlife and Countryside Act and the review that followed it made it a criminal offence for anyone to uproot a wild plant without the express permission of the owner or occupier of the land on which it grows. In addition, the rarest plants are protected by law from any disturbance – even picking the flowers or collecting seed. In any case you should not pick any flower without good reason, for a picked flower never produces seed.

It is just as important to protect the wild flowers' environment as it is to protect the plants themselves. Take extra care when walking in an area where a rare species grows: it is very easy to damage young, non-flowering plants without even seeing them, and compression of the soil by excessive trampling may prevent future seedlings of the species from becoming established. The bluebell, the glory of our woodlands in spring, is threatened as much by having its leaves trampled as by being picked.

White, cream or pale pink FLOWERS

CANADIAN WATERWEED

The little flowers of this waterweed on the surface of a quiet country stream appear quite harmless. Yet not long ago the plant was viewed with alarm. After this stranger from Canada first appeared in Europe in 1836 it spread with startling rapidity, choking ponds, canals and ditches all over Britain. Then suddenly, in the late 1860s, it stopped its all-conquering expansion.

Floating flowers on thread-like stems

Leaves in whorls of three

Stems submerged and rooting

ℹ️	
Canadian waterweed	
Elodea canadensis	
To 300cm	

| J | F | M | A | M | J |
| J | A | S | O | N | D |

Widespread in still or slow-moving fresh water.

Petals open wide as flower matures

WATER-PLANTAIN

In the muddy shallows of ponds and rivers the water-plantain is immediately recognisable by its tall, slender stem rising high above a thicket of broad leaves. The stem culminates in a pyramid of branching spikes tipped with tiny flowers. The name of arrowhead given to the related water plant found mainly in southern Britain refers only to the leaves growing above the water.

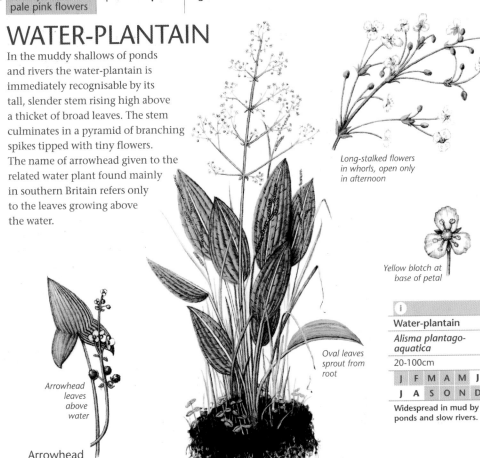

Long-stalked flowers in whorls, open only in afternoon

Yellow blotch at base of petal

Arrowhead leaves above water

Arrowhead
Sagittaria sagittifolia

Oval leaves sprout from root

Water-plantain
Alisma plantago-aquatica
20-100cm

J	F	M	A	M	J
J	A	S	O	N	D

Widespread in mud by ponds and slow rivers.

ENCHANTER'S NIGHTSHADE

Despite its name, enchanter's nightshade is not a nightshade but a member of the willowherb family. It bears its flowers in tall spikes and its leaves are pointed and lightly toothed. The leaves are in pairs set at right angles to each other up the hairy stem. Unlike other members of the willowherb family, the seeds of enchanter's nightshade are not dispersed by the wind. Instead, each egg-shaped fruit has hooked bristles which catch onto clothing or animal fur.

Flowers in long leafless spikes

Fruits droop down

Slightly toothed leaves

i

Enchanter's nightshade

Circaea lutetiana

20-60cm

| J | F | M | A | M | J |
| J | A | S | O | N | D |

Woods and shady places; rare in far north.

Two deeply notched petals

CLEAVERS

This tall, bright green plant is so common in our hedgerows that it is easily passed by without a second look. It is called cleavers because of the hooked bristles on its fruit which 'cleave' to clothes and animal hair. It is a favourite food of geese, and is also known as goosegrass.

Hedge bedstraw is a stouter scrambling or erect plant with smoother stems, and marsh bedstraw a related species of wet places.

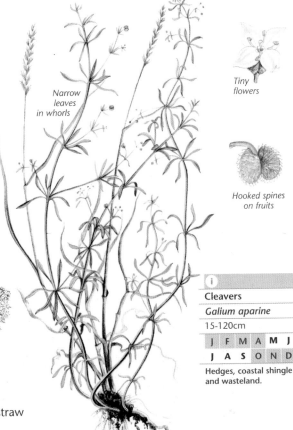

Narrow leaves in whorls

Tiny flowers

Hooked spines on fruits

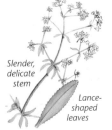

Slender, delicate stem

Lance-shaped leaves

Marsh bedstraw
Galium palustre

Hedge bedstraw
Galium mollugo

Cleavers

Galium aparine

15-120cm

J	F	M	A	M	J
J	A	S	O	N	D

Hedges, coastal shingle and wasteland.

WOODRUFF

This pretty woodland flower has no smell when fresh; but an hour or two after it is picked a magical scent – somewhere between vanilla and new-mown hay – emerges. The dried plant retains this smell for years, and used to be placed between bed linen.

Bedstraws are recognised by their slender, square stems, with whorls of 4-12 leaves and clusters of tiny flowers. Heath bedstraw is short and blackens when it is dried.

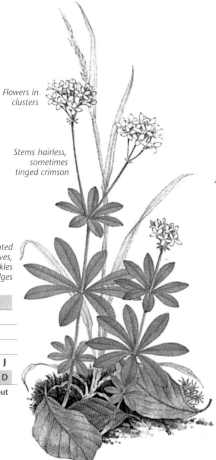

Flowers in clusters

Stems hairless, sometimes tinged crimson

Pointed leaves, prickles on edges

ℹ️					
Woodruff
Galium odoratum
15-45cm

| J | F | **M** | **A** | **M** | **J** |
| **J** | **A** | S | O | N | D |

Woodlands throughout much of British Isles.

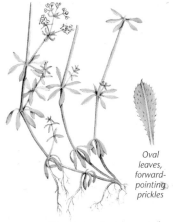

Oval leaves, forward-pointing prickles

Heath bedstraw
Galium saxatile

COWBERRY

Like its close relative the bilberry, the cowberry belongs to the heather family and grows on dry, acid soils. While the bilberry's flowers are reddish, those of cowberry are much paler, appearing almost white against the glossy evergreen leaves. They are also more deeply lobed than those of bilberry. Unlike the sweet, blue-black fruit of the bilberry, the cowberry's fruit is red and rather bitter.

Leaves often notched at tip

Edges of leaves rolled under; pale and dotted undersides

Bell-shaped flowers

Fruit a red berry

ⓘ					
Cowberry					
Vaccinium vitis-idaea					
15-30cm					
J	F	M	A	**M**	**J**
J	A	S	O	N	D

Widespread on upland moors and heaths mainly in northern and western Britain.

GIPSYWORT

A common sight by a shady river bank in summer is the tight little whorls of purple-dotted white flowers decorating the long, stiff stems of the gipsywort. The plant belongs to the mint family, and though completely odourless it shares many characteristics of other mints. Its leaves are set in pairs all the way up the square stem, each pair being capped with flowers.

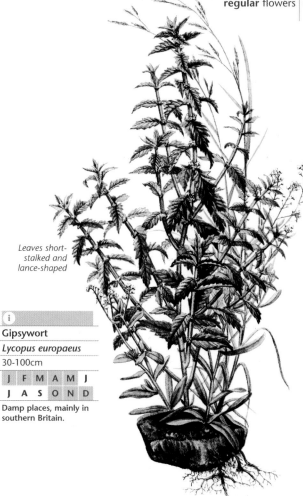

Leaves short-stalked and lance-shaped

ⓘ

Gipsywort

Lycopus europaeus

30-100cm

| J | F | M | A | M | J |
| J | A | S | O | N | D |

Damp places, mainly in southern Britain.

Flowers in whorls at base of leaves

COMMON WHITLOWGRASS

While whitlowgrass is very common on sandy ground throughout Britain, it is often overlooked. Historically it was believed to provide a cure for warts and whitlows. Hence the name, though strictly speaking it is not a grass but an annual herb of the cabbage family. It is a small plant, with deeply cleft petals at the end of long, leafless flower stems.

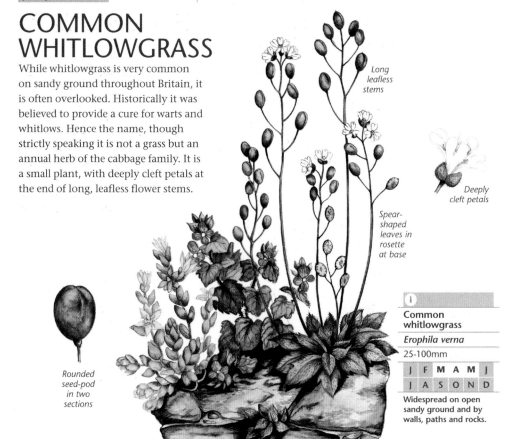

Long leafless stems

Deeply cleft petals

Spear-shaped leaves in rosette at base

Rounded seed-pod in two sections

Common whitlowgrass

Erophila verna

25-100mm

| J | F | **M** | **A** | **M** | **J** |
| **J** | **A** | **S** | **O** | **N** | D |

Widespread on open sandy ground and by walls, paths and rocks.

HORSE-RADISH

This large, distinctive plant was introduced in the 15th century and has spread far and wide beyond the vegetable garden, where it is cultivated for the sake of the pungent sauce made from its grated roots. The plant can be identified by its large, shiny leaves which at the base can grow to 60cm. The plant does not always flower but when it does it produces many small flowers which grow in dense, leafy panicles.

Flowers in dense leafy panicles

Lower leaves large, dark green and shiny

Petals twice as long as sepals

ⓘ

Horse-radish

Armoracia rusticana

30-150cm

| J | F | M | A | M | J |
| J | A | S | O | N | D |

Wasteland, river banks and road verges, especially in England.

GARLIC MUSTARD

Sometimes called hedge garlic, 'Jack-by-the-hedge' or 'poor man's mustard', this member of the cabbage family has small flowers and large, triangular leaves on a tall stem. The seeds are horn-shaped and almost black in colour, and the pods curve in at the base. The whole plant, but particularly the leaves when crushed, gives off a smell of garlic.

Leaves triangular and toothed

Petals twice as long as sepals

Ribbed cylindrical pods

Lower leaves more rounded

Garlic mustard
Alliaria petiolata
20-120cm

J	F	M	A	M	J
J	A	S	O	N	D

Wood margins and hedgerows, except in north-west, parts of south-west Scotland and western and south-west Ireland.

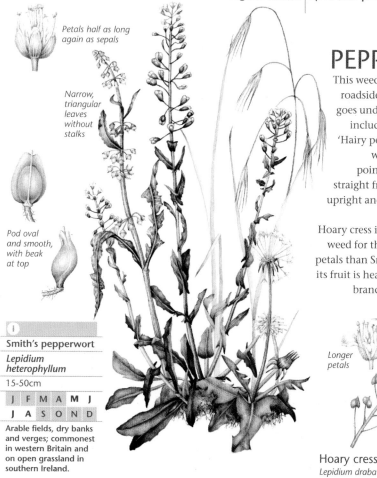

Petals half as long again as sepals

Narrow, triangular leaves without stalks

Pod oval and smooth, with beak at top

SMITH'S PEPPERWORT

This weed, commonly found on roadsides and by railway lines, goes under a number of names, including 'Smith's cress' and 'Hairy pepperwort'. The leaves, which are long, slender, pointed and toothed, grow straight from the stem, which is upright and often branched from the ground.

Hoary cress is another troublesome weed for the farmer. It has longer petals than Smith's pepperwort and its fruit is heart-shaped. The stem is branched in the upper part.

i

Smith's pepperwort

Lepidium heterophyllum

15-50cm

| J | F | M | A | M | J |
| J | A | S | O | N | D |

Arable fields, dry banks and verges; commonest in western Britain and on open grassland in southern Ireland.

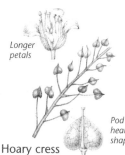

Longer petals

Pod heart-shaped

Hoary cress
Lepidium draba

FIELD PENNY-CRESS

The ripe yellowish fruit of field penny-cress brightens innumerable patches of wasteland throughout Britain. It is one of our five penny-cresses and is distinguished from its rarer relatives by the flat, almost circular, discs of its pods. The hairless plant has an upright, leafy stem, sometimes branched, that lengthens when it fruits. Apart from its fruit, the other distinctive feature of this plant is its unpleasant smell.

Flowers in clusters at top of stems

Leaves narrow, arrow-shaped at base

Petals twice as long as sepals

Pods winged, with notch

ⓘ
Field penny-cress
Thlaspi arvense
10-60cm

J	F	M	A	**M**	**J**
J	**A**	**S**	**O**	**N**	D

Wasteland and arable fields in much of Britain.

HAIRY ROCK-CRESS

Hirsuta means 'hairy', and the leaves and stem of this plant are unmistakably that. Its tall, erect seed-pods cluster round the upper stem, containing reddish-brown seeds which are slightly winged. The stem is long, slender and usually unbranching, culminating in a long spike of small flowers whose petals are narrow and not notched.

The much commoner Thale cress is also hairy, but its seed-pods and leaves slant away from the stem.

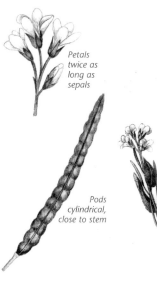

Petals twice as long as sepals

Pods cylindrical, close to stem

Stalkless upper leaves clasp stem

Lower leaves in rosette

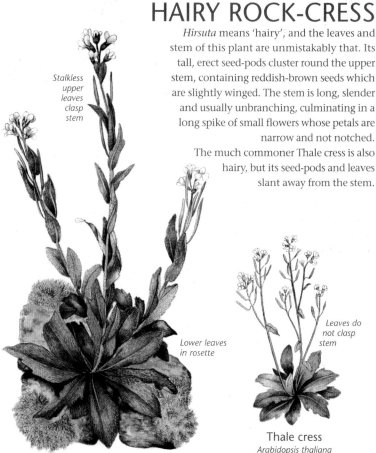

Hairy rock-cress

Arabis hirsuta

15-60cm

J	F	M	A	M	J
J	A	S	O	N	D

Widespread on limestone slopes, dunes, hedgebanks, walls and rocks.

Leaves do not clasp stem

Thale cress
Arabidopsis thaliana

WATERCRESS

The watercress plants that grow in streams in the wild are often just the same as those bred in water beds for market. Clusters of four-petalled flowers at the tips of the branches develop into long sausage-shaped seed-pods. Watercress is rich in vitamin C, and used to be prescribed for the treatment of scurvy. Plants should not be picked from stagnant water or streams flowing through pasture-land, where the eggs of liver fluke sometimes lie.

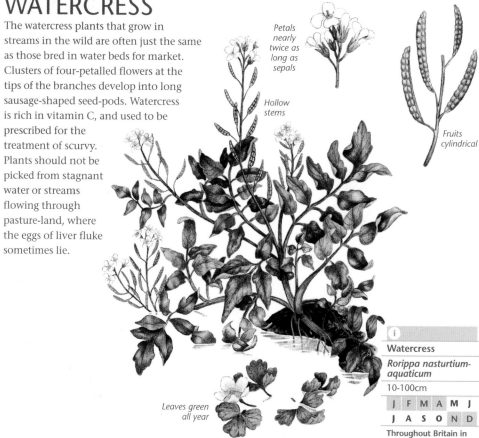

Petals nearly twice as long as sepals

Hollow stems

Fruits cylindrical

Leaves green all year

Watercress

Rorippa nasturtium-aquaticum

10-100cm

| J | F | M | A | M | J |
| J | A | S | O | N | D |

Throughout Britain in fast streams.

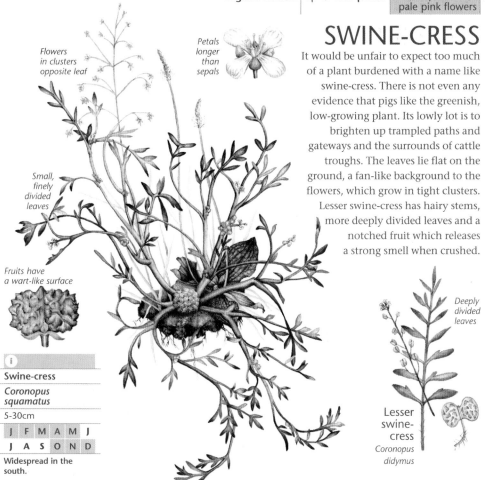

Flowers in clusters opposite leaf

Petals longer than sepals

Small, finely divided leaves

Fruits have a wart-like surface

ⓘ

Swine-cress

Coronopus squamatus

5-30cm

J	F	M	A	M	J
J	A	S	O	N	D

Widespread in the south.

SWINE-CRESS

It would be unfair to expect too much of a plant burdened with a name like swine-cress. There is not even any evidence that pigs like the greenish, low-growing plant. Its lowly lot is to brighten up trampled paths and gateways and the surrounds of cattle troughs. The leaves lie flat on the ground, a fan-like background to the flowers, which grow in tight clusters. Lesser swine-cress has hairy stems, more deeply divided leaves and a notched fruit which releases a strong smell when crushed.

Deeply divided leaves

Lesser swine-cress
Coronopus didymus

COMMON SCURVYGRASS

Spread like cream on top of a headland facing the sea, with plants such as thrift and sea campion, the flowers of common scurvygrass make a pretty sight. In the 17th century herbalists discovered that when taken in water the plant prevented scurvy, a disease caused by prolonged deficiency of vitamin C, and it became the fashion to drink a glass every day.

English scurvygrass has longer, toothed leaves. Diminutive Danish scurvygrass (*Cochlearia stanisar*) has spread along many roads and railway lines in recent years. Its lilac or white flowers appear in early spring, and the leaves are ivy-shaped and stalked.

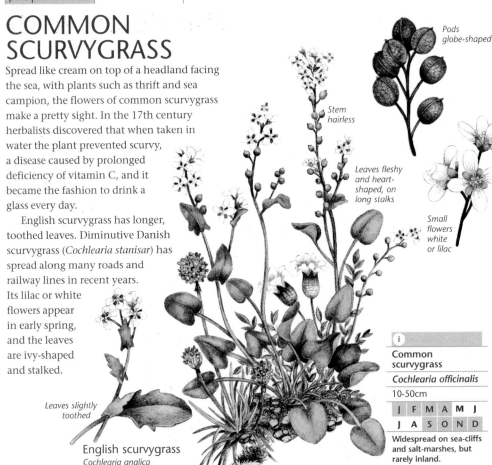

Pods globe-shaped

Stem hairless

Leaves fleshy and heart-shaped, on long stalks

Small flowers white or lilac

Leaves slightly toothed

English scurvygrass
Cochlearia anglica

ⓘ

Common scurvygrass

Cochlearia officinalis

10-50cm

| J | F | M | A | M | J |
| J | A | S | O | N | D |

Widespread on sea-cliffs and salt-marshes, but rarely inland.

SHEPHERD'S PURSE

There is no need to look out for shepherd's purse: it is difficult to avoid. One of the most common and persistent weeds in the world, shepherd's purse often appears in gardens. Its pretty flowers are tiny and the fruit has a distinctive heart shape which was likened hundreds of years ago to a shepherd's purse. When the pods are ripe the seeds tumble out, as from a purse. The rustic associations add to the plant's appeal.

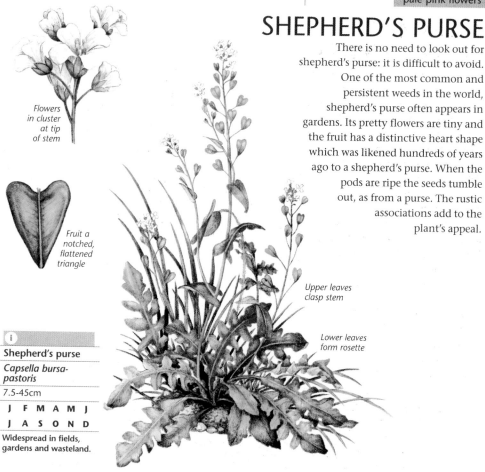

Flowers in cluster at tip of stem

Fruit a notched, flattened triangle

Upper leaves clasp stem

Lower leaves form rosette

Shepherd's purse

Capsella bursa-pastoris

7.5–45cm

J F M A M J
J A S O N D

Widespread in fields, gardens and wasteland.

HAIRY BITTERCRESS

This common garden weed has small flowers surrounded by long, cylindrical, upright pods and a neat rosette of leaves at the base. Its stems and leaves have hairs, but they are not very conspicuous. When the seed-pods are ripe they burst with surprising force.

Wavy bittercress (*Cardamine flexuosa*) differs from hairy bittercress in having wavy stems and six stamens instead of four.

Fruit upright, pinched between seeds

Stems arise from rosette of leaves

Petals twice as long as sepals

ⓘ		
Hairy bittercress		
Cardamine hirsuta		
7–30cm		

J	F	M	A	M	J
J	A	S	O	N	D

Widespread on bare ground, rocks, walls and dunes throughout British Isles.

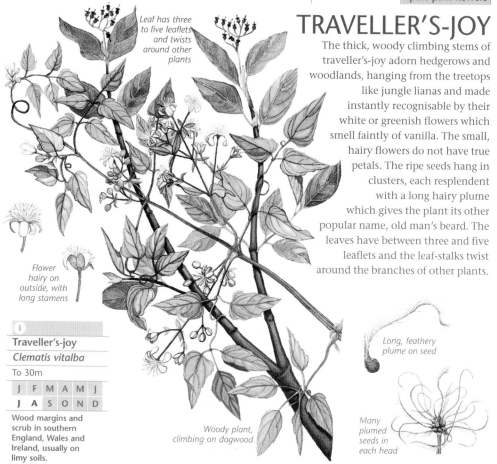

TRAVELLER'S-JOY

The thick, woody climbing stems of traveller's-joy adorn hedgerows and woodlands, hanging from the treetops like jungle lianas and made instantly recognisable by their white or greenish flowers which smell faintly of vanilla. The small, hairy flowers do not have true petals. The ripe seeds hang in clusters, each resplendent with a long hairy plume which gives the plant its other popular name, old man's beard. The leaves have between three and five leaflets and the leaf-stalks twist around the branches of other plants.

Leaf has three to five leaflets and twists around other plants

Flower hairy on outside, with long stamens

Long, feathery plume on seed

Many plumed seeds in each head

Woody plant, climbing on dogwood

i

Traveller's-joy

Clematis vitalba

To 30m

| J | F | M | A | M | J |
| J | A | S | O | N | D |

Wood margins and scrub in southern England, Wales and Ireland, usually on limy soils.

EYEBRIGHT

With its striking, purple-streaked flowers, sturdy branched stem and many-pointed leaves, eyebright is one of the prettiest semi-parasites in our countryside. It was formerly used as a treatment for eye disorders, hence its English name. It exists by attaching itself to the roots of plants such as clover and plantains. At least 20 species of *Euphrasia* are found in Britain. The different species are very difficult to identify.

Euphrasia micrantha has smaller, often purple, flowers and leaves. It is a northern species, found mainly in Scotland, near heather (page 238).

Leaves may have a purplish tinge

Branches start near base

Yellow blotch and purple lines on lower lip

Smaller, usually purple, flowers

Euphrasia micrantha

i					

Eyebright

Euphrasia nemorosa

2-30cm

J	F	M	A	M	J
J	A	S	O	N	D

Downs, pastures, heaths and woods, mainly in England and Wales.

TOOTHWORT

The whole toothwort plant is cream or pale pink, with no green leaves at all. It is a parasite which attaches itself to the roots of trees, mainly hazel and elm. Its upright, unbranched stems are covered with two rows of flowers which are pollinated by bumble-bees. The broad, ivory-coloured scale-like bracts beneath each flower look like teeth, giving the plant its common name.

Flowers in one-sided spike with scale-like bracts

Creamy oval scales

No green leaves

Toothwort	
Lathraea squamaria	
10-30cm	

J	F	M	A	M	J
J	A	S	O	N	D

Damp woods and shady hedgerows, except in northern Scotland.

Two-lipped flower, pink-tinged

WHITE DEAD-NETTLE

The large, open-mouthed flowers of the white dead-nettle, a great attraction to nectar-seeking bumble-bees, are a common sight in hedgerows. The flowers are set in a whorl round the square, upright, hairy stems, which often grow in large clumps. Its toothed, heart-shaped leaves are very similar to those of the true stinging nettle, but they are free of stinging hairs – hence the label 'dead'.

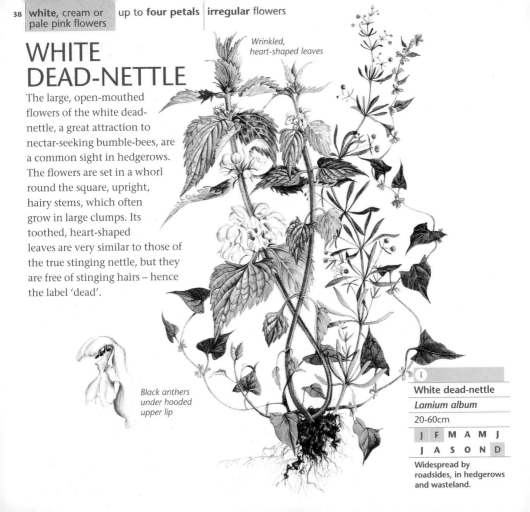

Wrinkled, heart-shaped leaves

Black anthers under hooded upper lip

ⓘ

White dead-nettle

Lamium album

20-60cm

| J | F | M | A | M | J |
| J | A | S | O | N | D |

Widespread by roadsides, in hedgerows and wasteland.

CLIMBING CORYDALIS

On a walk through a shady wood in summer, the careful observer may see the pale creamy-yellow flower of this plant scrambling though a tangle of bracken. While the flowers are small, their shape is distinctive. Unlike the closely related fumitories, the leaves of this species end in branched tendrils which enable it to climb other plants, such as grass or bracken.

The rare white ramping fumitory is also a scrambler, but has larger, creamy flowers tipped with dark red.

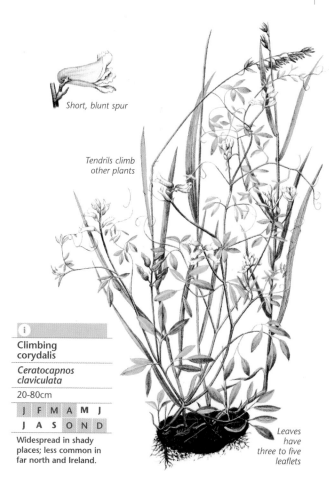

Short, blunt spur

Tendrils climb other plants

Leaves have three to five leaflets

J	F	M	A	M	J
J	A	S	O	N	D

ⓘ
Climbing corydalis
Ceratocapnos claviculata
20-80cm

Widespread in shady places; less common in far north and Ireland.

Dark red tip to flower

White ramping fumitory
Fumaria capreolata

WHITE CAMPION

This plant grows mainly on roadside verges and arable land, unlike the closely related red campion which is found more often in shady hedgerows and woodlands. Where the two plants grow together they often cross-breed and produce pink-flowered plants. The stems are upright, with hairy leaves, and bear large flowers that are faintly scented at night and attract moths. A ring of ten teeth surrounds the opening of the narrow seed capsule. Wreaths of campions were once used to crown the 'champion' in public games.

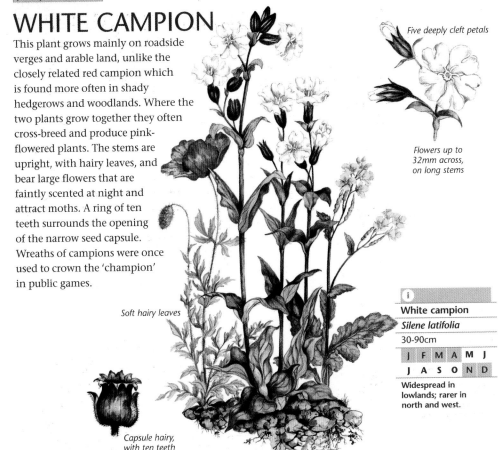

Five deeply cleft petals

Flowers up to 32mm across, on long stems

Soft hairy leaves

Capsule hairy, with ten teeth

i
White campion
Silene latifolia
30-90cm

J	F	M	A	M	J
J	A	S	O	N	D

Widespread in lowlands; rarer in north and west.

BLADDER CAMPION

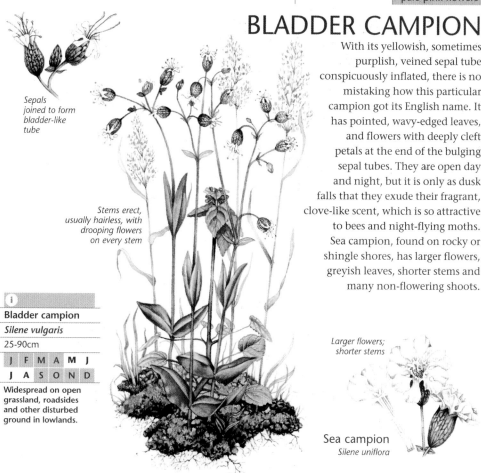

With its yellowish, sometimes purplish, veined sepal tube conspicuously inflated, there is no mistaking how this particular campion got its English name. It has pointed, wavy-edged leaves, and flowers with deeply cleft petals at the end of the bulging sepal tubes. They are open day and night, but it is only as dusk falls that they exude their fragrant, clove-like scent, which is so attractive to bees and night-flying moths. Sea campion, found on rocky or shingle shores, has larger flowers, greyish leaves, shorter stems and many non-flowering shoots.

Sepals joined to form bladder-like tube

Stems erect, usually hairless, with drooping flowers on every stem

Bladder campion

Silene vulgaris

25-90cm

| J | F | M | A | M | J |
| J | A | S | O | N | D |

Widespread on open grassland, roadsides and other disturbed ground in lowlands.

Larger flowers; shorter stems

Sea campion
Silene uniflora

FIELD MOUSE-EAR

Summer grassland is sometimes brightened by broad patches of field mouse-ear. The leaves are covered with short downy hairs, like the ears of a mouse. The 12 species of mouse-ear found in the British Isles are closely related to the stitchworts and chickweeds. Field mouse-ear is a low, hairy-stemmed plant with long, rooting shoots and erect flowering stems. Its leaves are paired at the top and form clusters at the base.

Common mouse-ear is a more abundant species, with smaller flowers and leaves. It grows on the same dry terrain as field mouse-ear.

Capsule cylindrical, with ten teeth

Petals deeply divided, twice as long as sepals

Non-flowering stems sprawl; flowering stems more upright

Leaves, narrow, lance-shaped

Petals and sepals about the same length

Common mouse-ear
Cerastium fontanum

ⓘ					
Field mouse-ear					
Cerastium arvense					
To 30cm					
J	F	**M**	**A**	**M**	**J**
J	**A**	**S**	**O**	**N**	D

Widespread on dry, sandy or chalky grassland, banks and waysides, mainly in eastern Britain; very rare in Ireland, Wales and Scotland.

STICKY MOUSE-EAR

The most obvious difference between sticky mouse-ear and other mouse-ears is that its flowers grow in tight, compact clusters, rather than separately. Sticky hairs cover the stems. The pale, yellowish-green leaves are almost oval and untoothed, and the petals are notched at the tip.

Little mouse-ear has similar leaves and petals. It has bracts and sepals with silvery tips and flowers from April to May.

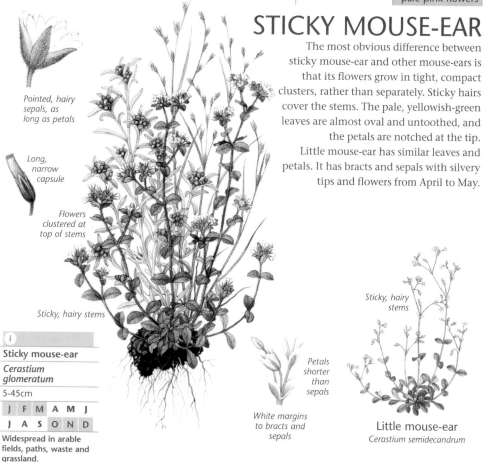

Pointed, hairy sepals, as long as petals

Long, narrow capsule

Flowers clustered at top of stems

Sticky, hairy stems

Sticky, hairy stems

Petals shorter than sepals

White margins to bracts and sepals

Little mouse-ear
Cerastium semidecandrum

Sticky mouse-ear

Cerastium glomeratum

5-45cm

J	F	M	A	M	J
J	A	S	O	N	D

Widespread in arable fields, paths, waste and grassland.

COMMON CHICKWEED

Five deeply notched petals make the flower of chickweed look like the 'star' of its scientific name. The reddish anthers on the stamens add a splash of colour. The stems have a single line of water-absorbing hairs that run down the line of the stem. Although it looks weak and straggly, chickweed can grow and flower even in the depths of winter and is one of the most widespread weeds across the world. Its English name comes from its long-standing use as poultry feed.

Upper leaves stalkless

Lower leaves stalked

Star-like petals, same length as sepals

Single line of hairs down one side of stem

Chickweed

Stellaria media

5-50cm

J F M A M J
J A S O N D

Widespread on waste and cultivated ground.

GREATER STITCHWORT

The big, star-like flowers of this plant are conspicuous in hedgerows in spring. Its petals are cleft halfway up and are longer than the sepals. The leaves are rough-edged and arranged in opposite pairs. Lesser stitchwort has smooth-edged leaves and petals cleft almost to the base. Bog stitchwort has long sepals forming a green star which extends beyond the petals.

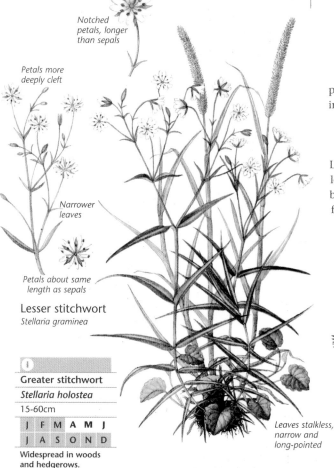

Notched petals, longer than sepals

Petals more deeply cleft

Narrower leaves

Petals about same length as sepals

Lesser stitchwort
Stellaria graminea

Greater stitchwort

Stellaria holostea

15-60cm

| J | F | M | A | M | J |
| J | A | S | O | N | D |

Widespread in woods and hedgerows.

Leaves stalkless, narrow and long-pointed

Petals much shorter than green sepals

Bog stitchwort
Stellaria uliginosa

THREE-NERVED SANDWORT

The undivided petals distinguish this plant from the superficially similar chickweeds and stitchworts, whose petals are cleft. Its leaves have three conspicuous veins or nerves on the underside – another distinctive feature. It has many delicate trailing branches, and is the only sandwort that grows in woodland. Its tiny seeds have an oily appendage that attracts ants, which help to distribute them.

Star-shaped flower; petals shorter than sepals

Flowers on long stalks

Leaves have three veins

Trailing stems

Three-nerved sandwort

Moehringia trinervia

10-40cm

J	F	M	A	**M**	**J**
J	**A**	S	O	N	D

Widespread in dry woods throughout Britain except for northern Scotland and western Ireland.

THYME-LEAVED SANDWORT

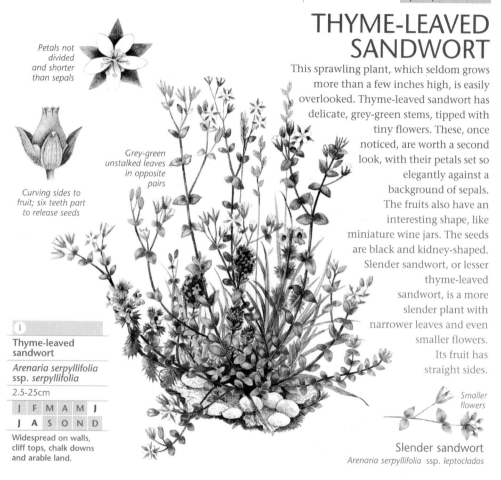

Petals not divided and shorter than sepals

Curving sides to fruit; six teeth part to release seeds

Grey-green unstalked leaves in opposite pairs

This sprawling plant, which seldom grows more than a few inches high, is easily overlooked. Thyme-leaved sandwort has delicate, grey-green stems, tipped with tiny flowers. These, once noticed, are worth a second look, with their petals set so elegantly against a background of sepals. The fruits also have an interesting shape, like miniature wine jars. The seeds are black and kidney-shaped. Slender sandwort, or lesser thyme-leaved sandwort, is a more slender plant with narrower leaves and even smaller flowers. Its fruit has straight sides.

i

Thyme-leaved sandwort

Arenaria serpyllifolia ssp. *serpyllifolia*

2.5-25cm

| J | F | M | A | M | J |
| J | A | S | O | N | D |

Widespread on walls, cliff tops, chalk downs and arable land.

Smaller flowers

Slender sandwort
Arenaria serpyllifolia ssp. *leptoclados*

SEA SANDWORT

This tough plant is a colonist of the seashore. It establishes itself on sand, stands up to rough weather and survives spells of immersion in salt water. In a setting where plants tend to be dull and greyish, the sea sandwort spreads carpets of glossy green among the dunes. The plant is hairless, with succulent, bright yellowish-green leaves which are edible. The globular fruits are also yellowish green.

Female flower has tiny petals

Male flower has large petals

Fleshy stalkless leaves

Flowering and non-flowering shoots from creeping stems

Flowers grow among leaves at ends of stems

Three teeth free seeds from fruit

ℹ️
Sea sandwort
Honckenya peploides
5-25cm
J F M A **M J**
J A S O N D
Around almost all coast of Britain.

COMMON WINTERGREEN

At a quick glance the flowers of the common wintergreen might easily be mistaken for lily of the valley although the leaves are very different. They hang like little bells on a tall stem, keeping their distance from the oval, glossy leaves, which remain green all year round, giving the plant its English name.

Long, leafless upper stem

Fruit in five segments

Leafy part of the stem very short

Flowers hang down, often pinkish

---

i

Common wintergreen

Pyrola minor

10-20cm

J F M A M J
J A S O N D

Locally in woods, moors and damp places in the north; less common in the south.

FAIRY FLAX

The thread-like stems of fairy flax, tipped with their dainty flowers, are often seen on moors and in grassland. The plant, shown here growing with horseshoe vetch, lacks the big blue flower which is the glory of pale flax and perennial flax. Although small and white, however, its flowers do develop into the typical five-celled seed-pod of the flax family. Unlike the other flaxes, the leaves of fairy flax are in opposite pairs. The flowers are in loose clusters. Also known by the less attractive name of Purging Flax, a translation of its Latin name *catharticum*, to denote its former use as a mild purgative.

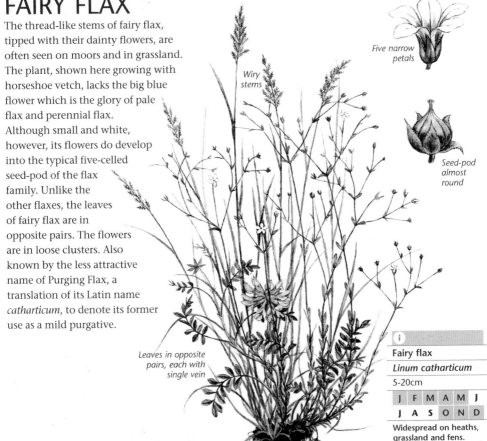

Wiry stems

Five narrow petals

Seed-pod almost round

Leaves in opposite pairs, each with single vein

i

Fairy flax

Linum catharticum

5-20cm

| J | F | M | A | M | J |
| J | A | S | O | N | D |

Widespread on heaths, grassland and fens.

CORN SPURREY

The most striking feature of this plant is not the flower, which opens prettily for a few hours from midday and emits an unpleasant smell, but its sticky leaves. They are long and narrow and arranged in whorl-like clusters at the swollen joints of the stems. When the fruits are ripe the flower-stalks turn downwards and the tops of the capsules open to release the seeds. Corn spurrey often grows with pineapple weed.

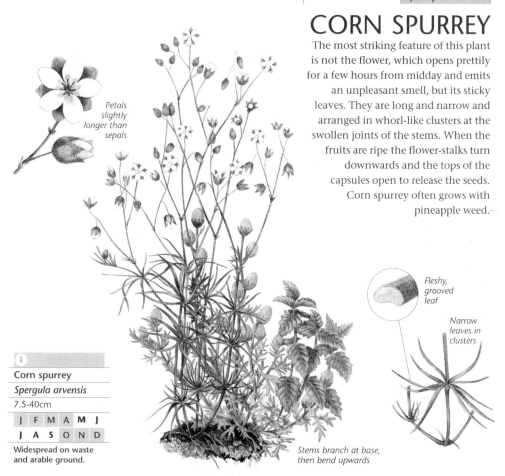

Petals slightly longer than sepals

Fleshy, grooved leaf

Narrow leaves in clusters

Stems branch at base, then bend upwards

Corn spurrey

Spergula arvensis

7.5-40cm

| J | F | M | A | M | J |
| J | A | S | O | N | D |

Widespread on waste and arable ground.

SPRING BEAUTY

An explosion of tiny flowers from a horn of leaves trumpets the presence of spring beauty. The flowers themselves are unexceptional, but they are presented in green cups, which later spread into curved plates, made by pairs of fused leaves surrounding the stems. The plant was introduced to Britain from western North America in the 18th century. Unlike the chickweeds and spurreys, spring beauty has two sepals instead of five. The plant is eaten in salads and as a vegetable.

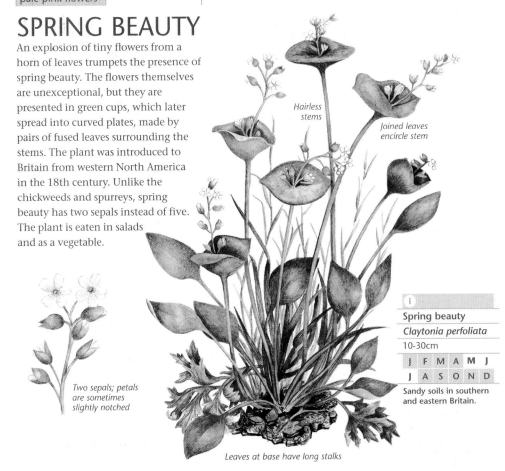

Hairless stems

Joined leaves encircle stem

Two sepals; petals are sometimes slightly notched

Spring beauty
Claytonia perfoliata
10-30cm

| J | F | M | A | **M** | **J** |
| **J** | **A** | **S** | **O** | **N** | D |

Sandy soils in southern and eastern Britain.

Leaves at base have long stalks

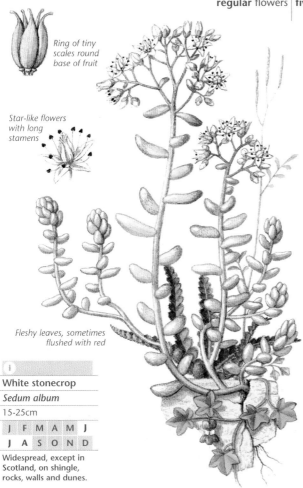

Ring of tiny scales round base of fruit

Star-like flowers with long stamens

Fleshy leaves, sometimes flushed with red

WHITE STONECROP

Walls, rocks and cliff faces are often adorned with white stonecrop. Its fleshy, cylindrical leaves grow out of the stems in alternate spirals, storing water to tide the plant over the frequent dry spells which are a natural hazard of living on brick and rock. The thick stems are topped by a broad head of small flowers. English stonecrop is smaller, with pink-tinged flowers and stubby red-tinged leaves.

Upper leaves flushed with crimson

English stonecrop
Sedum anglicum

ⓘ

White stonecrop

Sedum album

15-25cm

| J | F | M | A | M | J |
| J | A | S | O | N | D |

Widespread, except in Scotland, on shingle, rocks, walls and dunes.

MEADOW SAXIFRAGE

The tallest of the native saxifrages is an increasingly rare plant of old meadows. The straight, single stems are almost leafless and stickily hairy, and carry up to 12 flowers. But the most interesting feature is the tiny brown, nut-like bulbils between the stem and the stalks of the lower leaves.

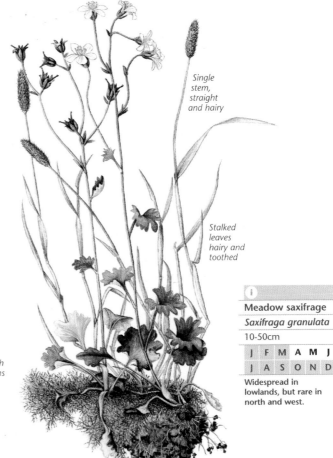

Single stem, straight and hairy

Stalked leaves hairy and toothed

Narrow petals with green veins

ⓘ

Meadow saxifrage

Saxifraga granulata

10-50cm

J	F	M	A	M	J
J	A	S	O	N	D

Widespread in lowlands, but rare in north and west.

MOSSY SAXIFRAGE

This plant is to be found most commonly on mountain ledges and screes where the soil is not acidic, and on open, grassy hillsides. It differs from the other saxifrages in having narrower leaves and prostrate, non-flowering shoots.

The tiny rue-leaved saxifrage has a reddish tinge, and stems which are sticky and hairy. It grows on the top of old walls and other dry, lime-rich places.

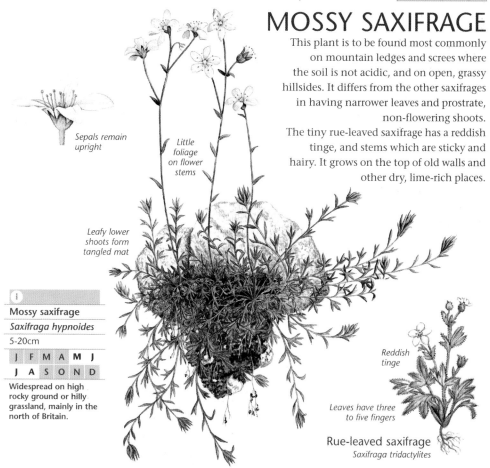

Sepals remain upright

Little foliage on flower stems

Leafy lower shoots form tangled mat

i
Mossy saxifrage
Saxifraga hypnoides
5-20cm

| J | F | M | A | M | J |
| J | A | S | O | N | D |

Widespread on high rocky ground or hilly grassland, mainly in the north of Britain.

Reddish tinge

Leaves have three to five fingers

Rue-leaved saxifrage
Saxifraga tridactylites

STARRY SAXIFRAGE

This attractive little plant thrives on wet, rocky ledges on high mountain-sides. But it can be seen at lower altitudes, provided the ground is rocky and well supplied with water from above. For all its toughness, it is a slender, graceful plant, sprouting clusters of star-like flowers with distinctive crimson anthers. The name saxifrage means 'stonebreaker', reflecting the old belief that the plant must somehow have caused the cracks in which it roots.

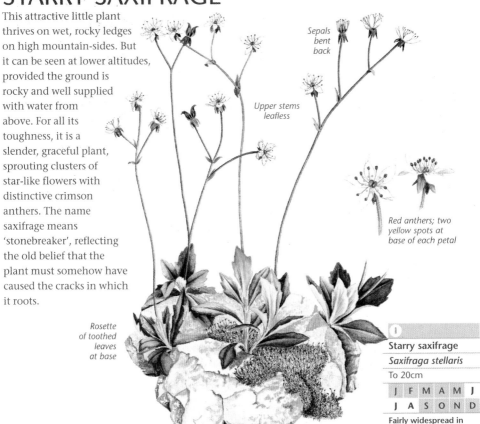

Sepals bent back

Upper stems leafless

Red anthers; two yellow spots at base of each petal

Rosette of toothed leaves at base

Starry saxifrage

Saxifraga stellaris

To 20cm

| J | F | M | A | M | J |
| J | A | S | O | N | D |

Fairly widespread in mountainous areas.

GRASS-OF-PARNASSUS

The plant's name comes from the Greek mountain where it was seen and written about as early as the 1st century AD. However, it is not a grass and does not look like one. The honey-scented flower has five modified stamens fringed with glands, distinguishing it from the saxifrages with which it is sometimes confused. The loose rosette of heart-shaped leaves on long stalks is the other main feature.

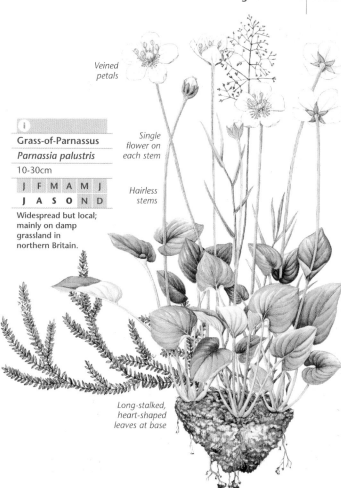

Grass-of-Parnassus

Parnassia palustris

10-30cm

| J | F | M | A | M | J |
| J | A | S | O | N | D |

Widespread but local; mainly on damp grassland in northern Britain.

Veined petals

Single flower on each stem

Hairless stems

Long-stalked, heart-shaped leaves at base

ROUND-LEAVED SUNDEW

The 'dew' of this plant is really a glue for catching insects, which are attracted by the shiny drops on the tips of the red hairs, mistaking them for water in which to lay eggs. They are held fast while the leaf curls to enclose and digest them. After a few days the leaf opens and the trap is set for the next meal. The insects make up for the lack of nutrients in the moorland soil. Great sundew has longer, narrower leaves.

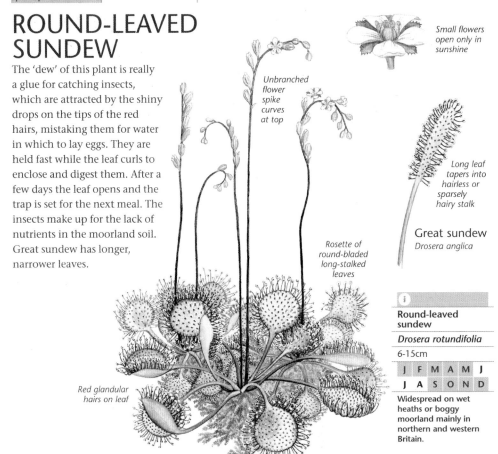

Small flowers open only in sunshine

Unbranched flower spike curves at top

Long leaf tapers into hairless or sparsely hairy stalk

Great sundew
Drosera anglica

Rosette of round-bladed long-stalked leaves

Red glandular hairs on leaf

ⓘ

Round-leaved sundew

Drosera rotundifolia

6-15cm

J	F	M	A	M	J
J	A	S	O	N	D

Widespread on wet heaths or boggy moorland mainly in northern and western Britain.

JAPANESE KNOTWEED

This plant was introduced in the first half of the 19th century and became a favourite with Victorian gardeners. It is now a persistent pernicious weed, often forming tall, dense thickets. It is fast-growing, with thick, often pinkish, zig-zag stems. The flowers are borne in branching spikes, growing from the base of leaves almost 15cm across. It has extensive underground creeping stems.

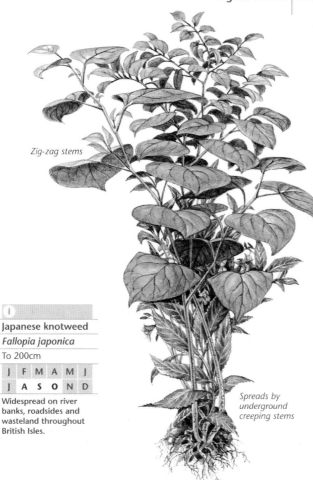

Zig-zag stems

Spreads by underground creeping stems

i
Japanese knotweed
Fallopia japonica
To 200cm

| J | F | M | A | M | J |
| J | A | S | O | N | D |

Widespread on river banks, roadsides and wasteland throughout British Isles.

Flowers in spikes

KNOTGRASS

One of the most common weeds of the British Isles, knotgrass is a member of the dock family. When found among corn it has upright stems, but on wasteland and seashores its stems are long and straggly and it lies flat on the ground. There is a marked difference in the size of the leaves, which are small on the flowering stems and much bigger on the main branches. Its flowers are small; birds eat the seeds. Equal-leaved knotgrass is almost as common and grows in similar habitats.

Oval leaves

Flowers in clusters at base of upper leaf-stalks

Knotgrass

Polygonum aviculare

To 100cm

J	F	M	A	M	J
J	A	S	O	N	D

Widespread on waste ground, arable fields and seashores.

WATER PEPPER

The narrow, unstalked leaves of water-pepper have a strong, acrid taste which gives the plant its name. This keeps the plant safe from grazing animals, and at one time it was put into beds to repel fleas. The tiny flowers are white, tinged green or pink, and grow in a slender, usually nodding, spike.
Black bindweed is distinguished from common bindweed (page 332) by its black fruits and its tiny pinkish-green flowers.

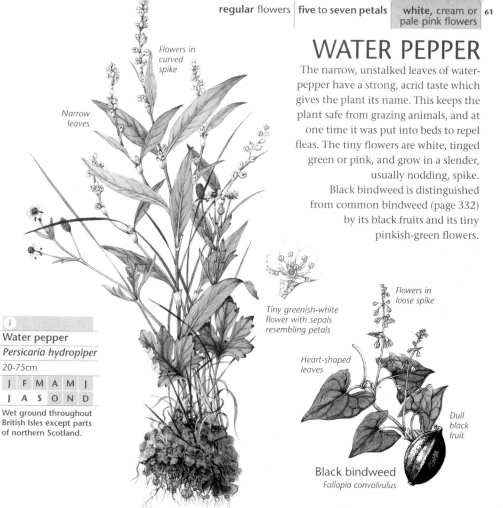

Flowers in curved spike

Narrow leaves

Tiny greenish-white flower with sepals resembling petals

Flowers in loose spike

Heart-shaped leaves

Dull black fruit

ⓘ

Water pepper
Persicaria hydropiper

20–75cm

| J | F | M | A | M | J |
| J | A | S | O | N | D |

Wet ground throughout British Isles except parts of northern Scotland.

Black bindweed
Fallopia convolvulus

CHICKWEED WINTERGREEN

This pretty little flower is best seen in its favourite setting, beneath tall Scots pines in a remote glen in Scotland. Occasionally it can be found in northern England on moist, mossy ground. Despite its name, it is neither a chickweed nor a wintergreen, but is a relative of the primrose (page 150). One or two delightful flowers rise on tall, thin stems from the middle of a whorl of broad, pale green leaves. The leaves in turn surmount a single, unbranched stem from which a few much smaller leaves grow below.

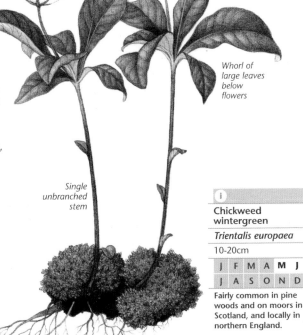

Whorl of large leaves below flowers

Single unbranched stem

Starry flower, five-nine petals (usually seven)

Ripe fruit splits into five parts

(i)					
Chickweed wintergreen					
Trientalis europaea					
10-20cm					

J	F	M	A	**M**	**J**
J	**A**	S	O	N	D

Fairly common in pine woods and on moors in Scotland, and locally in northern England.

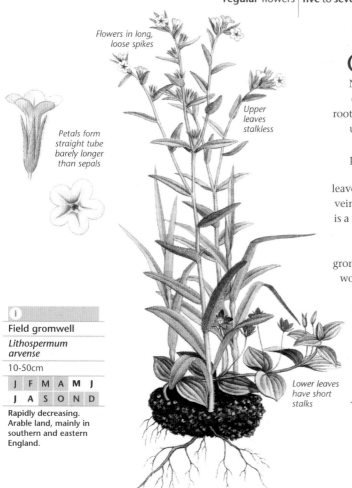

Flowers in long, loose spikes

Upper leaves stalkless

Petals form straight tube barely longer than sepals

Lower leaves have short stalks

Field gromwell

Lithospermum arvense

10-50cm

| J | F | M | A | M | J |
| J | A | S | O | N | D |

Rapidly decreasing. Arable land, mainly in southern and eastern England.

FIELD GROMWELL

Never a welcome sight to the cereal farmer, field gromwell roots in rich, arable land. It is an upright, roughly hairy plant, shown growing with scarlet pimpernel. The stem has few branches and widely spread leaves on which only the central vein is apparent. Field gromwell is a relative of the forget-me-not (page 226).

A related species, common gromwell, grows in long grass or woodland margins. It is leafier, taller and more branched, and the leaves have obvious lateral veins as well as a central vein.

Many leaves

Common gromwell

Lithospermum officinale

HEDGE BINDWEED

Given a free run, hedge bindweed can dress a hedge as if for a wedding with its brilliant trumpet flowers. Indeed, the blooms are so attractive it is easy to forget that they are the product of a very troublesome weed. The flowers are can be pink in some forms of the plant.

Common or field bindweed (page 332) has a smaller pink or white, often candy-striped, flower. Large bindweed bears flowers which are among the largest of all British wild flowers.

Stems twist upwards

Leaves shaped like arrowheads or hearts

Sepals partly hidden by two broad bracts

Flowers to 90mm across

Inflated bracts cover sepals

Large bindweed
Calystegia silvatica

<table>
<tr><td colspan="6">ⓘ</td></tr>
<tr><td colspan="6">Hedge bindweed</td></tr>
<tr><td colspan="6">Calystegia sepium</td></tr>
<tr><td colspan="6">To 3m or more</td></tr>
<tr><td>J</td><td>F</td><td>M</td><td>A</td><td>M</td><td>J</td></tr>
<tr><td>J</td><td>A</td><td>S</td><td>O</td><td>N</td><td>D</td></tr>
</table>

Hedges, woodland margins and fen throughout British Isles; sparser in northern England and Scotland.

BLACK NIGHTSHADE

In autumn, when the green berries of this nightshade ripen to black, they look very much like blackcurrants. But they contain the poisonous alkaloid solanine, and should not be eaten. The plant has dark, often blackish, stems and pointed, sometimes toothed, leaves. At a quick glance the little flowers look rather like those of its relative the potato, and the plant is often found growing between potato rows. But it occurs on waste ground as well as cultivated soil.

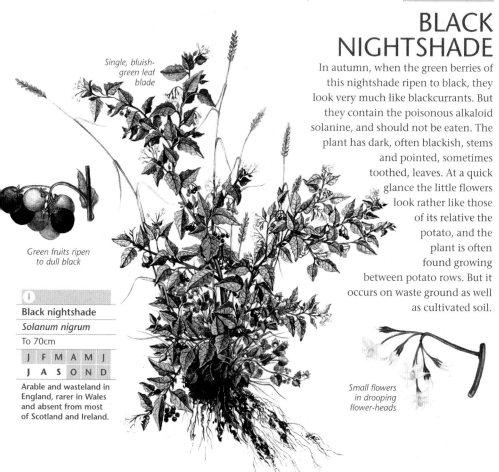

Single, bluish-green leaf blade

Green fruits ripen to dull black

i

Black nightshade

Solanum nigrum

To 70cm

| J | F | M | A | M | J |
| J | A | S | O | N | D |

Arable and wasteland in England, rarer in Wales and absent from most of Scotland and Ireland.

Small flowers in drooping flower-heads

WOOD-SORREL

The leaves of wood-sorrel look very much like clover, though the plants are not related. Wood-sorrel produces two sorts of flowers. One is the familiar, cup-shaped, lilac-veined flower which blooms in abundance on woodland floors, but produces very little seed. The other, found on short stalks close to the ground, is self-pollinating and fertile.

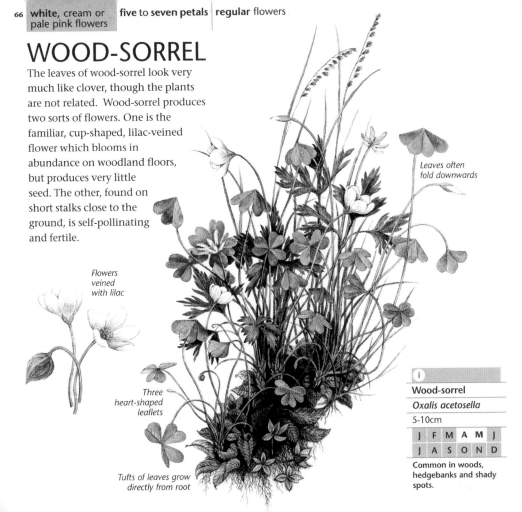

Leaves often fold downwards

Flowers veined with lilac

Three heart-shaped leaflets

Tufts of leaves grow directly from root

ⓘ

Wood-sorrel

Oxalis acetosella

5-10cm

J	F	**M**	**A**	**M**	J
J	**A**	**S**	O	N	D

Common in woods, hedgebanks and shady spots.

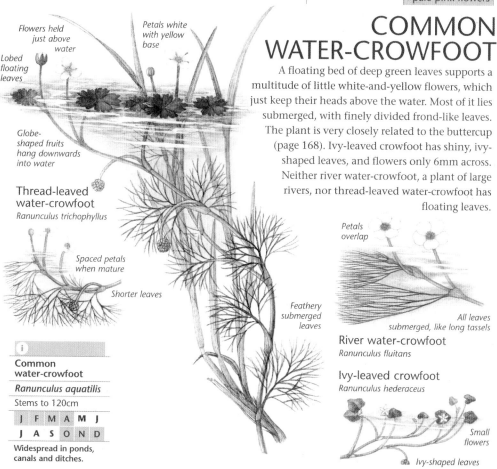

COMMON WATER-CROWFOOT

A floating bed of deep green leaves supports a multitude of little white-and-yellow flowers, which just keep their heads above the water. Most of it lies submerged, with finely divided frond-like leaves. The plant is very closely related to the buttercup (page 168). Ivy-leaved crowfoot has shiny, ivy-shaped leaves, and flowers only 6mm across. Neither river water-crowfoot, a plant of large rivers, nor thread-leaved water-crowfoot has floating leaves.

Flowers held just above water

Lobed floating leaves

Petals white with yellow base

Globe-shaped fruits hang downwards into water

Feathery submerged leaves

Thread-leaved water-crowfoot
Ranunculus trichophyllus

Spaced petals when mature

Shorter leaves

Petals overlap

All leaves submerged, like long tassels

River water-crowfoot
Ranunculus fluitans

Ivy-leaved crowfoot
Ranunculus hederaceus

Small flowers

Ivy-shaped leaves

Common water-crowfoot

Ranunculus aquatilis

Stems to 120cm

| J | F | M | A | M | J |
| J | A | S | O | N | D |

Widespread in ponds, canals and ditches.

DOG ROSE

Often thought of as the symbol of England, the dog rose is the commonest of our wild roses. It has the biggest flowers, blooming at the end of tall, sturdy stems which are liberally supplied with hooked thorns. The sweet-scented flowers, which have numerous yellow stamens, are white or pale pink and the fruit is the familiar red rose hip, from which syrup is made. The dog rose is cultivated by nurserymen to provide strong rootstocks onto which more delicate garden roses are grafted.

The field rose has trailing stems and curved thorns.

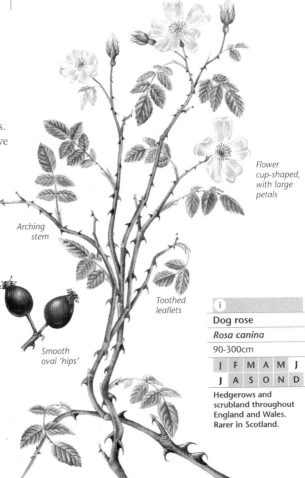

Flower cup-shaped, with large petals

Arching stem

Toothed leaflets

Smooth oval 'hips'

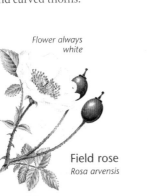

Flower always white

Field rose
Rosa arvensis

Dog rose	
Rosa canina	
90–300cm	

J	F	M	A	M	J
J	A	S	O	N	D

Hedgerows and scrubland throughout England and Wales. Rarer in Scotland.

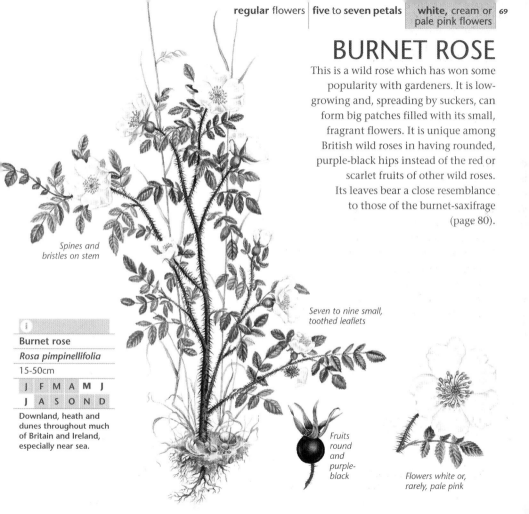

BURNET ROSE

This is a wild rose which has won some
popularity with gardeners. It is low-
growing and, spreading by suckers, can
form big patches filled with its small,
fragrant flowers. It is unique among
British wild roses in having rounded,
purple-black hips instead of the red or
scarlet fruits of other wild roses.
Its leaves bear a close resemblance
to those of the burnet-saxifrage
(page 80).

*Spines and
bristles on stem*

*Seven to nine small,
toothed leaflets*

Burnet rose

Rosa pimpinellifolia

15-50cm

J F M A M J
J A S O N D

Downland, heath and
dunes throughout much
of Britain and Ireland,
especially near sea.

*Fruits
round
and
purple-
black*

*Flowers white or,
rarely, pale pink*

RASPBERRY

The wild fruit is not as big as the cultivated varieties of raspberry, but the taste is at least as good. The tall, woody plant sends up shoots which bear fruit the following year and then die. Each fruit is made up of many globe-shaped segments, each growing round its own pip.

The related stone bramble is a smaller, low-growing plant found in hilly, mainly northern, districts. Its runners spread above ground.

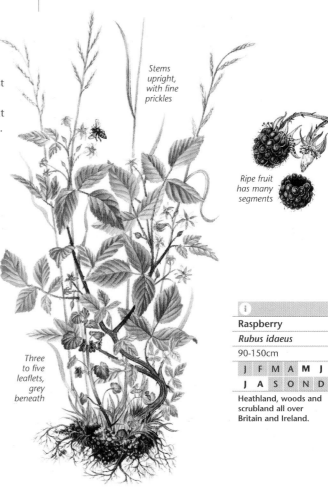

Stems upright, with fine prickles

Ripe fruit has many segments

Three to five leaflets, grey beneath

Fruit has few segments

Stone bramble
Rubus saxatilis

Raspberry	
Rubus idaeus	
90-150cm	

J	F	M	A	**M**	**J**
J	**A**	**S**	O	N	**D**

Heathland, woods and scrubland all over Britain and Ireland.

BRAMBLE

Rubus fruticosus is often used to refer to the scientific grouping of several hundred similar types, known as microspecies, each of which has its own pattern of thorns, leaf shape and flower colour varying from deep pink to white. In autumn, woods, hedges and scrubland are filled with the familiar sweet-tasting fruit, but not all varieties are equally good to eat. They are all popular with birds, which scatter the seed far and wide. The dewberry's fruit has fewer and larger segments, and is covered with a bluish bloom. It is absent from most of Scotland.

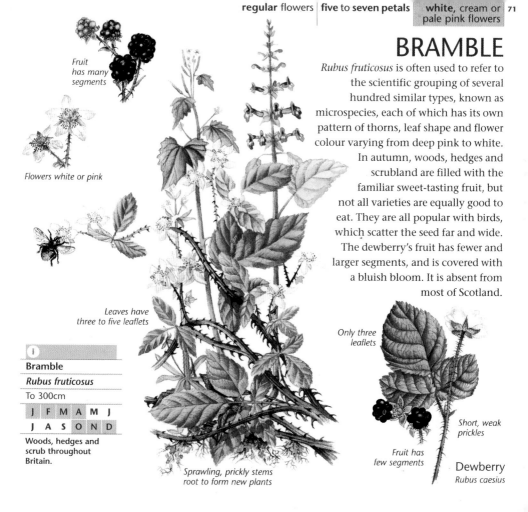

Fruit has many segments

Flowers white or pink

Leaves have three to five leaflets

i					

Bramble

Rubus fruticosus

To 300cm

J	F	M	A	M	J
J	A	S	O	N	D

Woods, hedges and scrub throughout Britain.

Sprawling, prickly stems root to form new plants

Only three leaflets

Short, weak prickles

Fruit has few segments

Dewberry
Rubus caesius

WILD STRAWBERRY

Small but superbly flavoured, the fruit of the wild strawberry is well worth seeking out when in season. It also has a curious feature. Its seeds or pips protrude from the surface of the fruit, while in cultivated strawberries the seeds are embedded in the surface of the fruit. The plant has clusters of bright green trefoil leaves, silky on the underside. The flowers of wild strawberry are on upright stalks and have petals which touch or overlap. By contrast the petals of the earlier-flowering barren strawberry do not touch, and the fruits are dry and fleshless.

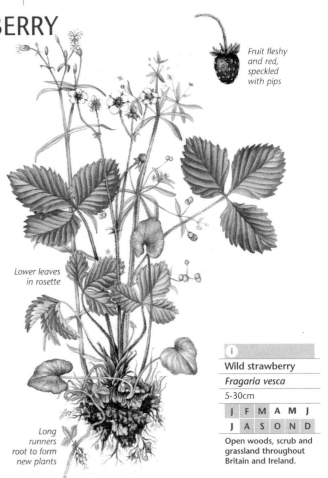

Fruit fleshy and red, speckled with pips

Lower leaves in rosette

Dry fleshless fruit

Wide gaps between notched petals

Barren strawberry
Potentilla sterilis

Long runners root to form new plants

ⓘ
Wild strawberry
Fragaria vesca
5-30cm

J	F	M	A	M	J
J	A	S	O	N	D

Open woods, scrub and grassland throughout Britain and Ireland.

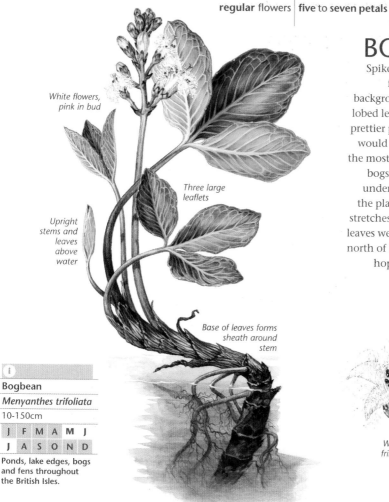

White flowers, pink in bud

Three large leaflets

Upright stems and leaves above water

Base of leaves forms sheath around stem

BOGBEAN

Spikes of feathery, white flowers set against a background of large, three-lobed leaves make this a far prettier plant than its name would suggest, and one of the most attractive plants of bogs and fens. Creeping underwater stems enable the plant to colonise large stretches of marshland. The leaves were once used in the north of England in place of hops to impart a bitter flavour to beer.

White hairs fringe petals

ⓘ

Bogbean

Menyanthes trifoliata

10-150cm

| J | F | M | A | M | J |
| J | A | S | O | N | D |

Ponds, lake edges, bogs and fens throughout the British Isles.

DROPWORT

This plant is similar to meadowsweet (see opposite), but its flowers are creamy-white, with a less yellowish tinge. Unlike the meadowsweet, the dropwort's sprays of flowers are hardly scented, and the blooms fewer but larger. Its leaves are divided into numerous, heavily toothed dark green leaflets. The common name refers to the plant's roots, which are swollen in places into pea-sized tubers – the 'drops'.

Flowers in clusters

Undersides of petals bright pink

Swollen tubers on roots

Many leaflets, heavily toothed

Dropwort

Filipendula vulgaris

15-50cm

J	F	M	A	M	J
J	A	S	O	N	D

Widespread on dry grassland, especially on chalk and limestone in England; rare elsewhere.

MEADOWSWEET

A flower with such an attractive name cannot fail to win friends. It smells good and, seen in great drifts by a river bank in summer, it looks superb. In medieval and Tudor times the flowers were often strewn among the rushes on the floors of houses to sweeten the domestic air. Queen Elizabeth much approved of this practice. But the flowers are best seen in a natural setting, where the dense clusters of blossom sprout like creamy foam at the end of tall, hairless, branching stems. Meadowsweet is in fact a corruption of an older name, mede-sweete, given to it by the Anglo-Saxons who used it to flavour their mead.

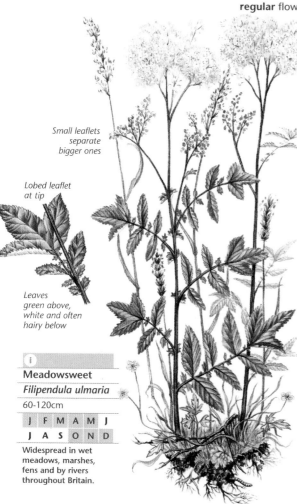

Small leaflets separate bigger ones

Lobed leaflet at tip

Leaves green above, white and often hairy below

ⓘ

Meadowsweet

Filipendula ulmaria

60-120cm

| J | F | M | A | M | J |
| J | A | S | O | N | D |

Widespread in wet meadows, marshes, fens and by rivers throughout Britain.

Five bent-back sepals and five petals

Fruits twisted spirally

ROUGH CHERVIL

Roadsides and hedgebanks are dominated by the 'big four' of the parsley family during the summer months. First on the scene is cow parsley, followed by rough chervil, upright hedge-parsley and hogweed (page 93). Rough chervil differs from the others in having a purple-spotted stem, which is also coarsely hairy. The other main difference is the conspicuous swelling where the leaf-stalks join the stem. They all have big umbrella-shaped heads of flowers.

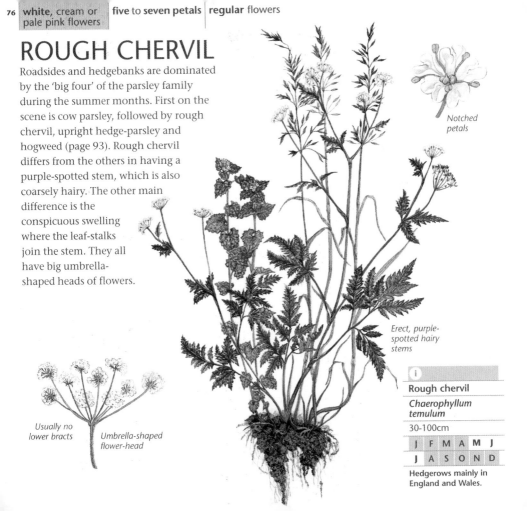

Notched petals

Erect, purple-spotted hairy stems

Usually no lower bracts

Umbrella-shaped flower-head

Rough chervil

Chaerophyllum temulum

30-100cm

J	F	M	A	**M**	**J**
J	**A**	**S**	**O**	**N**	D

Hedgerows mainly in England and Wales.

SANICLE

Most people would recognise this plant as a member of the parsley family; but many would find it hard to explain the name. Sanicle is happiest in beech woods, on chalk or limestone soils, where it is often found in extensive patches. The plant is hairless and its lobed leaves are shiny and deeply toothed. The fruit is covered with hooked bristles which catch on to the fur of any passing animals, spreading the seeds.

Upper and lower bracts present

Umbrella-shaped flower-heads on tall stalks

Flower-head made up of several smaller heads

Stems upright and hairless

Bisexual flowers stalkless, in centre of flower-head

Leaves arise from base

Male flowers on stalks, at edge of flower-head

ⓘ

Sanicle

Sanicula europaea

20-40cm

J	F	M	A	M	J
J	A	S	O	N	D

Dry deciduous woodland; rare in Scotland.

UPRIGHT HEDGE-PARSLEY

A fruit which looks like some unpleasant little insect has earned upright hedge-parsley the local name of 'Devil's nightcap'. The hooked spines ensure that the fruit is carried away on the back of any passing animal to grow elsewhere, most commonly by the roadside. Of the three main roadside varieties of parsley, much alike in appearance, upright hedge-parsley flowers last (from July to August), after cow parsley (April to June) and rough chervil (May to July).

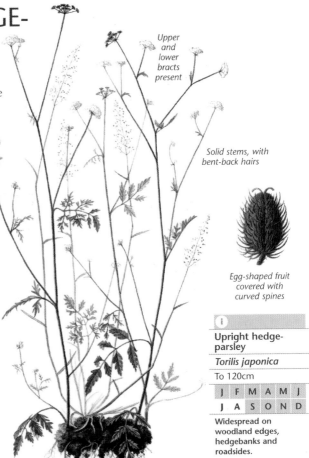

Upper and lower bracts present

Solid stems, with bent-back hairs

Egg-shaped fruit covered with curved spines

Many stalked flowers on each main branch of flower-head

Upright hedge-parsley	
Torilis japonica	
To 120cm	

J	F	M	A	M	J
J	A	S	O	N	D

Widespread on woodland edges, hedgebanks and roadsides.

BUR CHERVIL

This plant is much less common than the three main hedgebank parsleys – upright hedge-parsley, rough chervil and cow parsley – and tends to confine itself to certain areas, particularly East Anglia. It is a distinctive plant, smaller and more delicate than cow parsley, with much more finely cut leaves and hairless, hollow stems. The flower-heads are small, umbrella-like clusters on stalks opposite the leaves, which are hairy on the underside. The fruits are covered with very short, hooked bristles.

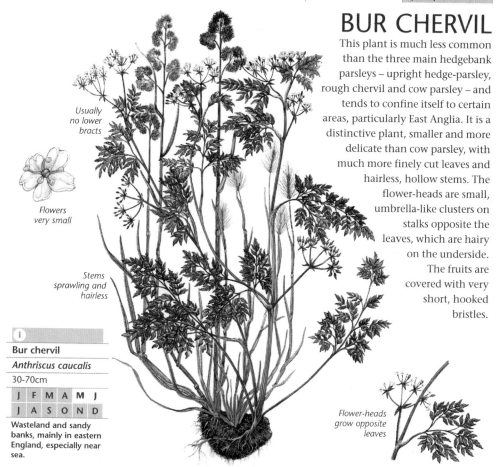

Usually no lower bracts

Flowers very small

Stems sprawling and hairless

Flower-heads grow opposite leaves

i

Bur chervil

Anthriscus caucalis

30-70cm

| J | F | M | A | M | J |
| J | A | S | O | N | D |

Wasteland and sandy banks, mainly in eastern England, especially near sea.

BURNET-SAXIFRAGE

Despite its name, this is neither a burnet nor a saxifrage but a member of the parsley family, with its characteristic branched 'umbrella' of flowers. It is an upright, elegant plant with tough, almost solid stems which are rounded and sometimes covered in downy hairs. All the leaves are divided into leaflets, but those on the stem are much more finely cut than those growing from the base.

Greater burnet-saxifrage is darker green and much taller, growing to 120cm. It is a more robust plant, with larger leaflets and longer fruits.

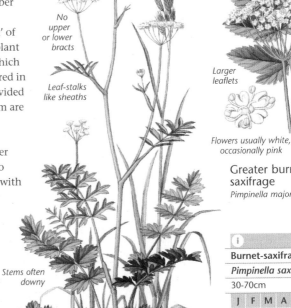

No upper or lower bracts

Leaf-stalks like sheaths

Stems often downy

Larger leaflets

Stem prominent ridged

Flowers usually white, occasionally pink

Greater burnet-saxifrage
Pimpinella major

Flower-head has 10-20 branches

Fruit round and shiny

ⓘ

Burnet-saxifrage

Pimpinella saxifraga

30-70cm

J	F	M	A	M	J
J	A	S	O	N	D

Scattered in dry grassy places; absent from much of northern and western Scotland.

PIGNUT

This relative of the carrot is best known for its edible, swollen brown tubers, which have a pleasantly nutty flavour eaten raw or cooked. Pigs are certainly fond of them, hence the name. But they were also popular among country children in the days when sweets were scarce. Slender, hairless stems rise from the tubers and end in little umbrellas of flowers, with fewer branches than those of burnet-saxifrage. The leaves are much divided, those growing from the base withering before the plant flowers. Another difference from burnet-saxifrage is the shape of the seed-pod.

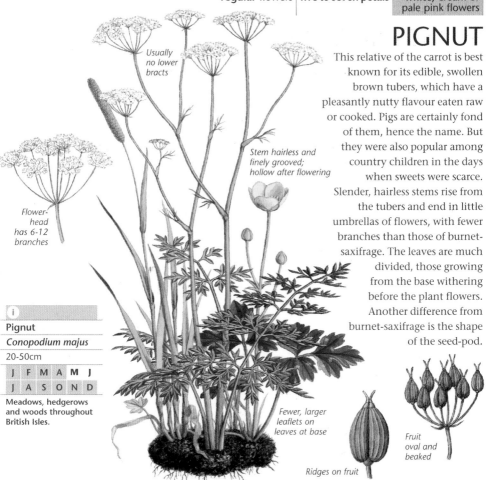

Usually no lower bracts

Stem hairless and finely grooved; hollow after flowering

Flower-head has 6-12 branches

ⓘ

Pignut

Conopodium majus

20-50cm

| J | F | M | A | **M** | **J** |
| **J** | **A** | **S** | **O** | **N** | D |

Meadows, hedgerows and woods throughout British Isles.

Fewer, larger leaflets on leaves at base

Ridges on fruit

Fruit oval and beaked

GROUND ELDER

Gardeners have good reason for disliking this plant, which in Northern Ireland is known, appropriately, as garden plague. Its most striking feature is the bright green leaves which form a canopy shutting out all light from anything attempting to grow below, though taller plants like rosebay willowherb often grow alongside it. Ground elder also has long, white, underground runners, enabling it to spread rapidly. Its flowers are minute, in dense heads which can have up to 20 slender umbrella-like branches. Its English name refers to the similarity of the leaves to those of elder trees.

Usually no upper or lower bracts

Prominent yellow stamens

Pod egg-shaped and ridged

Up to nine leaflets on each leaf

Stems hollow, grooved and hairless

Ground elder

Aegopodium podagraria

30-100cm

| J | F | M | A | M | J |
| J | A | S | O | N | D |

Common throughout British Isles in cultivated and waste ground.

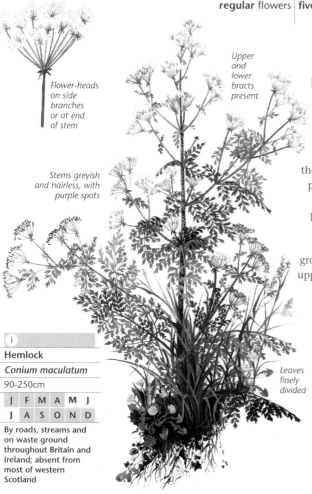

Flower-heads on side branches or at end of stem

Upper and lower bracts present

Stems greyish and hairless, with purple spots

HEMLOCK

One of the tallest members of the parsley family, with hairless, purple-blotched stems, fern-like leaves and an unpleasant smell, hemlock is fortunately an easy plant to identify. Every part of the plant is poisonous, but the seeds contain the biggest concentration of alkaloids, particularly coniine, which paralyses the respiratory nerves. Socrates was poisoned by hemlock, and the plant formed part of the witches' brew in Shakespeare's *Macbeth*. The flowers grow in dense little umbrellas, and the upper bracts are on the outer side only.

Hemlock

Conium maculatum

90-250cm

| J | F | M | A | M | J |
| J | A | S | O | N | D |

By roads, streams and on waste ground throughout Britain and Ireland; absent from most of western Scotland

Leaves finely divided

Fruits round, with wavy ridges

FOOL'S WATERCRESS

The leaves of this plant are similar to those of watercress (hence its common name), though the leaflets of fool's watercress have shallow teeth. Although less tasty than true watercress it can be eaten safely. The plant could also be mistaken for lesser water-parsnip though, unlike that plant, it usually has no lower bracts below the flower-head. The main feature that distinguishes the plant from lesser water-parsnip is the way the short stalks bearing the flower-heads sprout from the stem opposite a leaf.

Entire plant is hairless

Flower-head short-stalked, opposite leaf

Sprawling stems hollow and finely furrowed

Fruit oval, with thick ridges

Leaflets shiny, stalkless, with toothed edges

Fool's watercress

Apium nodiflorum

30-100cm

| J | F | M | A | M | J |
| J | A | S | O | N | D |

Marshy places, ditches and slow streams; absent from much of Scotland.

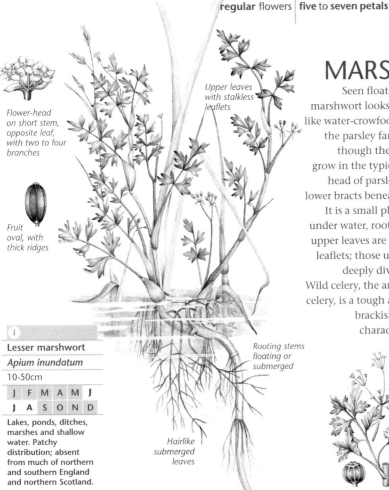

Flower-head
on short stem,
opposite leaf,
with two to four
branches

Upper leaves
with stalkless
leaflets

Fruit
oval, with
thick ridges

Rooting stems
floating or
submerged

Hairlike
submerged
leaves

LESSER MARSHWORT

Seen floating in a pond, lesser marshwort looks at first glance more like water-crowfoot than a member of the parsley family. But its flowers, though they are small and few, grow in the typical umbrella-shaped head of parsleys and there are no lower bracts beneath the flower-head. It is a small plant, growing in and under water, rooting as it creeps. The upper leaves are divided into narrow leaflets; those under the water have deeply divided, hairlike lobes. Wild celery, the ancestor of cultivated celery, is a tough and hairless plant of brackish places and has the characteristic celery smell.

ⓘ

Lesser marshwort

Apium inundatum

10-50cm

| J | F | M | A | M | J |
| J | A | S | O | N | D |

Lakes, ponds, ditches, marshes and shallow water. Patchy distribution; absent from much of northern and southern England and northern Scotland.

Grooved,
upright
stems

Leaflets of
lower leaves
on separate
stalks

Wild celery
Apium graveolens

LESSER WATER-PARSNIP

Though often mistaken for fool's watercress, lesser water-parsnip has leaves that are more coarsely toothed and have a distinct purple ring towards the bottom of the stalks of the lower leaves. Unlike fool's watercress, there are leaf-like bracts below the lower flower-stalks. The umbrella-shaped flower-heads grow on stalks opposite the leaves. The lower leaves have long stalks with five to nine pairs of leaflets. The plant spreads by means of stolons – sprawling stems which bend to the ground or below the water and take root. Its roots were once used to make a poultice to cleanse sores and disperse swellings.

Fruit constricted in middle

Leaflets coarsely toothed

Leaf-like upper and lower bracts below flower-heads

ⓘ

Lesser water-parsnip

Berula erecta

30–100cm

J	F	M	A	M	J
J	A	S	O	N	D

Fens, ditches and marshes; rare in western and northern Britain.

FOOL'S PARSLEY

This hairless plant contains an alkaloid called coniine, the main active ingredient of hemlock, which is extremely poisonous. Its most striking feature is the presence of long, streamer-like little leaves called bracteoles, hanging beneath the umbrella-shaped flower-heads. The flower-heads themselves are always at the end of a branch, opposite a leaf. The fruit is egg-shaped and deeply ridged.

Bracteoles (upper bracts) below flower-heads but usually no lower bracts

Finely ribbed stems

Leaves triangular, finely divided

Fruit deeply ridged

Fool's parsley

Aethusa cynapium

5-100cm

| J | F | M | A | M | J |
| J | A | S | O | N | D |

Cultivated and wasteland; widespread, but absent from much of Scotland and Ireland.

HEMLOCK WATER-DROPWORT

It smells of parsley and has the characteristic umbrella-shaped flower-head of the parsley family. But hemlock water-dropwort is also one of Britain's most poisonous plants, dangerous to humans and animals. It is often seen in broad clumps in or on the edge of fresh water. A stout, hairless plant, it has large flower-heads and deep green leaves made up of broad, triangular, heavily toothed leaflets.

Fine-leaved water-dropwort has leaves that are paler as well as finer. It is found most commonly in eastern England in slow or still fresh water.

Fruit cylindrical, with two upright styles

Upper and lower bracts below flower-head

Up to 40 branches on fruiting head

Leaf-stalks form sheath around stem

Heavily toothed leaflets form triangular leaf

Finer leaflets

Usually no lower bracts

Fine-leaved water-dropwort
Oenanthe aquatica

ⓘ

Hemlock water-dropwort

Oenanthe crocata

30-150cm

J	F	M	A	M	J
J	A	S	O	N	D

By fresh water, mainly in south and west.

PARSLEY WATER-DROPWORT

A close relative of the hemlock water-dropwort, parsley water-dropwort also bears some similarity to it. The main difference in appearance between the two plants is in the leaves – parsley water-dropwort has long, narrow leaflets, greyish in colour, compared with the triangular, deeper green leaves of hemlock water-dropwort. Tubular water-dropwort is a plant of marshes, ditches and other wet places, and is absent from most of Scotland. The flower-heads become dense and globular when the angular fruits ripen.

Up to 10 branches in flower-head, with bracts

Fruit oval and ridged

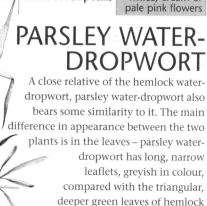

Long, narrow leaflets

Parsley water-dropwort

Oenanthe lachenalii

30-100cm

| J | F | M | A | M | J |
| J | A | S | O | N | D |

Fresh water and brackish marsh, especially near coast.

Leaves divided

Flower-head has up to five branches, with no bracts

Tubular water-dropwort

Oenanthe fistulosa

WILD ANGELICA

A mass of blossom, often pink-tinged, at the top of tall stems makes wild angelica easy to identify. It is also notable for the broad sheathing of the stalks on the upper leaves, which are much smaller than the lower leaves. The 17th-century herbalist Nicholas Culpeper recommended angelica against 'all epidemical diseases' and also as a candy, for which the stalks of the related garden angelica are still crystallised today.

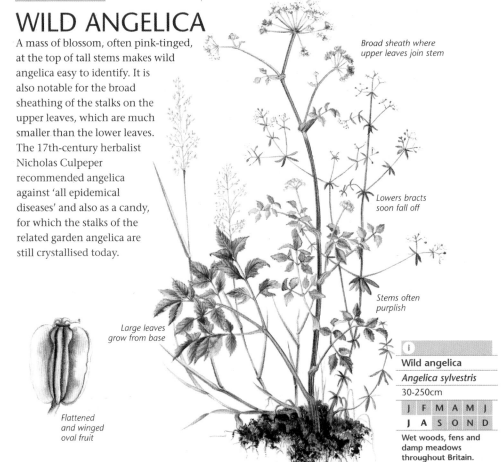

Broad sheath where upper leaves join stem

Lowers bracts soon fall off

Stems often purplish

Large leaves grow from base

Flattened and winged oval fruit

i						

Wild angelica

Angelica sylvestris

30-250cm

J	F	M	A	M	J
J	A	S	O	N	D

Wet woods, fens and damp meadows throughout Britain.

COW PARSLEY

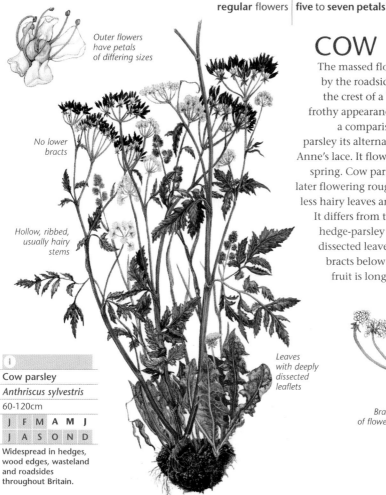

The massed flowers of cow parsley by the roadside seem to foam like the crest of a breaking wave. This frothy appearance long ago inspired a comparison which gave cow parsley its alternative name of Queen Anne's lace. It flowers in abundance in spring. Cow parsley differs from the later flowering rough chervil in having less hairy leaves and unspotted stems. It differs from the still later upright hedge-parsley in its broader, more dissected leaves, and in having no bracts below the flower-head. Its fruit is long, smooth and black.

Outer flowers have petals of differing sizes

No lower bracts

Hollow, ribbed, usually hairy stems

Leaves with deeply dissected leaflets

Branches of flower-head hairless

ⓘ

Cow parsley

Anthriscus sylvestris

60-120cm

| J | F | M | A | M | J |
| J | A | S | O | N | D |

Widespread in hedges, wood edges, wasteland and roadsides throughout Britain.

WILD CARROT

A tall, roughly hairy plant, the wild carrot is recognisable by the single purplish-red flower usually seen at the centre of each densely packed flower-head. The finely divided bracts under the flower-head are also distinctive. The fruits have long barbed spines which attach themselves to passing animals.

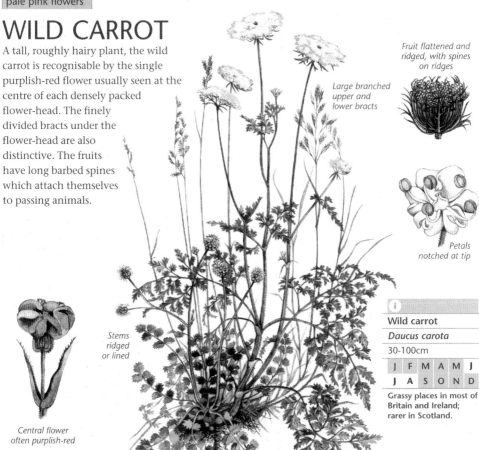

Fruit flattened and ridged, with spines on ridges

Large branched upper and lower bracts

Petals notched at tip

Stems ridged or lined

Central flower often purplish-red

Stout root

Leaf very finely divided

Wild carrot

Daucus carota

30-100cm

| J | F | M | A | M | J |
| J | A | S | O | N | D |

Grassy places in most of Britain and Ireland; rarer in Scotland.

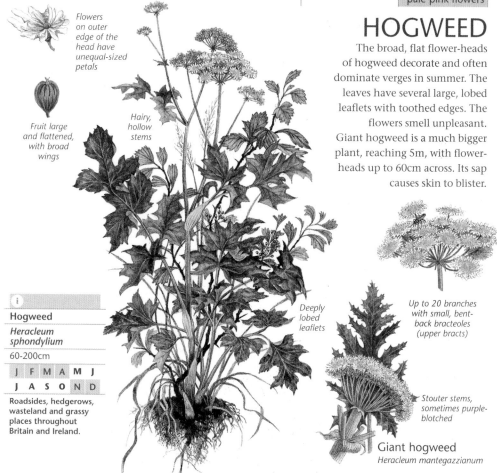

Flowers on outer edge of the head have unequal-sized petals

Fruit large and flattened, with broad wings

Hairy, hollow stems

HOGWEED

The broad, flat flower-heads of hogweed decorate and often dominate verges in summer. The leaves have several large, lobed leaflets with toothed edges. The flowers smell unpleasant. Giant hogweed is a much bigger plant, reaching 5m, with flower-heads up to 60cm across. Its sap causes skin to blister.

Deeply lobed leaflets

Up to 20 branches with small, bent-back bracteoles (upper bracts)

Stouter stems, sometimes purple-blotched

Giant hogweed
Heracleum mantegazzianum

ℹ

Hogweed

Heracleum sphondylium

60-200cm

J F M **A** **M** **J**
J **A** **S** **O** N D

Roadsides, hedgerows, wasteland and grassy places throughout Britain and Ireland.

SWEET CICELY

The crushed leaves of sweet cicely give off a strong smell of aniseed, for which it was once cultivated as a flavouring for food. Its flowers are densely packed together in tight, many-branched heads, while its leaves are large, bright green and much divided, often with small white blotches. The stalks of the stem leaves form a sheath round the hairy stem. The fruits are long and slender with ridges.

Many-branched flower-head

Usually no lower bracts

Stems hollow and downy

Bisexual flowers large, on thick stems

Male flowers on thin stems

ⓘ					

Sweet cicely

Myrrhis odorata

60-180cm

J	F	M	A	**M**	**J**
J	**A**	S	O	N	D

Probably introduced. Widespread, particularly in north, in shady and grassy places.

BROOKWEED

With its long, hairless flower spikes and leafy stems rising from a rosette at the base, it is all too easy to mistake this plant for one of the many small cresses of the cabbage family. But it has five petals instead of their four, and the petals are joined at the base. It is usually found on or near the coast, where a small stream runs out to the sea, and on damp cliffs above a beach.

Tiny leaf-like bract on flower-stalk

ⓘ

Brookweed

Samolus valerandi

5-45cm

J	F	M	A	M	J
J	A	S	O	N	D

Wet places, especially near sea. Rare in Scotland and northern England.

Leafy stems, few branches

Oval untoothed leaves

YARROW

The Greek warrior-hero Achilles was said to have used yarrow to purge and heal wounds made by iron weapons – hence the plant's generic name *Achillea*. Its ancient role now forgotten, yarrow still thrives as a roadside plant, thanks to its deep, water-gathering roots. The broad, flat flower-heads and numerous dark green feathery leaves – the *millefolium* (thousand leaf) of the plant's species name – make it an easy plant to identify. The flowers are usually white but can be pale or deep pink.

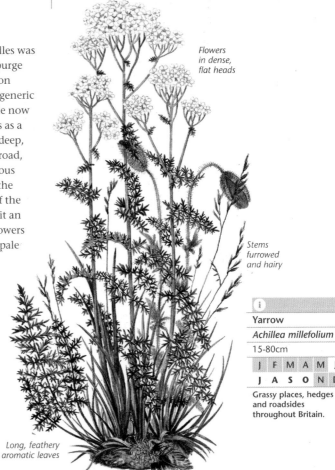

Flowers in dense, flat heads

Stems furrowed and hairy

Each flower has many tiny florets instead of petals

Long, feathery aromatic leaves

Yarrow

Achillea millefolium

15–80cm

J	F	M	A	M	J
J	A	S	O	N	D

Grassy places, hedges and roadsides throughout Britain.

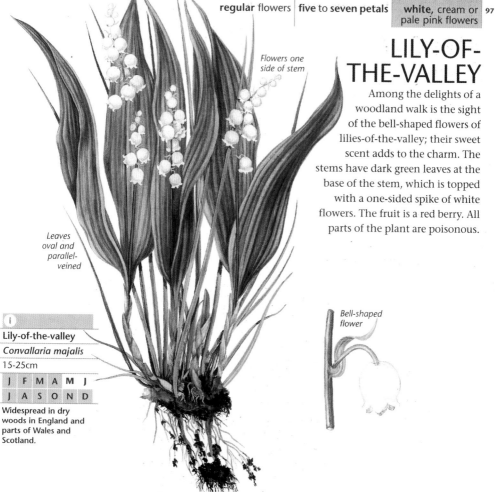

LILY-OF-THE-VALLEY

Among the delights of a woodland walk is the sight of the bell-shaped flowers of lilies-of-the-valley; their sweet scent adds to the charm. The stems have dark green leaves at the base of the stem, which is topped with a one-sided spike of white flowers. The fruit is a red berry. All parts of the plant are poisonous.

Flowers one side of stem

Leaves oval and parallel-veined

Bell-shaped flower

Lily-of-the-valley

Convallaria majalis

15-25cm

| J | F | M | A | M | J |
| J | A | S | O | N | D |

Widespread in dry woods in England and parts of Wales and Scotland.

SOLOMON'S-SEAL

Though not so conspicuously pretty as lily-of-the-valley, Solomon's-seal is attractive in a more subdued way. The arching stem carries broad, spreading leaves beneath which hang the slender-waisted flowers. The fruit is a blue-black berry. The use of its powdered roots as a cure for bruises may have had the approval of King Solomon.

The stem of the rarer, shorter Solomon's-seal is angled, with a single fragrant flower to each leaf.

Drooping flowers

Leaves stalkless and parallel-veined

Long, arching stems

Long, bell-shaped flower, waisted in middle

Flowers larger, not waisted

Angular Solomon's-seal
Polygonatum odoratum

ⓘ
Solomon's-seal
Polygonatum multiflorum
30–80cm

J	F	M	A	**M**	**J**
J	**A**	S	O	N	D

Woods, usually on chalk or limestone, mainly southern Britain.

RAMSONS

Crush the stems or leaves of ramsons and the smell of garlic can be overpowering. But the plant has other attractions. Its flower-heads can carry up to 25 little star-like flowers which rise above broad, bright green leaves with winged, triangular stalks. Ramsons is a vigorous plant, tending to dominate its habitat to the exclusion of everything else.

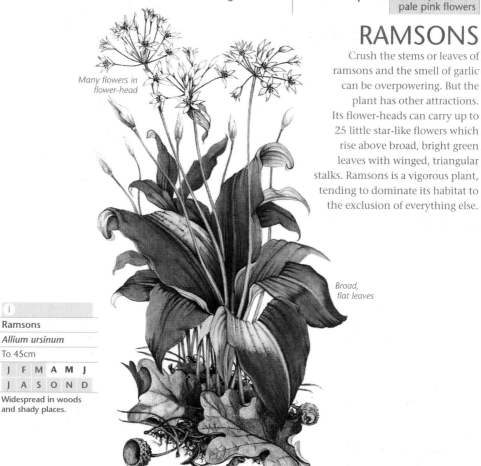

Many flowers in flower-head

Broad, flat leaves

Ramsons

Allium ursinum

To 45cm

J F **M A M** J
J **A** S O N D

Widespread in woods and shady places.

SNOWDROP

Perhaps more than any other flower, the snowdrop signals that winter will soon be at an end. A small leaf-like sheath covers the top of the flower stem as it forces its way through the snow. Two bluish-green leaves appear first, followed by the flower, the inner sepals of which are notched. The snowdrop was probably introduced from central Europe in medieval times.

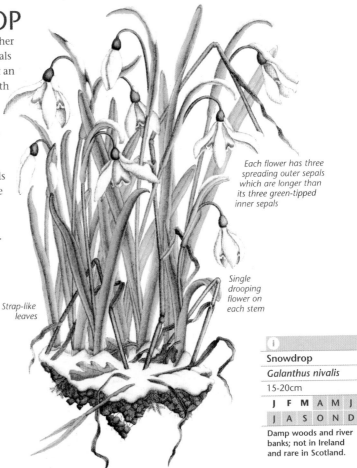

Each flower has three spreading outer sepals which are longer than its three green-tipped inner sepals

Single drooping flower on each stem

Strap-like leaves

i

Snowdrop

Galanthus nivalis

15-20cm

J	F	M	A	M	J
J	A	S	O	N	D

Damp woods and river banks; not in Ireland and rare in Scotland.

WOOD ANEMONE

One of the delights of a spring walk in deciduous woodland is to find a carpet of wood anemones. The big, demurely drooping flowers respond immediately to the sun and raise their heads, petals wide open, to take it in, only to close again as soon as cloud or evening comes. But they wither quickly if picked. After the plant has flowered, one or two long-stalked leaves grow direct from the underground stem.

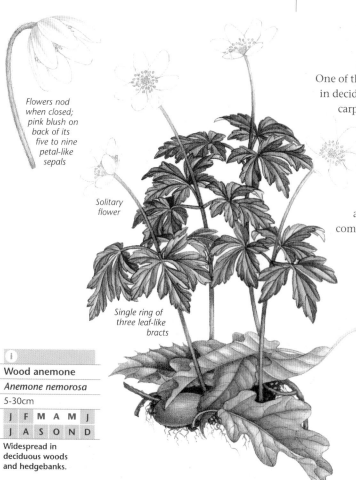

Flowers nod when closed; pink blush on back of its five to nine petal-like sepals

Solitary flower

Single ring of three leaf-like bracts

Wood anemone

Anemone nemorosa

5-30cm

| J | F | M | A | M | J |
| J | A | S | O | N | D |

Widespread in deciduous woods and hedgebanks.

WHITE CLOVER

In flower, white clover makes a pretty sight carpeting a meadow. It is easily identified by the white bands on its leaves and by its tight, single flower-heads waving in the breeze at the top of long stems. The scented flowers are a rich and early source of nectar for bees. This species of clover is the one most commonly cultivated for fodder. The creeping stems take root as they progress and can be difficult to eradicate.

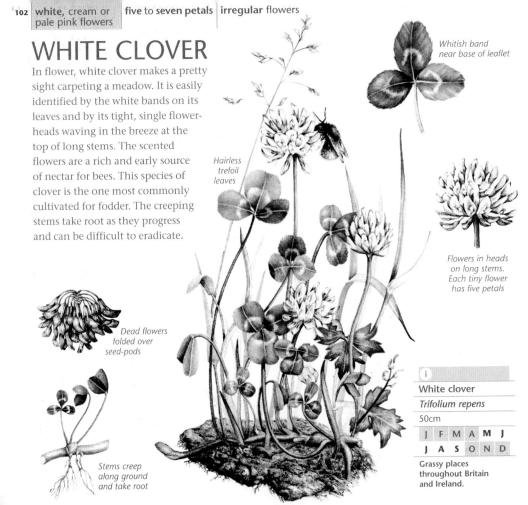

Whitish band near base of leaflet

Hairless trefoil leaves

Flowers in heads on long stems. Each tiny flower has five petals

Dead flowers folded over seed-pods

Stems creep along ground and take root

White clover

Trifolium repens

50cm

J F M A M J
J A S O N D

Grassy places throughout Britain and Ireland.

HARE'S-FOOT CLOVER

Hold the soft, downy flower-head of this plant in your hand and its common name suddenly seems apt. From a distance the long, cylindrical flower-heads look just as distinctive, but call a different image to mind. They are like bottle brushes, waving on the ends of their long stalks. The flowers have a pinkish tinge with pale brown pointed teeth on the sepals, which are masked by a covering of long white hairs. The leaflets are narrow and slightly toothed.

Pointed stipules at base of leaf

---

i

Hare's-foot clover

Trifolium arvense

10-20cm

| J | F | M | A | M | J |
| J | A | S | O | N | D |

Dry, grassy places, commonest in southern and eastern England and absent from most of Scotland and Ireland.

Flowers with five petals, in cylindrical heads on long stalks

In fruit, the brown teeth of sepal tube spread widely

BIRD'S-FOOT

The seed-pods of this small downy plant do bear a remarkable resemblance to a bird's foot. The plant differs from bird's-foot trefoil in having smaller flowers and different leaves. It also differs from most other species of the pea family in that its pods do not split open to release their seeds but break into separate segments, each of which then splits to release its seed.

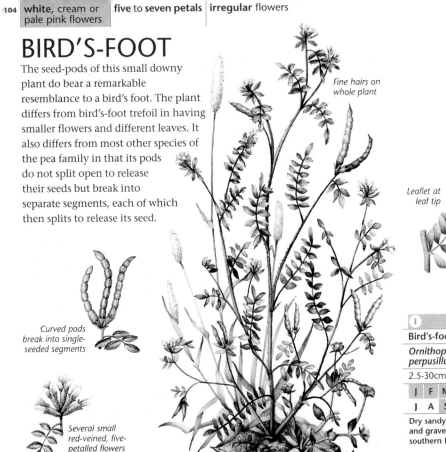

Fine hairs on whole plant

Leaflet at leaf tip

Curved pods break into single-seeded segments

Several small red-veined, five-petalled flowers on each flower-stalk

Bird's-foot

Ornithopus perpusillus

2.5-30cm

| J | F | M | A | M | J |
| J | A | S | O | N | D |

Dry sandy grassland and gravel, mainly in southern Britain.

GREATER BUTTERFLY ORCHID

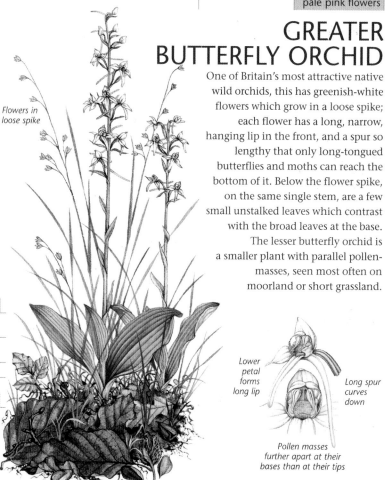

One of Britain's most attractive native wild orchids, this has greenish-white flowers which grow in a loose spike; each flower has a long, narrow, hanging lip in the front, and a spur so lengthy that only long-tongued butterflies and moths can reach the bottom of it. Below the flower spike, on the same single stem, are a few small unstalked leaves which contrast with the broad leaves at the base.

The lesser butterfly orchid is a smaller plant with parallel pollen-masses, seen most often on moorland or short grassland.

Flowers in loose spike

Greater butterfly orchid

Platanthera chlorantha

20-60cm

| J | F | M | A | M | J |
| J | A | S | O | N | D |

Widespread in woods and pastures on lime-rich soils.

Lower petal forms long lip

Long spur curves down

Pollen masses further apart at their bases than at their tips

AUTUMN LADY'S TRESSES

This wild orchid is often plentiful on downland and dry pastureland, where its fragrance scents the evening air. But it is a small plant with less showy flowers than most orchids, and so is easily overlooked among the abundance of tall grasses. The rosette of leaves at the base of the plant dies back in June, when a flowering spike starts to grow. Unusually among orchids, the buds sprout spirally in a single row up the stem, which has a few, scale-like leaves. Autumn lady's tresses sometimes disappears for several years then suddenly reappears.

Flowers set spirally up stem

Single, upright stem

Lance-shaped scale-leaves on stem

Oval leaves in rosette

Lower lip with frilled edge

---

i

Autumn lady's tresses

Spiranthes spiralis

7.5-15cm

J	F	M	A	M	J
J	A	S	O	N	D

Dry grassy places, especially on chalk in southern areas.

WHITE WATER-LILY

The spectacular flower of the white water-lily is, at 10-20cm across, the largest produced by any British wild plant. Typical of its many local names is that used in Cheshire, where it is known as the 'lady of the lake'. But it needs a sunny day to catch its full beauty: the flowers which float on the surface of the water, at the end of long stems, only open fully in sunshine and start to close as soon as the sun begins to wane.

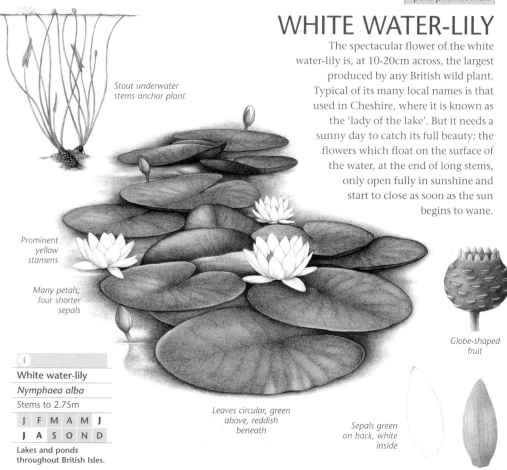

Stout underwater stems anchor plant

Prominent yellow stamens

Many petals; four shorter sepals

Globe-shaped fruit

Leaves circular, green above, reddish beneath

Sepals green on back, white inside

White water-lily

Nymphaea alba

Stems to 2.75m

| J | F | M | A | M | J |
| J | A | S | O | N | D |

Lakes and ponds throughout British Isles.

MOUNTAIN AVENS

This beautiful evergreen, often found in garden rockeries, is rarely seen in the wild, because it favours inaccessible rocky ledges. Each attractive flower rises on a separate stem from a fan of leaves. It has a mass of golden stamens and is clasped by long, green sepals. As the Latin name *octopetala* suggests, it usually has eight petals. The leaves are distinctive, being dark green and very oak-like, with a silvery underside.

Long green sepals

Yellow stamens

Fruit has long feathery styles

Single flower on stem

Leaves dark green above, silvery beneath

i

Mountain avens

Dryas octopetala

2.5-50cm

| J | F | M | A | M | J |
| J | A | S | O | N | D |

Rare in England. Local on limestone rock ledges and steep slopes in Scotland, north Wales and western Ireland.

DAISY

Gardeners may sometimes wonder how the daisy survived before lawns were invented. In fact the daisy grows prolifically, if less noticeably, in short grassland everywhere. It is a very pretty flower whose attractions tend to be overlooked because it is so common. Its genius for survival is perhaps best exemplified by the flat rosette of leaves, which spreads too close to the ground for animals to bite or for mowers to cut.

Oval, downy seed

Short yellow disc floret

Long strap-like ray floret

Leafless, hairy flower-stalk with a single flower-head

Yellow disc ringed by white rays, often tipped red

ⓘ

Daisy

Bellis perennis

To 12cm

J F M A M J J A S O N D

Common everywhere in short grassland, especially on lawns.

Leaves spoon-shaped, slightly toothed

Rosette of leaves at base

SNEEZEWORT

In the Middle Ages the roots of sneezewort were used to quell the pain of toothache and relieve cold symptoms. It is a greyish, erect plant with a creeping root and attractive, creamy-white blooms – similar to the yarrow, to which it is related, but larger and fewer. Unlike the yarrow, its leaves are long, narrow and undivided, with a saw-toothed edge.

Stiff, erect stems, hairy near top

Leaves narrow, finely toothed and stalkless

Ring of bracts surrounds greenish-white ring of petal-like florets

Sneezewort

Achillea ptarmica

20-60cm

| J | F | M | A | M | J |
| J | A | S | O | N | D |

Damp grassland, usually on acid soils, throughout British Isles; rarer in Ireland.

MOUNTAIN EVERLASTING

As its name suggests, this is a plant of mountain slopes, though it is also found on dry pasture and heathland. Its leaves are silvery-white and woolly underneath and grey-green on top. It spreads by creeping, rooting runners as well as by seeds, which travel far on a 'parachute' of long white hairs. The male flowers have a ring of bracts like the ray florets of a daisy, while the female flowers (on a separate plant) are bigger, with long pink or white bracts.

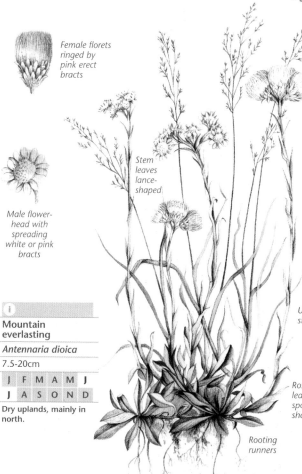

Female florets ringed by pink erect bracts

Male flower-head with spreading white or pink bracts

Stem leaves lance-shaped

Unbranched stems

Rosette leaves spoon-shaped

Rooting runners

Parachute of long white hairs

Mountain everlasting

Antennaria dioica

7.5-20cm

| J | F | M | A | M | J |
| J | A | S | O | N | D |

Dry uplands, mainly in north.

SEA MAYWEED

The big, daisy-like flowers of scentless mayweed make a happy sight by roadsides and on wasteland in summer. It is also a common weed of arable fields.

Sea mayweed is stouter with fleshy leaves, and grows in bare places near the sea. Scented mayweed is more slender and upright, with smaller flowers; it has a pleasant, chamomile smell. It is most common in southern Britain.

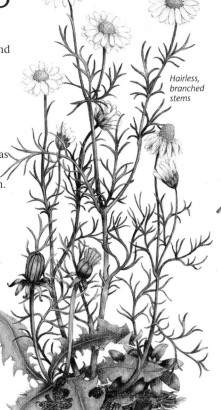

Hairless, branched stems

Solitary flat flower-head

More slender, with drooping rays

Leaves deeply divided

Scented mayweed
Matricaria recutita

(i)
Sea mayweed
Tripleurospermum inodorum
15-60cm

J	F	M	A	M	J
J	A	S	O	N	D

Waste and cultivated bare ground throughout British Isles.

STINKING CHAMOMILE

Compared with scentless mayweed, stinking chamomile has shorter, broader leaf segments on slightly hairy stems and downy-white bracts with a narrow, green midrib. It also has a strong, sickly sweet and unpleasant smell. In fruit the flat yellow centre of the flower becomes a solid cone of seeds.

Corn chamomile is a decreasing arable weed. It is slightly scented, with grey, downy stems and leaves downy-white underneath.

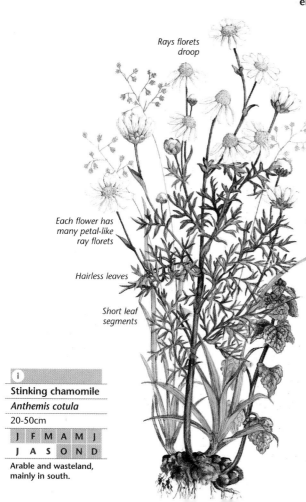

Rays florets droop

Each flower has many petal-like ray florets

Hairless leaves

Short leaf segments

Stinking chamomile

Anthemis cotula

20-50cm

| J | F | M | A | M | J |
| J | A | S | O | N | D |

Arable and wasteland, mainly in south.

Leaves downy beneath

Greyish downy stems

Corn chamomile
Anthemis arvensis

OX-EYE DAISY

Countless young lovers have pulled off the petals of ox-eye daisy one by one, wondering whether 'he (or she) loves me, he (or she) loves me not'. Far from imperilling its existence, this treatment seems to have encouraged the ox-eye daisy to thrive, since it decorates grassy places everywhere. The solitary flowers are certainly eye-catching, like giant daisies up to 60mm across.

Long white outer florets

Sparsely hairy unbranched stems

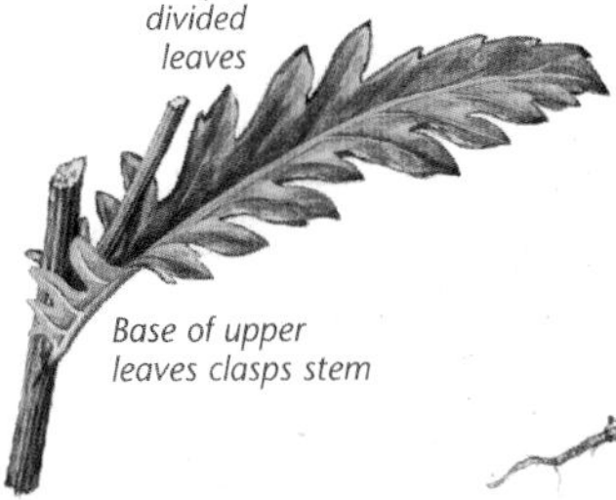

Deeply divided leaves

Base of upper leaves clasps stem

i

Ox-eye daisy

Leucanthemum vulgare

20-75cm

| J | F | M | A | M | J |
| J | A | S | O | N | D |

Widespread on most good soil; less common in northern Scotland.

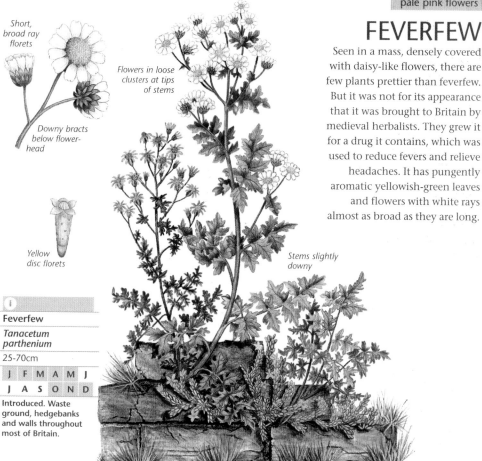

Short, broad ray florets

Flowers in loose clusters at tips of stems

Downy bracts below flower-head

Yellow disc florets

Stems slightly downy

FEVERFEW

Seen in a mass, densely covered with daisy-like flowers, there are few plants prettier than feverfew. But it was not for its appearance that it was brought to Britain by medieval herbalists. They grew it for a drug it contains, which was used to reduce fevers and relieve headaches. It has pungently aromatic yellowish-green leaves and flowers with white rays almost as broad as they are long.

ⓘ

Feverfew

Tanacetum parthenium

25-70cm

| J | F | M | A | M | J |
| J | A | S | O | N | D |

Introduced. Waste ground, hedgebanks and walls throughout most of Britain.

COMMON MEADOW-RUE

The flowers of this perennial plant, a relative of the anemones, have four small sepals and many long, rigid, pollen-bearing stamens which give the head a fluffy look. Its stem is grooved and hairless and usually has no branches. The leaves are dark green above and paler below, and divided into numerous segments. Lesser meadow-rue is more slender and has drooping stamens. It grows in grassland or on dunes.

Leaves much divided

The petal-like sepals are whitish but the many stamens make clusters look yellow

Lesser meadow-rue
Thalictrum minus

Stamens droop

i

Common meadow-rue

Thalictrum flavum

60-120cm

J F M A M J
J A S O N D

Wet ground, mainly in southern and eastern England.

GREATER CELANDINE

Ants feed on the oil glands of the plant's black seeds and carry off the seeds stuck to their bodies. The flowers, up to 25mm across, grow in clusters on leafy stems. The leaves, which are blue-green underneath, are almost hairless and the terminal leaf is usually three-lobed. The caustic orange sap of greater celandine has been used since ancient times for burning away warts and corns.

Stems leafy

Flowers in clusters

Rounded leaflets, blue-green beneath

i

Greater celandine

Chelidonium majus

30-90cm

| J | F | M | A | **M** | **J** |
| **J** | **A** | **S** | O | N | D |

Hedgerows and banks, usually near habitation; uncommon in Scotland and western Ireland.

YELLOW HORNED POPPY

The horned poppy is one of the most colourful of Britain's seashore plants. Its flowers are up to 90mm across. These are pollinated by small flies of the shingle and sand-dunes, and are followed in autumn by long, narrow seed-pods – the 'horns' of its name. These grow up to 30cm long and are more like the pods of some members of the cabbage family than those of cornfield poppies. The yellow sap is foul-smelling, and all parts of the plant are poisonous.

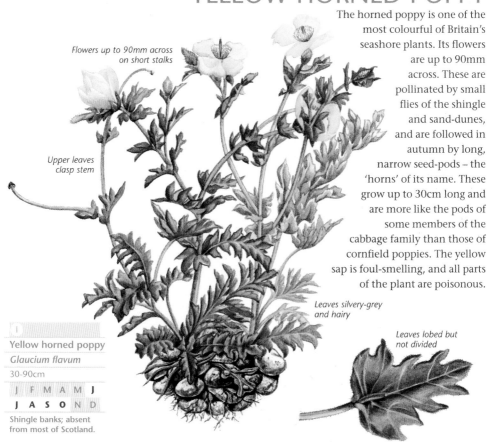

Flowers up to 90mm across on short stalks

Upper leaves clasp stem

Leaves silvery-grey and hairy

Leaves lobed but not divided

i

Yellow horned poppy

Glaucium flavum

30-90cm

| J | F | M | A | M | J |
| J | A | S | O | N | D |

Shingle banks; absent from most of Scotland.

WELSH POPPY

The Welsh poppy still grows in the wild in damp upland woods and rocky places, but is now more commonly found as a garden escape. It has many branches on its sparsely hairy stem. The leaves at the base have long stalks while the upper ones are much shorter. Each stem is crowned by a single flower. The ripe seed capsule opens by flaps at the top. The sap is yellow.

Ripe capsule has ribs

Flowers up to 75mm across on long stalks

Bright green leaves divided into many leaflets

Welsh poppy

Meconopsis cambrica

30-60cm

J	F	M	A	**M**	**J**
J	**A**	S	O	N	D

Damp, shady soil in most of the British Isles.

LADY'S BEDSTRAW

Legend says the Virgin Mary lay on a bed of this plant in Bethlehem, hence the name and the belief that it led to safe and easy childbirth. The dried plant, which smells of new-mown hay, was commonly used to stuff mattresses. The stems, upright or sprawling, are often tinged light brown, with short hairs. They bear whorls of unstalked leaves, which are single-veined, also with short hairs. The related crosswort has similar flowers, but its sprawling stem is yellow-green and its very hairy broader leaves have three veins.

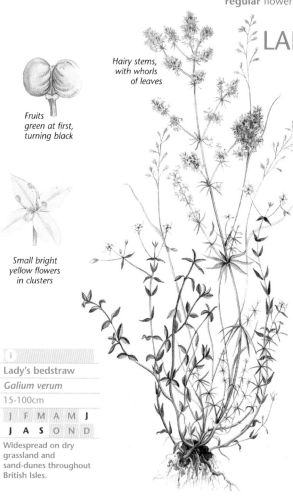

Fruits green at first, turning black

Hairy stems, with whorls of leaves

Small bright yellow flowers in clusters

i

Lady's bedstraw

Galium verum

15-100cm

J F M A M J
J A S O N D

Widespread on dry grassland and sand-dunes throughout British Isles.

Leaves in whorls of four

Crosswort
Cruciata laevipes

LARGE-FLOWERED EVENING PRIMROSE

The flowers of large-flowered evening primrose open at dusk and emit a delicate fragrance which attracts night-flying moths. The blooms are up to 80mm across and arranged in spikes on a sturdy stem. The leaves are set alternately round the stem. The large-flowered evening primrose was introduced from North America as a garden flower, but escaped. Evening primroses are related to the willowherb rather than the primrose family. Several species are naturalised in southern Britain, and these cross-breed making identification very difficult.

Large cup-shaped flowers in spike

Red hairs on stem

Narrow-toothed leaves

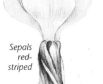

Sepals red-striped

i						

Large-flowered evening primrose

Oenothera glazioviana

50-180cm

J	F	M	A	M	**J**
J	**A**	**S**	O	N	D

Dunes and waste ground in England, Wales and a few parts of southern Scotland.

WELD

The greenish-yellow flowers of weld turn on their stalks during the day to follow the sun. The upright, hairless stem bears narrow leaves with wavy edges. A brilliant yellow dye produced from weld, or dyer's rocket, has been used since the Stone Age.

Wild mignonette is a shorter plant, growing to only 75cm, and differs from weld in having divided leaves and flowers with six petals, arranged in shorter broader spikes.

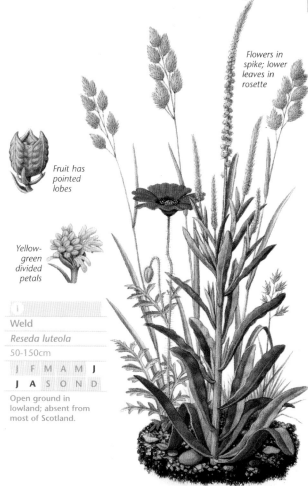

Fruit has pointed lobes

Yellow-green divided petals

Flowers in spike; lower leaves in rosette

i
Weld
Reseda luteola
50-150cm

J	F	M	A	M	**J**
J	**A**	S	O	N	D

Open ground in lowland; absent from most of Scotland.

Divided leaves

Wild mignonette
Reseda lutea

YELLOW BIRD'S-NEST

This waxy-looking plant grows in the darkest parts of woods, usually among pine and beech. It does not need sunlight and feeds on the decaying vegetable matter that covers the woodland floor. The simple, unbranched stem bears unstalked scale-like leaves. The plant's common name comes from the tangle of short, fleshy branched roots which look something like a bird's nest. No part of the plant is green.

Flower-head upright when fruits ripen

Whole plant brownish-yellow or ivory-coloured

Bell-shaped flowers sometimes have five petals instead of four

Yellow bird's-nest

Monotropa hypopitys

7.5-30cm

J	F	M	A	M	**J**
J	**A**	S	O	N	D

Very local in woodlands and on sand-dunes, mainly in southern England.

ANNUAL WALL-ROCKET

A common alternative name for annual wall-rocket is stinkweed, because its stem contains sulphuretted hydrogen, the 'rotten eggs' chemical beloved by schoolboys for making stink-bombs. Its unbranched stem carries upright seed-pods, each half of which contains two rows of yellow-brown seeds – the Latin name *diplotaxis* means 'double row'. The petals are twice as long as the sepals, which sometimes spread slightly.

Few leaves on stem

Fruit cylindrical with two rows of seeds in each half

Annual wall-rocket

Diplotaxis muralis

15-60cm

J F **M A M J**
J A S O N D

Common on walls, and waste and sandy ground, mainly in southern and eastern England.

Lobed leaves form rosette at base

Petals almost twice as long as sepals

TREACLE MUSTARD

Herbalists used treacle mustard to counteract animal bites and poison in the 16th century, and its seeds were given to children to drive out intestinal worms. Its leaves may be smooth-edged or have shallow teeth; the lower ones have stalks but the upper ones do not. The young flower-head is flat-topped and the seed-pods are downy.

A close relation, the wallflower is easily identified by its much larger, fragrant flowers and hairy fruits, which are round in cross-section.

Fruit square in cross-section

Erect, leafy stem

Petals almost twice as long as sepals

Fruit round in cross-section

Wallflower
Cheiranthus cheiri

Treacle mustard

Erysimum cheiranthoides

15-60cm

J F M **A M J**
J A S O N D

Probably introduced. Cultivated and waste ground; rare in north and west of Britain.

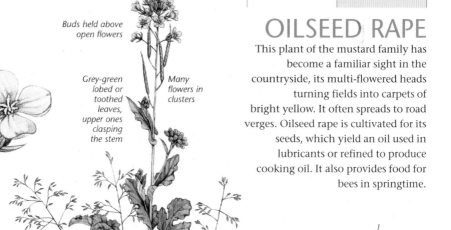

Buds held above open flowers

Grey-green lobed or toothed leaves, upper ones clasping the stem

Many flowers in clusters

Petals open flat

OILSEED RAPE

This plant of the mustard family has become a familiar sight in the countryside, its multi-flowered heads turning fields into carpets of bright yellow. It often spreads to road verges. Oilseed rape is cultivated for its seeds, which yield an oil used in lubricants or refined to produce cooking oil. It also provides food for bees in springtime.

Long, narrow seed-pods project at angle from stem

ⓘ

Oilseed rape

Brassica napus ssp. *oleifera*

To 150cm

| J | F | M | A | M | J |
| J | A | S | O | N | D |

Widespread on farmland and roadsides throughout Britain; rare in Ireland.

BLACK MUSTARD

The flower-heads of black mustard used to paint splashes of yellow across the countryside much as oilseed rape does today. It was grown for its black-brown seeds, which are still used to make mustard and the oil from the seeds is used in soap and some medicines. Today, however, rape is a more profitable crop, and fields of black mustard are much rarer. The plant persists as a weed, however, long after fields have been cleared. The long seed-pods grow upright and hug the stem.

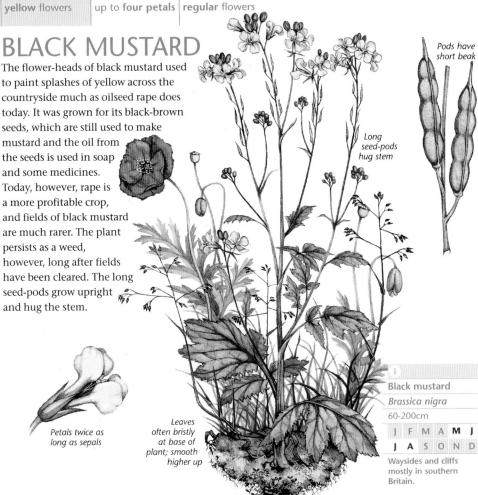

Pods have short beak

Long seed-pods hug stem

Petals twice as long as sepals

Leaves often bristly at base of plant; smooth higher up

Black mustard

Brassica nigra

60–200cm

J	F	M	A	**M**	**J**
J	**A**	S	O	N	D

Waysides and cliffs mostly in southern Britain.

CHARLOCK

A choking weed which has been in the past a serious menace to arable land, charlock today is becoming rarer as a result of the use of weed-killers. The pods hold one row of black or dark brown seeds in each half. These seeds can persist in the soil for up to 50 years and may burst forth when old pastures are ploughed. The sepals usually spread out horizontally below the flowers. Charlock was once sold as a vegetable in Ireland.

Sepals usually spread horizontally below flower

Pods held away from stem

Hairy plant

Pods cylindrical with long beak

Charlock

Sinapis arvensis

15-100cm

J F M A **M J**
J A S O N D

Field margins, roadsides and wasteland all over British Isles.

HEDGE MUSTARD

The branches of this common wasteland plant, seen growing with poppies, protrude almost at right angles from the rigid stem, and its upper leaves have their lowest leaflets bent downwards towards the stem. The small flowers produce seed-pods which are held upright, pressed close to the stem. In 16th and 17th-century France, actors, singers and politicians used infusions from this plant as a gargle. In Britain its sap was mixed with honey as a cure for asthma.

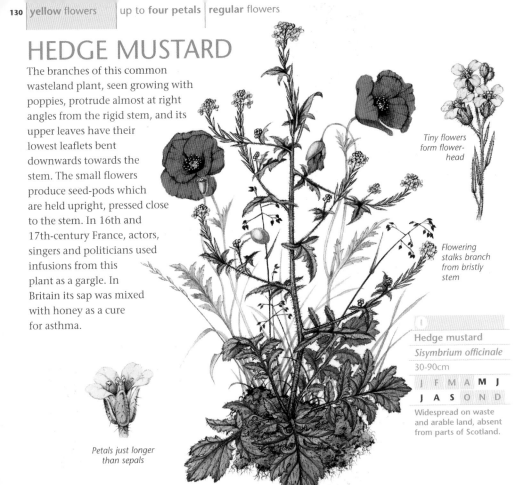

Tiny flowers form flower-head

Flowering stalks branch from bristly stem

Petals just longer than sepals

Hedge mustard
Sisymbrium officinale
30-90cm

| J | F | M | A | M | J |
| J | A | S | O | N | D |

Widespread on waste and arable land, absent from parts of Scotland.

MARSH YELLOW-CRESS

This plant likes a site which is under water in winter but which dries out in summer. The stem is hollow and its leaves are strongly lobed; the base of some leaf-stalks half-clasps the stem. The petals are the same length as the sepals, and the small brown seeds are held in a pointed pod which is about the same length as its stalk. Though a relative of salad cresses, marsh yellow-cress is itself inedible.

Lower leaves stalked, upper ones stalkless

Marsh yellow-cress

Rorippa palustris

25–60cm

J F M A M J
J A S O N D

Widespread on pond sides and river banks; absent from much of Scotland and Wales.

Petals same length as sepals

Fruit oblong and squat

WILD RADISH

This persistant annual was once an irksome weed of arable land. The colour of its flowers varies. Usually they are yellow, but may be white or lilac. The stems are rough and hairy. The fruit bears up to ten seeds in a pod about 50mm long.

The rarer seaside sea radish has leaves divided into many overlapping and crowded leaflets. Its fruit contains no more than five seeds. The flowers are always yellow.

Dark veins on petals

'Waisted' and jointed pod

Lower leaves have up to seven pairs of leaflets; fewer leaflets on upper leaves

Up to ten leaflets

Sea radish
Raphanus raphanistrum
ssp. *maritimus*

Wild radish

Raphanus raphanistrum ssp. *raphanistrum*

20-75cm

| J | F | M | A | M | J |
| J | A | S | O | N | D |

Cultivated and wasteland, rarer in Scotland and Ireland.

WINTER-CRESS

The wallflower-like dense flower spikes of common winter-cress brighten the banks of ditches, streams and ponds in early summer. The hairless plant has a branched stem and the lower leaves are deeply lobed, while the upper ones clasp the stem. The plant is a rich source of vitamin C. Its Latin name comes from St Barbara, the patron saint of gunners, quarrymen and miners, because the leaves were once used to cover wounds caused by explosives.

Petals twice as long as sepals

Flower-head lengthens as fruits develop

Seed-pod with one row of seeds in each half

Hairless plant with shiny leaves

Winter-cress

Barbarea vulgaris

30-90cm

| J | F | M | A | M | J |
| J | A | S | O | N | D |

Hedgebanks and damp places, rarer in Scotland.

TORMENTIL

The four-petalled flower of tormentil distinguishes it from the five-petalled creeping tormentil (page 154). Its upper leaves are stalkless and have three leaflets and two leaf-like appendages called stipules. The sprawling, non-rooting, flowering stems grow from a rosette of leaves that often wither before the flowers appear. Tormentil's astringent roots were the source of a herbal remedy which was used in the 17th century to relieve the 'torment' of toothache and abdominal pains.

Trailing tormentil has four-five petalled flowers and stems which root in early summer.

Stalkless leaves with three leaflets and two leaf-like stipules

Stems grow from rosette of leaves

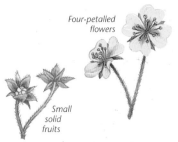

Four-petalled flowers

Small solid fruits

i

Tormentil

Potentilla erecta

5-50cm

J F M **A** **M** **J** **J** **A** **S** O **N** D

Widespread on heaths, moors, grassland and bogs throughout the British Isles.

HONEYSUCKLE

The scent of this climbing plant, also called woodbine, perfumes the air on summer evenings, attracting moths which pollinate the flowers. Its reddish-purple stems climb by twining spirally clockwise around the stems of shrubs and trees in woods and hedges, although they often trail close to the ground. As many as 12 individual creamy-yellow trumpet-shaped flowers cluster in each flower-head. The seeds are contained in bright red berries.

Oval leaves light green on top, bluish below; in opposite pairs

Four-lobed upper lip

Tongue-like lower lip

Woody climbing stems

Honeysuckle

Lonicera periclymenum

Up to 6m

J F M A M **J**
J **A S** O N D

Widespread in woods, hedgerows and scrub throughout the British Isles.

YELLOW ARCHANGEL

Many parts of the yellow archangel resemble white dead-nettle (page 38), but its striking yellow flowers, red-streaked on the lower lip, are a major point of difference. The square flowering stem carries hairy, toothed leaves, and flowers and leaves give off an unpleasant smell when they are bruised. A garden version with white-blotched leaves often escapes into the wild.

The related large-flowered hemp-nettle has a hairier stem and violet-blotched lip on flowers.

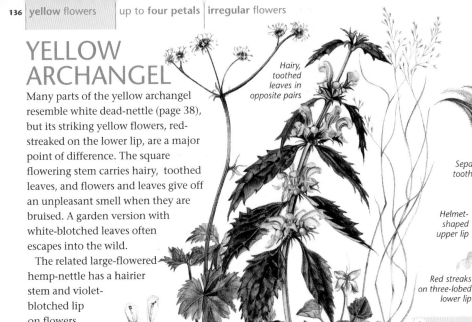

Hairy, toothed leaves in opposite pairs

Sepals form toothed tube

Helmet-shaped upper lip

Red streaks on three-lobed lower lip

Violet-blotched lip

Hairy stem

Large-flowered hemp-nettle
Galeopsis speciosa

Yellow archangel

Lamiastrum galeobdolon

20-60cm

J	F	M	A	**M**	**J**
J	A	S	O	N	D

Old woodland in England and Wales; very rare in Scotland and Ireland.

COMMON BROOMRAPE

This parasitic plant obtains its food by attaching its underground stems to the roots of other plants, especially clovers, wild carrot and some members of the daisy family. It has no green leaves, but the stem has numerous overlapping leaf-like scales. The whole plant is often tinged with red and is in every way smaller than its close relative, greater broomrape, which lives on gorse and broom. The two lips of its petal tube have toothed edges. The plant often damages clover crops.

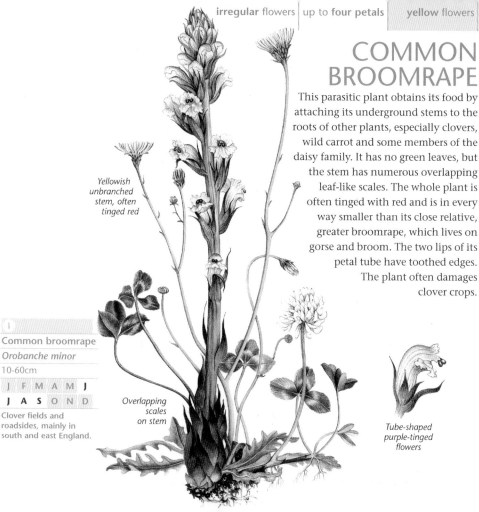

Yellowish unbranched stem, often tinged red

Overlapping scales on stem

Tube-shaped purple-tinged flowers

i

Common broomrape

Orobanche minor

10-60cm

J F M A M **J**
J A S O N D

Clover fields and roadsides, mainly in south and east England.

COMMON TOADFLAX

The plant's name partly derives from its similarity to flax – its leaves are narrow and grow spirally up the stems. But it is the unusual shape of the flowers which attracts the attention. These grow in long spikes of 20 or more, and each has two lips; when the sides of the flower are squeezed, the lips open like a mouth. The flowers are pale yellow, with a distinctive orange swelling on the lower lip.

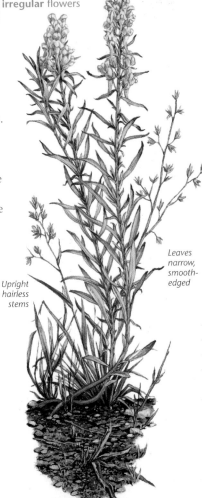

Leaves narrow, smooth-edged

Upright hairless stems

Orange bulge on lower lip closes end of flower tube

Spur at base of flower

Common toadflax

Linaria vulgaris

23-80cm

J	F	M	A	M	J
J	**A**	**S**	O	**N**	D

Road verges, banks and waste ground; absent from most of Ireland and northern Scotland.

MONKEYFLOWER

Not many plants have been introduced into Britain from Alaska, but this is one. It was brought in 1812 from Unalaska Island, where it often rains for 250 days a year. It quickly made itself at home here and now adds a welcome splash of colour to many river banks, with its distinctive, bright yellow petals and red-spotted bulges at the opening to the flower tube. It spreads by means of leafy runners, often choking small streams.

Red-spotted bulges in petal tube

Leaves in pairs

Monkeyflower

Mimulus guttatus

20-75cm

J F M A M **J**
J **A** **S** O N D

By streams and in marshy meadows throughout most of Britain and parts of Ireland.

Lower leaves stalked

Flowers between stem and leaf

Creeping roots

YELLOW RATTLE

Another name for this bright, attractive plant is 'hay rattle' because of the sound produced by the ripe seeds inside their capsule. It is a partly parasitical plant, which fixes its roots on to the root system of an adjoining grass, and extracts water and minerals from it. The stem is covered in short hairs and the narrow, unstalked leaves are regularly toothed. The flower is two-lipped, with two rounded, usually violet teeth on the upper lip and joined, inflated sepals. The fruit is round and flattened.

Stems black-spotted with pairs of narrow, toothed leaves

Two toothed bracts below each pair of flowers

Violet teeth on upper lip

Yellow rattle

Rhinanthus minor

10-50cm

| J | F | M | A | M | J |
| J | A | S | O | N | D |

Grassy places throughout British Isles.

COMMON COW-WHEAT

It was once believed that cows which fed on this plant would produce the finest and yellowest butter, and that pregnant women would bear male children if they ate a flour prepared from the wheat-like seeds. The usually hairless stem carries opposite pairs of untoothed leaves which vary from oval to lance-shaped. Flowers grow in pairs in the angle between a leaf-like bract and the stem and both flowers face the same direction. The petal tube is two-lipped, often with the mouth closed and the lower lip pointing forwards.

Fruit flattened, with up to four smooth, wheat-like seeds

i

Common cow-wheat

Melampyrum pratense

7.5-60 cm

J F M A M J
J A S O N D

Woods, heaths and grassy places throughout Britain.

Stems upright, usually branched

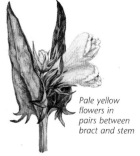

Pale yellow flowers in pairs between bract and stem

GREATER BLADDERWORT

Although a shy flowerer, the greater bladderwort produces attractive flowers which may speckle the surface of deep still waters in summer; but beneath this innocent display lurks a sinister world where tiny bladders wait to trap insects. The bladders, borne on leaves, have hairs at one end. When a water insect brushes these hairs, a trap door is triggered and the insect is drawn into the bladder on the inrush of water. The trap closes and the insect is left to die. The plant absorbs the mineral salts left by its decomposed victim.

Lesser bladderwort has smaller flowers and some shoots bearing only bladders with no leaves. It grows in boggy pools, mainly in northern and western Britain.

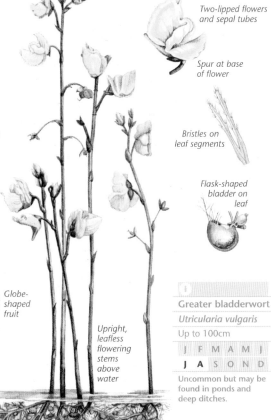

Two-lipped flowers and sepal tubes

Spur at base of flower

Bristles on leaf segments

Flask-shaped bladder on leaf

Globe-shaped fruit

Upright, leafless flowering stems above water

Feathery leaves below water

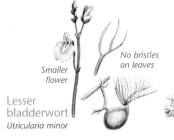

Smaller flower

No bristles on leaves

Lesser bladderwort
Utricularia minor

Greater bladderwort
Utricularia vulgaris
Up to 100cm

J F M A M J
J A S O N D

Uncommon but may be found in ponds and deep ditches.

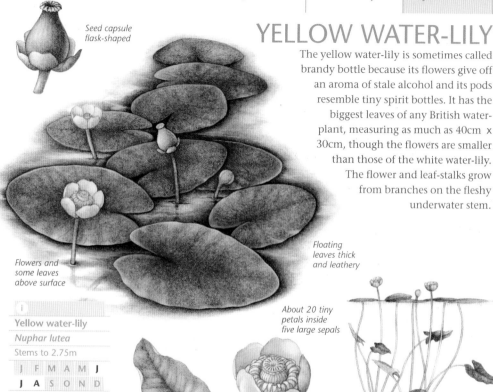

Seed capsule
flask-shaped

YELLOW WATER-LILY

The yellow water-lily is sometimes called brandy bottle because its flowers give off an aroma of stale alcohol and its pods resemble tiny spirit bottles. It has the biggest leaves of any British water-plant, measuring as much as 40cm x 30cm, though the flowers are smaller than those of the white water-lily. The flower and leaf-stalks grow from branches on the fleshy underwater stem.

Floating leaves thick and leathery

Flowers and some leaves above surface

About 20 tiny petals inside five large sepals

Yellow water-lily

Nuphar lutea

Stems to 2.75m

J F M A M **J**
J A S O N D

Still and slow-flowing water; absent from much of northern Scotland and northern England.

Submerged leaves crinkly

Flower yellowish-green on outside

Stout, branched stem

COMMON ROCK-ROSE

Despite its name, common rock-rose is not a rose at all, and has neither scent nor nectar. However, it has abundant pollen to attract insects, and can also pollinate itself. The yellow shade of the flowers can vary, and some forms have an orange spot at the base of each petal. Its narrow leaves have leaf-like stipules at the base.

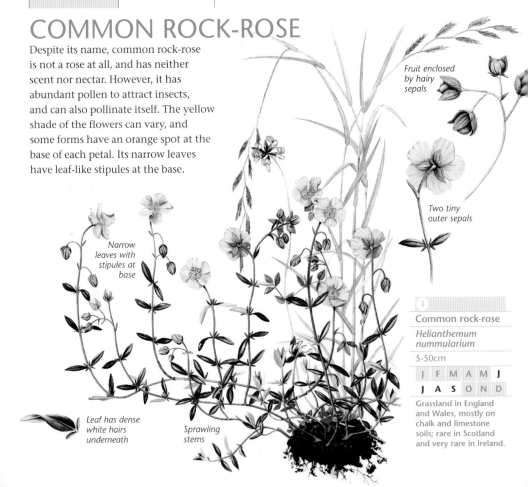

Fruit enclosed by hairy sepals

Two tiny outer sepals

Narrow leaves with stipules at base

Leaf has dense white hairs underneath

Sprawling stems

Common rock-rose

Helianthemum nummularium

5-50cm

J F M A M **J**
J **A** **S** O N D

Grassland in England and Wales, mostly on chalk and limestone soils; rare in Scotland and very rare in Ireland.

TUTSAN

Stamens bristle like pins in a pin-cushion in the flowers of tutsan, which rise in small clusters above large stalkless leaves. Medieval herbalists laid these leaves across flesh wounds to help them to heal, because of the plant's genuine antiseptic properties; its name is derived from the French *toute-saine*, 'all healthy'. When dried, the leaves give off a pleasant smell and they were once used as bookmarks, particularly for Bibles. Unlike other members of the St John's-wort family, the fruit is a berry.

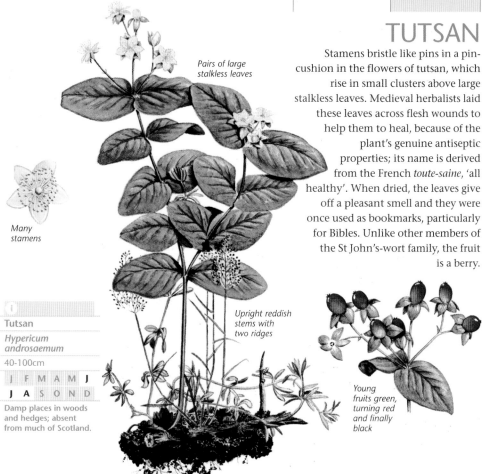

Pairs of large stalkless leaves

Many stamens

Upright reddish stems with two ridges

Young fruits green, turning red and finally black

Tutsan

Hypericum androsaemum

40–100cm

| J | F | M | A | M | J |
| J | A | S | O | N | D |

Damp places in woods and hedges; absent from much of Scotland.

PERFORATE ST JOHN'S-WORT

Translucent glands on the leaves, which look like perforations when held up to the light, give this plant its common and Latin names. It differs from most other similar St John's-worts in having two narrow ridges along its hairless stem. Its flowers are up to 25mm across, with black dots at the edge of the petals and with the stamens grouped in three bundles. During the crusades, the Knights of St John of Jerusalem used the leaves of this plant to heal wounds received in battle.

Imperforate St John's-wort lacks the translucent leaf spots but has square stems, blunt sepals and black spots on the leaves.

Stalkless clear-spotted leaves

Hairless stems, woody at base

Leaves with black spots but no clear dots

Imperforate St John's-wort
Hypericum maculatum

Perforate St John's-wort

Hypericum perforatum

30-80cm

J	F	M	A	M	**J**
J	**A**	**S**	O	N	D

Grassland, hedges and open woods throughout most of Britain.

Black dots at edge of petals

Sepals pointed

SQUARE-STALKED ST JOHN'S-WORT

As its name implies, the shape of the stem is the main distinguishing feature of this species; the squared appearance comes from four narrow wings which run along it. The flowers are similar to those of perforate St John's-wort but only half as large. The petals may have a very few black glands at the edges, while the leaves are stalkless, with many small translucent glands. Marsh St John's-wort has unwinged stems and is covered in white down. Hairy St John's-wort has hairy stems and leaves. It has translucent glands on the leaves and black glands on the flowers and sepals.

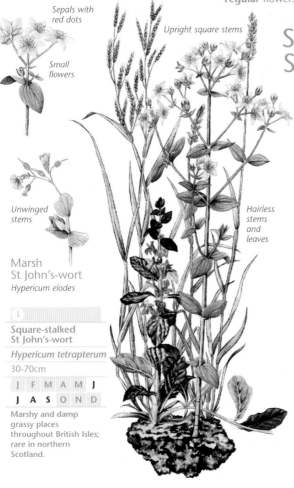

Sepals with red dots

Small flowers

Upright square stems

Hairless stems and leaves

Unwinged stems

Marsh
St John's-wort
Hypericum elodes

**Square-stalked
St John's-wort**

Hypericum tetrapterum

30-70cm

| J | F | M | A | M | J |
| J | A | S | O | N | D |

Marshy and damp grassy places throughout British Isles; rare in northern Scotland.

Black glands on sepals and some petals

Hairy St John's-wort
Hypericum hirsutum

SLENDER ST JOHN'S-WORT

Unlike perforate St John's-wort, slender St John's-wort dislikes lime-rich soils and grows mainly on acid heaths and commons. Its heart-shaped, hairless leaves grow in pairs, their bases clasping the slender, smooth stems. The sepals are rounded and fringed with black glands, and the golden petals have dark red spots at their edges.

Trailing St John's-wort, commonest in the south and west, has sprawling, two-ridged stems and much smaller flowers. Its pale green leaves are oval, with black and transparent dots.

Rounded sepals with black glands

Heart-shaped leaves with transparent dots

Smaller flowers with a few black dots

Sprawling stems

Trailing St John's-wort
Hypericum humifusum

Smooth, unridged stems

i

Slender St John's-wort

Hypericum pulchrum

15-60cm

J	F	M	A	M	J
J	A	S	O	N	D

Woodland fringes and rough grassland, on acid soils, throughout British Isles.

BITING STONECROP

This diminutive plant is sometimes known as wall-pepper because of the sharp taste of its yellowish-green leaves, best avoided because they are poisonous in quantity. Its short stalks are very numerous, some bearing star-like flowers, others with overlapping and succulent leaves. The flowers have broad-based golden petals. The young leaves are tipped with crimson and the young fruits are yellowish, turning brown when they spread apart. Superstition says that if the stonecrop is planted on the roof of a house it will ward off thunderstorms.

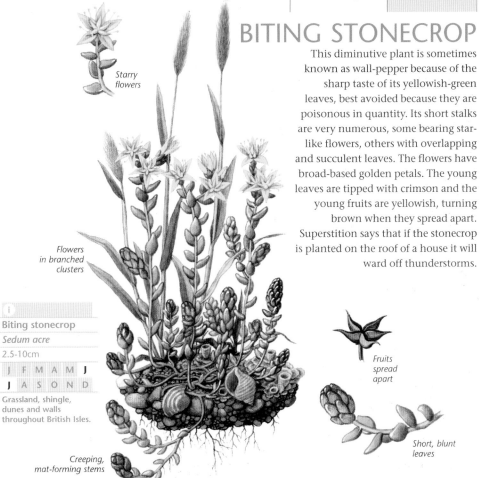

Starry flowers

Flowers in branched clusters

i

Biting stonecrop

Sedum acre

2.5-10cm

| J | F | M | A | M | **J** |
| **J** | A | S | O | N | D |

Grassland, shingle, dunes and walls throughout British Isles.

Fruits spread apart

Short, blunt leaves

Creeping, mat-forming stems

PRIMROSE

Flowering early in the New Year in the West Country, the unmistakable 'first rose' is the herald of spring. Its species name of *vulgaris* means 'common', but unfortunately the plant is less common than it used to be because of over-picking. Primroses produce two kinds of flower, and seeds are produced only when pollen is transferred from one to the other.

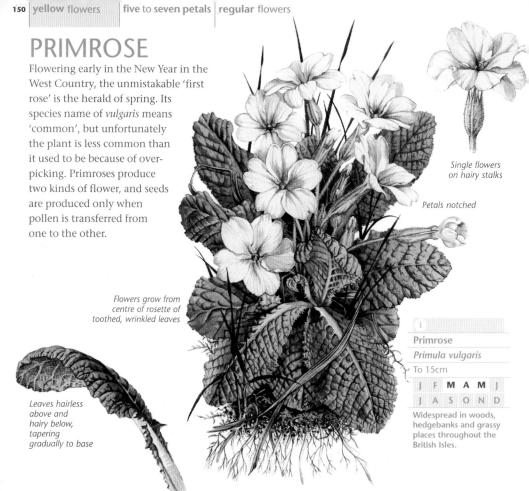

Single flowers on hairy stalks

Petals notched

Flowers grow from centre of rosette of toothed, wrinkled leaves

Leaves hairless above and hairy below, tapering gradually to base

i		
Primrose		
Primula vulgaris		
To 15cm		

J	F	**M**	**A**	**M**	J
J	A	S	O	N	D

Widespread in woods, hedgebanks and grassy places throughout the British Isles.

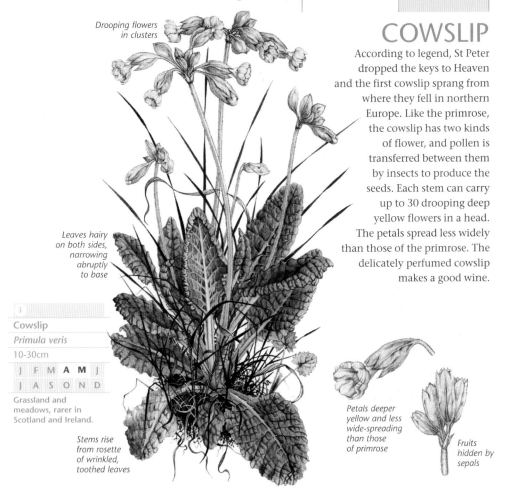

Drooping flowers in clusters

COWSLIP

According to legend, St Peter dropped the keys to Heaven and the first cowslip sprang from where they fell in northern Europe. Like the primrose, the cowslip has two kinds of flower, and pollen is transferred between them by insects to produce the seeds. Each stem can carry up to 30 drooping deep yellow flowers in a head. The petals spread less widely than those of the primrose. The delicately perfumed cowslip makes a good wine.

Leaves hairy on both sides, narrowing abruptly to base

Cowslip

Primula veris

10-30cm

J F **M A M** J
J A S O N D

Grassland and meadows, rarer in Scotland and Ireland.

Stems rise from rosette of wrinkled, toothed leaves

Petals deeper yellow and less wide-spreading than those of primrose

Fruits hidden by sepals

AGRIMONY

A scent of apricots attracts flies and bees to agrimony's slender, crowded spike of little starry flowers. In pagan times the plant was thought to have magical properties; nowadays its leaves, deeply divided into coarsely toothed leaflets, are still used as a stimulating alternative to tea. Fragrant agrimony is a stouter plant, with more branches and fragrant leaves which have many sticky glands underneath.

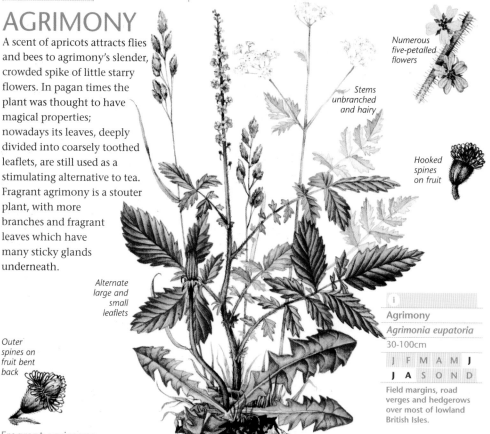

Numerous five-petalled flowers

Stems unbranched and hairy

Hooked spines on fruit

Alternate large and small leaflets

Outer spines on fruit bent back

Fragrant agrimony
Agrimonia procera

i		
Agrimony		
Agrimonia eupatoria		
30-100cm		

J	F	M	A	M	J
J	A	S	O	N	D

Field margins, road verges and hedgerows over most of lowland British Isles.

WOOD AVENS

The alternative name of herb bennet derives from the flower's association with St Benedict. In the 15th century it was widely used to ward off evil spirits. It has downy stems and deeply divided leaves which have a large lobed leaflet at the end. Little leaf-like stipules grow in pairs at the junction of the stem and leaf-stalk.

The flowers are small and widely spread, with a long, hooked hairy style which is retained on the fruit. This catches on the fur of passing animals, dispersing the seeds.

Stipules at base of leaf-stalks

Upper leaves three-lobed

Lower leaves grow from root

Five yellow petals, not overlapping

Fruit with long hooked spine

Fruits form head

Wood avens

Geum urbanum

30–70cm

J F M A M J J A S O N D

Widespread in damp shady places, rarer in Scotland.

SILVERWEED

The long-stalked solitary flowers and the silvery silky-hairy leaves of its many leaflets make silverweed easy to identify. The plant spreads by overground runners, often forming large patches. It was once eaten in western Scotland – its edible roots were said to taste like parsnips.

Creeping tormentil is a related but bigger species, often found in hedgerows. It flowers from June to September.

Large, solitary flowers

Leaflets silvery beneath, or on both sides

Small and large leaflets alternate

Stems spread from rosette of leaves

Creeping tormentil
Potentilla reptans

Silverweed	
Potentilla anserina	
5-25cm	

J F M A **M J**
J A S O N D

Widespread in damp, grassy and waste places, and by roadsides throughout British Isles.

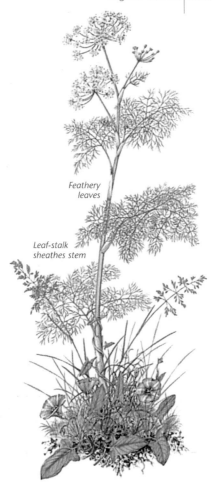

Feathery leaves

Leaf-stalk sheathes stem

FENNEL

With its hairless leaves divided into long thread-like lobes and its distinctive, aniseed smell, fennel is easy to recognise. It is a tall plant, with feathery sprays of bright green leaves, whose stalks sheathe the stems. The plant has no upper or lower bracts. The Romans probably brought it to Britain as a medicine – particularly for indigestion – and to flavour their food.

Fennel

Foeniculum vulgare

60-250cm

J F M A M **J**
J A S O N D

Roadsides, cliffs and waste places especially near sea; mainly in southern and eastern Britain.

GARDEN PARSLEY

Any plant of this species, growing wild in Britain, will have escaped from cultivated stock, which was brought into Britain from the Mediterranean in the Middle Ages. It differs from the presentday cultivated form in not having the deeply curled or frilled leaves which give a delicate feathery quality to the kitchen garden plant. It has, however, the characteristic umbrella-shaped flower-head of the parsley family, with up to 20 branches. The leaf-stalks clasp the stem at their base like a sheath.

Corn parsley has smaller white flower-heads, but bigger, toothed greyish-green leaflets in rows on either side of the stem.

Corn parsley
Petroselinum segetum

Toothed leaflets; large fruits

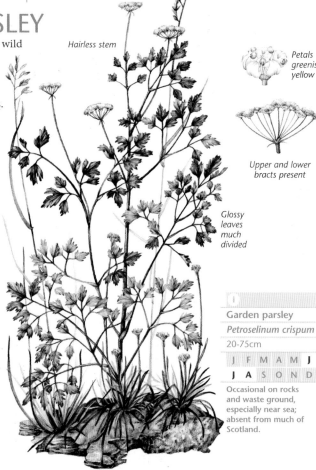

Hairless stem

Glossy leaves much divided

Petals greenish-yellow

Upper and lower bracts present

Garden parsley

Petroselinum crispum

20-75cm

| J | F | M | A | M | J |
| J | A | S | O | N | D |

Occasional on rocks and waste ground, especially near sea; absent from much of Scotland.

PEPPER-SAXIFRAGE

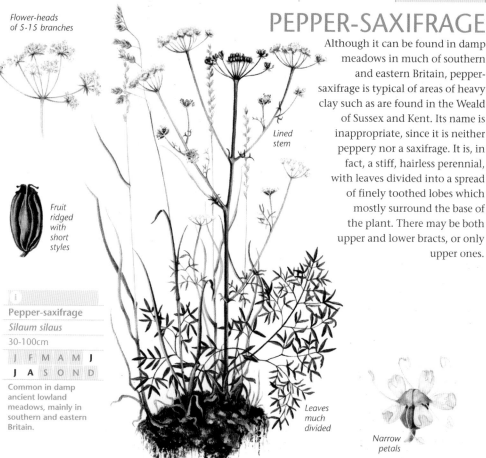

Although it can be found in damp meadows in much of southern and eastern Britain, pepper-saxifrage is typical of areas of heavy clay such as are found in the Weald of Sussex and Kent. Its name is inappropriate, since it is neither peppery nor a saxifrage. It is, in fact, a stiff, hairless perennial, with leaves divided into a spread of finely toothed lobes which mostly surround the base of the plant. There may be both upper and lower bracts, or only upper ones.

Flower-heads of 5-15 branches

Lined stem

Fruit ridged with short styles

i	
Pepper-saxifrage	
Silaum silaus	
30-100cm	

J F M A M **J**
J **A** S O N D

Common in damp ancient lowland meadows, mainly in southern and eastern Britain.

Leaves much divided

Narrow petals

WILD PARSNIP

Like the carrot, the garden parsnip has been developed by long and careful cultivation from its wild and fairly inedible ancestor. The 16th-century herbalist John Gerard described the root of the wild parsnip as 'small, hard, woodie, and not fit to be eaten'. Apart from the root, however, the wild parsnip looks much like its cultivated relation. It is a tall, hairy, strong-smelling plant, with leaves divided into toothed and lobed leaflets. The flowers are clustered at the top of long, branching stems, in large, umbrella-shaped flower-heads.

Angled, rough-haired stem

Flower-heads of 5-10 branches

Upper and lower bracts absent, or few and soon falling

Tiny flowers, petals rolled inwards

Fruits narrowly winged

Leaflets lobed and toothed

Wild parsnip

Pastinaca sativa

30-120cm

| J | F | M | A | M | J |
| J | A | S | O | N | D |

Widespread on dry, grassy and waste ground and on roadsides, mainly in southern and eastern Britain.

ALEXANDERS

A stout, bushy plant with hairless, ridged stems, alexanders often colonises waste ground near the sea, decorating the cliffs with its greenish-yellow flowers in spring and early summer. Its unusual name is a reference to its origins in Macedonia, the country of Alexander the Great. All the plant is edible. The dark green leaves are used as a herb and to flavour a white sauce; the young stems can be cooked and eaten like asparagus; the flower-buds are sometimes used in salads and even the roots can be cooked and eaten as a substitute for parsnip. The fruits are black when ripe.

Many-branched flower-head

Curved petals

Leaf-stalks sheathe stem

Ridged stem

Toothed, glossy leaflets

Alexanders

Smyrnium olusatrum

45-150cm

J F **M A M J**
J A S O N D

Widespread in hedgebanks and on waste ground near sea.

YELLOW PIMPERNEL

A creeping plant which is a member of the primrose family, yellow pimpernel has oval leaves, with very short stalks, in opposite pairs. The five-petalled flowers grow singly from the base of leaf-stalks. The sepals are long and narrow but lack the orange margin found on yellow loosestrife. The seed capsules are globe-shaped.

Creeping Jenny thrives in similar conditions to yellow pimpernel and is also grown in rock gardens and hanging baskets. Its leaves are rounder and its flowers only half open, with broader sepals. The flowers and leaves are black-dotted.

Long, narrow sepals, with no orange margin

Flowers fully open

Slender, sprawling stems

Flowers grow singly from base of leaf-stalk

Fruit globe-shaped

Bright green, pointed leaves, in pairs

Flowers only half open

Sepals broader

Rounded leaves

Creeping Jenny
Lysimachia nummularia

Yellow pimpernel

Lysimachia nemorum

To 40cm

| J | F | M | A | M | J |
| J | A | S | O | N | D |

Woods and shady hedges, throughout most of British Isles.

YELLOW LOOSESTRIFE

The willow-like leaves on this plant grow either in pairs or in whorls of three to four, their upper surface dotted with minute orange or black glands. The tops are bright green and the undersides rather bluish-green. Yellow loosestrife often grows in large colonies, spread by strong underground and overground stems. Dotted loosestrife often escapes from gardens into the wild. The flowers grow in tight groups at the base of leaves up most of the stem, and the sepals have no orange edge.

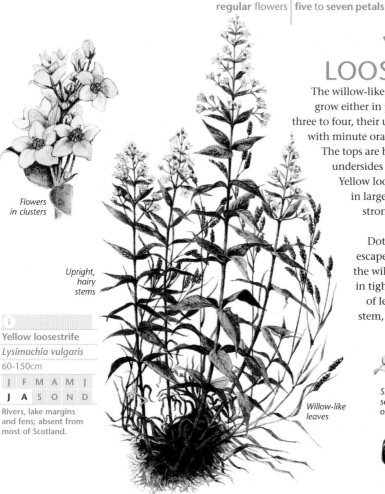

Flowers in clusters

Upright, hairy stems

Willow-like leaves

Yellow loosestrife

Lysimachia vulgaris

60-150cm

J F M A M J
J A S O N D

Rivers, lake margins and fens; absent from most of Scotland.

Short sepals with orange margins

Fruit globe-shaped

GREAT MULLEIN

The tall stems of great mullein are sturdy and usually unbranched. The leaves are grey from their dense covering of white hairs, and their edges run down the stem. Yellow five-petalled flowers are borne tightly packed in spikes at the tops of the stems. The three upper stamens are woolly, the lower two hairless. Great mullein is a biennial, producing a rosette of woolly leaves in the first year and a tall flowering stem the following year. The plant then dies. The is the commonest of the British mulleins.

Densely packed flowers in single spike

Edges of upper leaves run down stem

Leaves covered with dense white hairs

Upper stamens have hairy filaments

Great mullein

Verbascum thapsus

30–200cm

J	F	M	A	M	J
J	A	S	O	N	D

Waste ground and sunny banks, rarer in Scotland and Ireland.

DARK MULLEIN

The flower spikes of dark mullein are less compact than those of great mullein, and the stems carry smaller, darker leaves, which are hairy but not woolly. The bases of the lower leaves are heart-shaped. Between five and ten flowers rise from the base of each bract. There are purple spots at the base of the petals, and all five stamens are densely covered with purple hairs.

Looser flower spike, stems often branched

Hairy stem and leaves

Dark green leaves have long stalk

Flowers in clusters; purple spots at base of petals

i
Dark mullein
Verbascum nigrum
50-120cm

J	F	M	A	M	J
J	A	S	O	N	D

Waysides and open banks, mainly in southern and eastern England; absent from Ireland and most of Scotland.

TUBEROUS COMFREY

The name refers to the plant's stout, tuber-like root; but above ground it differs from common comfrey (page 255) also in having a smaller, more slender outline and an upright, hairy stem that has few branches. The middle leaves are larger than those near the base and the edges of the upper leaves run a short distance down the stem.

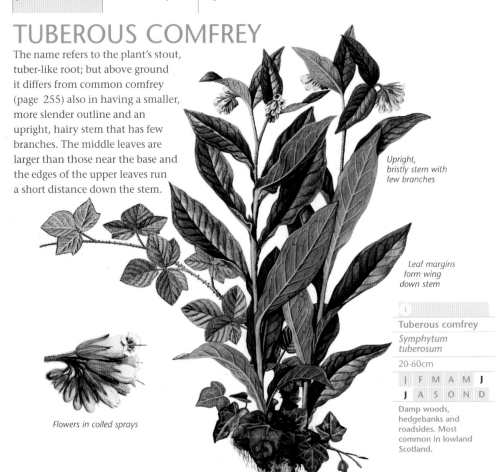

Upright, bristly stem with few branches

Leaf margins form wing down stem

Flowers in coiled sprays

i

Tuberous comfrey

Symphytum tuberosum

20-60cm

J	F	M	A	M	**J**
J	A	S	O	N	D

Damp woods, hedgebanks and roadsides. Most common in lowland Scotland.

MARSH-MARIGOLD

As early as March, Marsh-marigolds light up damp places with their brilliant golden flowers and glossy leaves. The plants continue flowering well into summer and are at their most luxuriant in partial shade. The flowers are sometimes as much as 50mm across, with as many as 100 stamens. The heart-shaped leaves have long stalks and are dark green. What seem to be five petals are in fact glossy yellow sepals. The whole plant is hairless.

Leaves heart-shaped, dark green and shiny

i						
Marsh-marigold

Caltha palustris

30-60cm

| J | F | **M** | **A** | **M** | **J** |
| **J** | **A** | S | O | N | D |

Marshes, ditches and beside ponds and streams all over Britain and Ireland.

Many stamens

GOLDILOCKS BUTTERCUP

A striking feature of this buttercup is the flawed appearance of many of its flowers, which give the impression of having been pecked by birds. One flower may have up to five petals while others have none at all, and many of the petals are small and malformed. Goldilocks has deeply divided upper leaves, but the lower ones vary greatly in shape. Overall, it looks like a smaller and less hairy meadow buttercup. It is the main British woodland species.

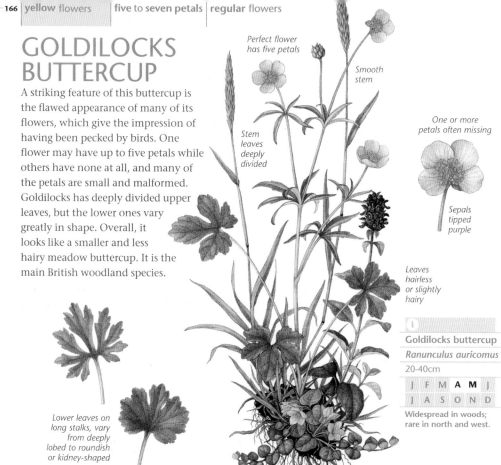

Perfect flower has five petals

Smooth stem

Stem leaves deeply divided

One or more petals often missing

Sepals tipped purple

Leaves hairless or slightly hairy

Lower leaves on long stalks, vary from deeply lobed to roundish or kidney-shaped

i

Goldilocks buttercup

Ranunculus auricomus

20-40cm

| J | F | **M** | **A** | **M** | J |
| J | A | S | O | N | D |

Widespread in woods; rare in north and west.

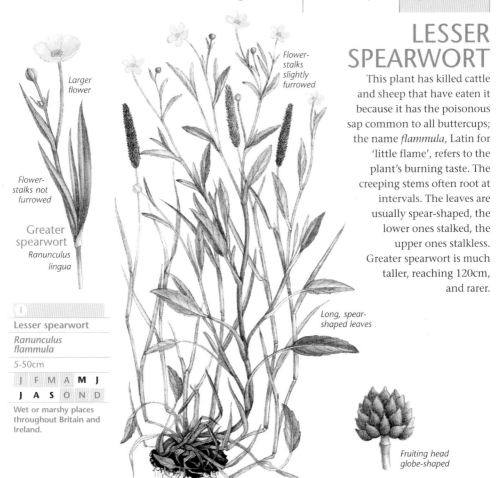

Larger flower

Flower-stalks not furrowed

Greater spearwort
Ranunculus lingua

Flower-stalks slightly furrowed

LESSER SPEARWORT

This plant has killed cattle and sheep that have eaten it because it has the poisonous sap common to all buttercups; the name *flammula*, Latin for 'little flame', refers to the plant's burning taste. The creeping stems often root at intervals. The leaves are usually spear-shaped, the lower ones stalked, the upper ones stalkless. Greater spearwort is much taller, reaching 120cm, and rarer.

Long, spear-shaped leaves

i

Lesser spearwort

Ranunculus flammula

5–50cm

| J | F | M | A | M | J |
| J | A | S | O | N | D |

Wet or marshy places throughout Britain and Ireland.

Fruiting head globe-shaped

MEADOW BUTTERCUP

Fields bright with meadow buttercups are a less common sight than they once were, as traditional meadows are ploughed and resown with grass and clover. But where they still occur they are one of the most delightful sights of early summer. The meadow buttercup is taller than bulbous and creeping buttercups. The leaves are hairy and deeply cut, while the flowers are on smooth stalks on a branching stem.

The bulbous buttercup flowers earlier than the meadow species, from March onwards, and prefers drier grassland. It is rarer in northern and western Britain.

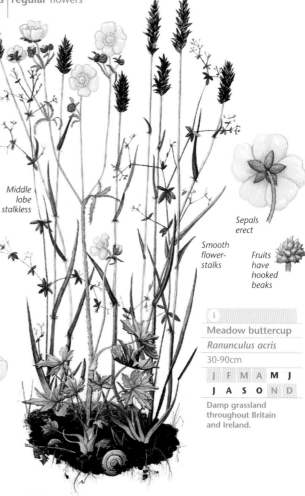

Middle lobe stalkless

Sepals erect

Smooth flower-stalks

Fruits have hooked beaks

i		
Meadow buttercup		
Ranunculus acris		
30-90cm		

J	F	M	**A**	**M**	**J**
J	**A**	**S**	O	N	D

Damp grassland throughout Britain and Ireland.

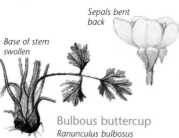

Sepals bent back

Base of stem swollen

Bulbous buttercup
Ranunculus bulbosus

Stem and leaves hairy

Flowers with erect sepals

Fruits in globe-shaped head

Three leaflets, middle one stalked

i
Creeping buttercup
Ranunculus repens
5-50cm
J F M A **M** **J**
J **A** S O N D

Widespread on disturbed land, damp pasture and roadsides.

CREEPING BUTTERCUP

This might well be called the problem buttercup, for its creeping overground runners can spread rapidly, in time taking over whole fields. In pastureland this can be serious, for like all buttercups it is poisonous. Cattle avoid it, but as they eat the grass around the buttercup, so they make room for it to spread, until the whole field is covered. The glossy-petalled flowers are borne on furrowed stalks, and the sepals are erect. Celery-leaved buttercup has smaller flowers with down-turned sepals and hairless, shiny, pale green leaves without a stalked middle lobe.

Smaller flowers

Celery-leaved buttercup
Ranunculus sceleratus

Long fruit

BOG ASPHODEL

The bog asphodel brings welcome splashes of colour to many sombre moors throughout Britain. In fact, it offers more than one colour, depending on the season. When its flowers are out, growing at the top of the stem in short spikes, they are a brilliant orange-yellow. Then in autumn, after flowering, the fruits, leaves and flower-stalks take on a peachy tint before turning deep orange. Its flattened leaves are like those of the iris, and its seeds have long tails at each end which help them to float during periods of flooding.

Flowers in spike at top of stem

Fruit has brown seeds with tail

Short leaves sheathe stem

Stamens woolly, with orange tips

i		
Bog asphodel		
Narthecium ossifragum		
5-45cm		

J	F	M	A	M	J
J	**A**	**S**	O	N	D

Bogs, moors and mountains, mainly in the north and west.

WILD DAFFODIL

The poet William Wordsworth made the wild daffodil very much his own. It is rare in Scotland and absent from most of Ireland. Even in England it has suffered from the depredations of drainage schemes. But its bright, nodding flowers can still be seen in abundance in damp woods in parts of England and Wales. They are smaller than most of the 10,000 cultivated forms, with a darker yellow 'trumpet' as long as the outer lobes of the flower.

Single flower on stem

Fruit splits into three parts when ripe

---

i

Wild daffodil

Narcissus pseudonarcissus

To 36cm

J **F M A** M J
J A S O N D

Widespread in damp open woodland, heathland, common and meadow in southern and western England and Wales.

Bluish-green leaves, all growing from base

Outer lobes of flower pale yellow around darker yellow trumpet

Papery spathe protects bud

YELLOW IRIS

This handsome flower is also called yellow flag, possibly recalling Clovis, the 5th-century king of the Franks, who first wore the iris as a heraldic device. Its leaves are sharp-edged and sword-shaped, and can cut if not handled carefully. But it is the flower which makes this such a striking plant, especially when seen in large clumps, usually on the edge of pools and streams. Each stem bears two or three flower buds, wrapped in a papery spathe. The huge green seed capsules are almost as conspicuous as the flowers, and last well into autumn.

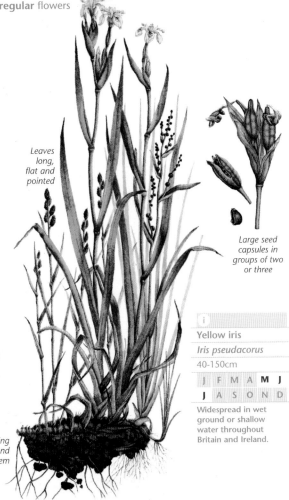

Leaves long, flat and pointed

Large seed capsules in groups of two or three

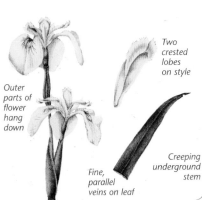

Outer parts of flower hang down

Two crested lobes on style

Fine, parallel veins on leaf

Creeping underground stem

Yellow iris

Iris pseudacorus

40-150cm

J	F	M	A	**M**	**J**
J	A	S	O	N	D

Widespread in wet ground or shallow water throughout Britain and Ireland.

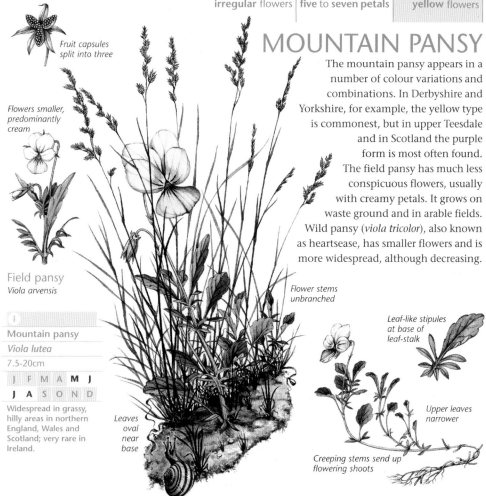

Fruit capsules split into three

Flowers smaller, predominantly cream

Field pansy
Viola arvensis

i

Mountain pansy

Viola lutea

7.5–20cm

J F M A **M J**
J A S O N D

Widespread in grassy, hilly areas in northern England, Wales and Scotland; very rare in Ireland.

Leaves oval near base

MOUNTAIN PANSY

The mountain pansy appears in a number of colour variations and combinations. In Derbyshire and Yorkshire, for example, the yellow type is commonest, but in upper Teesdale and in Scotland the purple form is most often found. The field pansy has much less conspicuous flowers, usually with creamy petals. It grows on waste ground and in arable fields. Wild pansy (*viola tricolor*), also known as heartsease, has smaller flowers and is more widespread, although decreasing.

Flower stems unbranched

Leaf-like stipules at base of leaf-stalk

Upper leaves narrower

Creeping stems send up flowering shoots

DYER'S GREENWEED

Resembling a dwarf broom, dyer's greenweed was used in the 14th century by Flemish immigrants for the yellow dye it produced. Cloth dipped in the dye turns bright yellow, then green when dipped again in a solution of blue woad. The dye was known as Kendal green, after the Cumbrian town where it was developed. The plant's smooth stems carry stalkless, undivided leaves and flowers in spikes at their tips.

The less common petty whin has much smaller flowers and fruit, and usually has a spiny stem. It flowers in May and June on moors and heaths scattered over much of mainland Britain.

Spikes of flowers at tips of shoots

Flat, hairless pods

Smooth green stems

Smooth leaves

Pods swollen

Spiny stem

Petty whin
Genista anglica

Dyer's greenweed

Genista tinctoria

30-60cm

J	F	M	A	M	**J**
J	**A**	S	O	N	D

Clay grassland in England, Wales and southern Scotland.

Many flowers in globe-shaped head

Dark spot on leaflet

Spotted medick
Medicago arabica

Rounded leaflets, with tiny points

Black medick

Medicago lupulina

5-60cm

J	F	M	A	**M**	**J**
J	**A**	S	O	N	D

Grassy places in Britain and Ireland; rarer in Scotland.

BLACK MEDICK

The name of black medick, here seen growing with silverweed, has nothing to do with medicine: it means plant of the Medes, a people of ancient Persia. It has trefoil leaves, and is distinguished from the similar lesser trefoil (page 177) by a tiny pointed tip in the rounded end of each toothed leaflet. The flower-head contains between 10 and 50 separate flowers, and the black pods are coiled, unlike the straight pods of clover. Spotted medick has a spot on each leaflet, no more than five flowers in each head and a seed-pod that is spirally coiled and spiny.

Seed-pods black and coiled

COMMON BIRD'S-FOOT TREFOIL

The word trefoil suggests that each leaf has only three leaflets. In bird's-foot trefoil, however, each leaf has an extra pair of leaflets close to the stem. The red streaks sometimes seen on the flowers give the plant the alternative common name of 'bacon-and-eggs'. The seed-pods are arranged like the toes of a bird's foot. Greater bird's-foot trefoil has a hollow and more upright stem. It prefers damper ground.

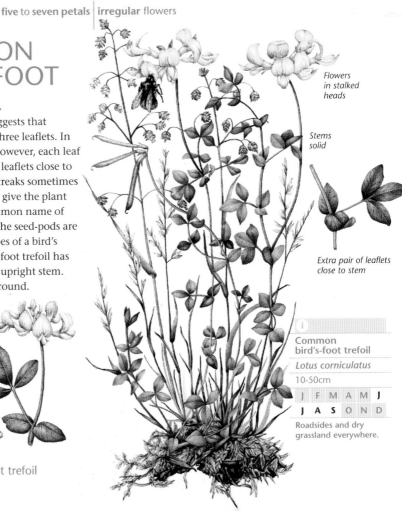

Flowers in stalked heads

Stems solid

Extra pair of leaflets close to stem

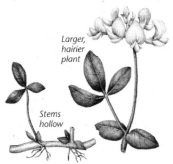

Larger, hairier plant

Stems hollow

Greater bird's-foot trefoil
Lotus pedunculatus

i		
Common bird's-foot trefoil		
Lotus corniculatus		
10-50cm		

J	F	M	A	M	**J**
J	**A**	**S**	O	N	D

Roadsides and dry grassland everywhere.

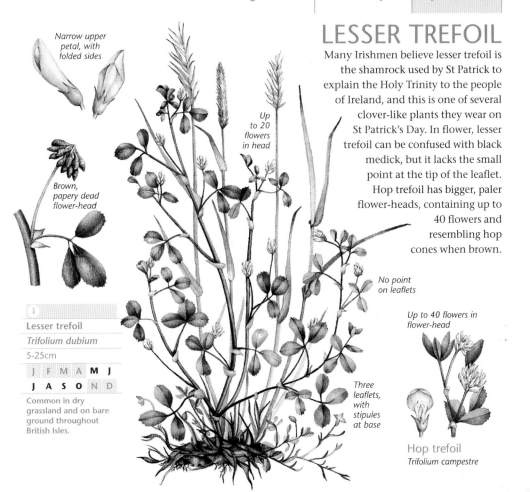

Narrow upper petal, with folded sides

Brown, papery dead flower-head

LESSER TREFOIL

Many Irishmen believe lesser trefoil is the shamrock used by St Patrick to explain the Holy Trinity to the people of Ireland, and this is one of several clover-like plants they wear on St Patrick's Day. In flower, lesser trefoil can be confused with black medick, but it lacks the small point at the tip of the leaflet. Hop trefoil has bigger, paler flower-heads, containing up to 40 flowers and resembling hop cones when brown.

Up to 20 flowers in head

No point on leaflets

Three leaflets, with stipules at base

Lesser trefoil

Trifolium dubium

5-25cm

J	F	M	A	**M**	**J**
J	**A**	**S**	**O**	N	D

Common in dry grassland and on bare ground throughout British Isles.

Up to 40 flowers in flower-head

Hop trefoil
Trifolium campestre

TALL MELILOT

The two yellow-flowered melilots can be most easily distinguished by the shape of their flowers. In that of tall melilot the lower petal, or keel, is the same length as the wing petals on each side and the petal above; in ribbed melilot the lower petal is shorter than the others. Tall melilot has golden-yellow coloured flowers, while those of ribbed melilot are lemon-yellow. The flowers of both species are a rich source of nectar for honey-bees. The seed-pods of tall melilot are egg-shaped, hairy and black. The name 'tall melilot' is misleading as ribbed melilot tends to be the taller of the two plants.

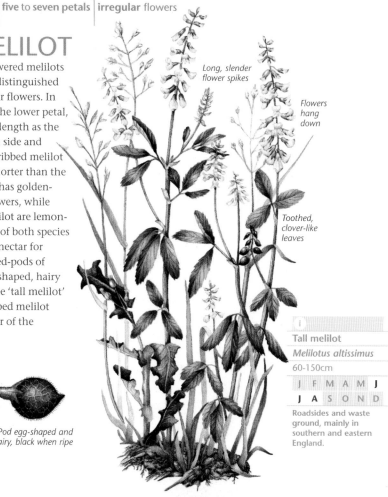

Long, slender flower spikes

Flowers hang down

Toothed, clover-like leaves

Pod egg-shaped and hairy, black when ripe

Tall melilot

Melilotus altissimus

60-150cm

| J | F | M | A | M | J |
| J | A | S | O | N | D |

Roadsides and waste ground, mainly in southern and eastern England.

RIBBED MELILOT

Although the leaves of ribbed melilot resemble those of clover, the flowers are quite different, being borne in long spikes. They develop into brown, hairless pods with the wrinkles that give the species its name. The lower petal or 'keel' is shorter than that of tall melilot. Melilots were introduced from Europe in the 16th century as a fodder crop. The dried plant smells of new-mown hay.

Flowers in long tapering spikes

Trefoil leaves

Ribbed melilot

Melilotus officinalis

60-150cm

| J | F | M | A | M | J |
| J | A | S | O | N | D |

Common on roadsides and embankments, especially in the south and east.

Seed-pod wrinkled and hairless, brown when ripe

Short lower petal

HORSESHOE VETCH

The golden mat of horseshoe vetch that spreads beneath a walker's feet hides a cunning natural mechanism for perpetuating the species. The weight of a bee landing on the joined lower petals causes a string of pollen to be ejected onto the insect, which it then carries to another flower. The plant's flowers are occasionally red-veined.

Flowers in clusters of four to eight

Base of each petal narrow and extended

Each leaf has 7 to 25 leaflets

Two stipules at leaf base

Seed-pods have horseshoe-shaped segments which separate when ripe

J	F	M	A	**M**	**J**
J	**A**	**S**	**O**	**N**	D

Horseshoe vetch

Hippocrepis comosa

10-30cm

Chalk and limestone grassland and cliffs in England and Wales.

Many trailing stems from woody rootstock

KIDNEY VETCH

The old idea that kidney vetch could cure kidney diseases is now known to be false. There is more aptness in the plant's alternative name of lady's fingers, a reference to the silky, finger-like bracts which appear just below the flower-heads. The seeds are borne in pods enclosed by the woolly, purple-tipped sepals. Each leaf carries pairs of leaflets with a terminal leaflet, all of which are green above and silky white beneath. Although the flowers are usually yellow, they may be red, orange or pink.

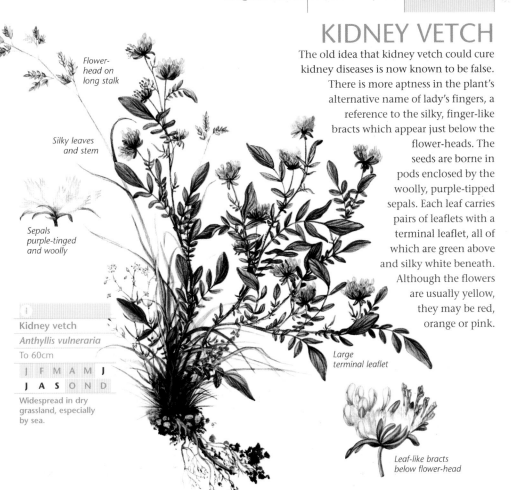

Flower-head on long stalk

Silky leaves and stem

Sepals purple-tinged and woolly

Large terminal leaflet

Leaf-like bracts below flower-head

i

Kidney vetch

Anthyllis vulneraria

To 60cm

| J | F | M | A | M | J |
| J | A | S | O | N | D |

Widespread in dry grassland, especially by sea.

MEADOW VETCHLING

Farmers once encouraged this slender, scrambling plant to grow in their meadows because the nodules of its roots draw nitrogen from the air and thus increase the richness of the soil. The plant, particularly its seeds, is also rich in protein so it adds to the food value of pasturage and hay. Although a tendril for climbing springs from each pair of leaflets, meadow vetchling tends not to be a great climber. Instead, the angular stems rise from the rootstock in profusion, relying on each other and surrounding plants for support. Five to twelve flowers are borne on a stalk that is longer than the leaves.

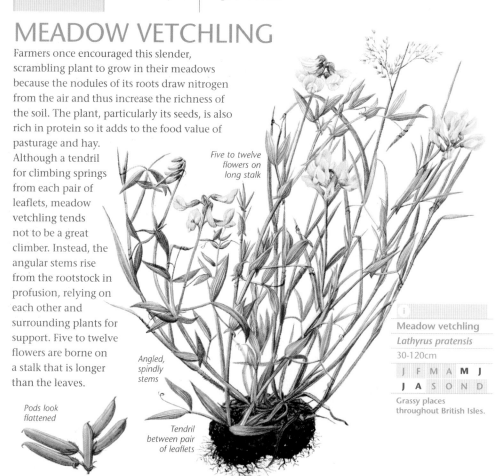

Five to twelve flowers on long stalk

Angled, spindly stems

Pods look flattened

Tendril between pair of leaflets

Meadow vetchling

Lathyrus pratensis

30-120cm

| J | F | M | A | **M** | **J** |
| **J** | **A** | S | O | N | D |

Grassy places throughout British Isles.

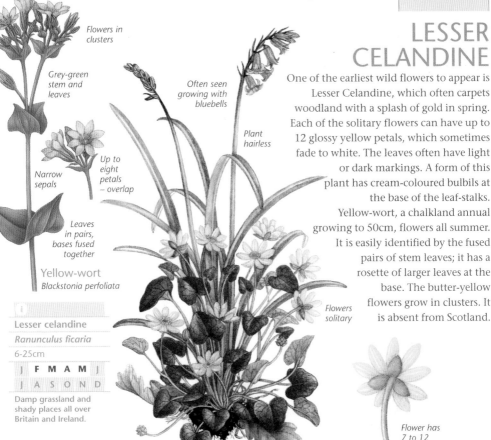

Flowers in clusters

Grey-green stem and leaves

Narrow sepals

Up to eight petals – overlap

Leaves in pairs, bases fused together

Yellow-wort
Blackstonia perfoliata

Lesser celandine

Ranunculus ficaria

6–25cm

J **F M A M** J
J A S O N D

Damp grassland and shady places all over Britain and Ireland.

Often seen growing with bluebells

Plant hairless

Flowers solitary

Heart-shaped leaves on long stalks

Leaves may be mottled

LESSER CELANDINE

One of the earliest wild flowers to appear is Lesser Celandine, which often carpets woodland with a splash of gold in spring. Each of the solitary flowers can have up to 12 glossy yellow petals, which sometimes fade to white. The leaves often have light or dark markings. A form of this plant has cream-coloured bulbils at the base of the leaf-stalks. Yellow-wort, a chalkland annual growing to 50cm, flowers all summer. It is easily identified by the fused pairs of stem leaves; it has a rosette of larger leaves at the base. The butter-yellow flowers grow in clusters. It is absent from Scotland.

Flower has 7 to 12 petals and three sepals

NODDING BUR-MARIGOLD

The tightly packed flower-heads of this plant really do nod on their slender stalks, giving a certain charm to an otherwise undistinguished wild flower. A member of the daisy family, it has a compact flower-head which looks like a single flower, but is in fact made up of many tiny individual flowers, surrounded by a ring of green leaf-like bracts. The flowers are unscented and the leaves unstalked and undivided.

Trifid bur-marigold, which grows in similar places, has leaves with three spear-shaped lobes, the middle one being the longest.

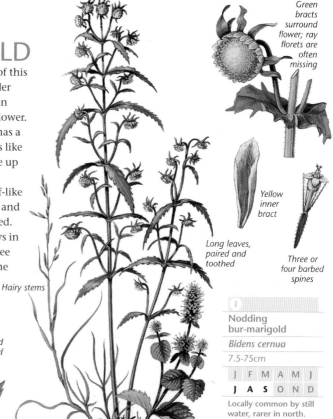

Green bracts surround flower; ray florets are often missing

Yellow inner bract

Long leaves, paired and toothed

Three or four barbed spines

Hairy stems

Flowers erect, not nodding

Three-lobed leaf

Usually two barbed spines on fruit

Trifid bur-marigold
Bidens tripartita

i
Nodding bur-marigold
Bidens cernua
7.5–75cm

J	F	M	A	M	J
J	**A**	**S**	O	N	D

Locally common by still water, rarer in north.

COLT'S-FOOT

As winter subsides, colt's-foot is so eager to burst into flower that it does not wait for its leaves to form: they appear later. The flowers comprise both disc and ray florets, and are borne singly. Then there are the many overlapping, fleshy, purple scales which cover the stems right up to the flower-heads. Finally, there are the large, toothed leaves, which appear after the flowers; their hoof-like shape gives the plant its name. The 'parachutes' by which the seeds are spread need only the slightest of draughts to keep them airborne.

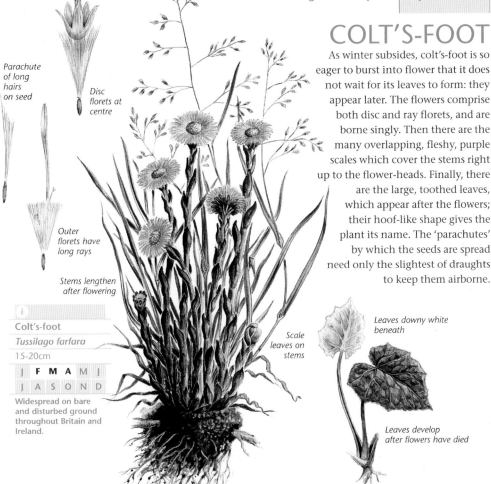

Parachute of long hairs on seed

Disc florets at centre

Outer florets have long rays

Stems lengthen after flowering

Scale leaves on stems

Leaves downy white beneath

Leaves develop after flowers have died

Colt's-foot

Tussilago farfara

15-20cm

J **F M A** M J
J A S O N D

Widespread on bare and disturbed ground throughout Britain and Ireland.

COMMON FLEABANE

The best way to identify this plant is by the leaf rather than the flower. The upper leaves are stalkless and heart-shaped at the base, so that they half-clasp the stem. All the leaves are wrinkled, wavy-edged and woolly, and the whole plant is greyish in colour. The flower is daisy-like, with up to 600 separate florets packed into each golden-yellow flower-head. When the plant was burnt, the smoke was said to drive away fleas.

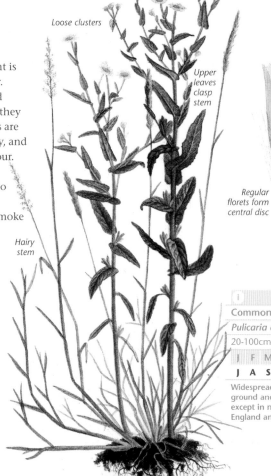

Loose clusters

Upper leaves clasp stem

Regular florets form central disc

Hairy stem

Ray florets form outer ring

Common fleabane	
Pulicaria dysenterica	
20-100cm	

J F M A M J
J A S O N D

Widespread on marshy ground and meadows, except in northern England and Scotland.

COMMON CUDWEED

The little flowers of the common cudweed are easily overlooked, half-hidden behind a thicket of silver-grey woolly hairs and spreading side branches. The flowers are gathered in small ball-like clusters of 20-40 at the tips of tough, wiry stems. These clusters look yellow from the tips of the bracts, but the actual florets are white, tipped with red. Blunt, narrow, woolly grey leaves overlap all the way up the stems. Medieval farmers gave the plant to cattle that had stopped ruminating, to replace their 'cud'.

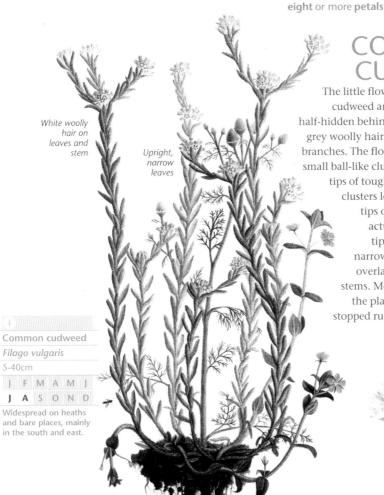

White woolly hair on leaves and stem

Upright, narrow leaves

i

Common cudweed

Filago vulgaris

5-40cm

J F M A M J
J A S O N D

Widespread on heaths and bare places, mainly in the south and east.

Dense clusters

GOLDENROD

The Elizabethans failed to notice that this bright and brilliant plant was native to this country, and instead spent large sums of money importing it for use in the treatment of wounds. As soon as its presence was noticed on Hampstead Heath its market price crashed. The flower-heads have short rays and grow in branched spikes. The narrow, surrounding bracts look like sepals and are greenish-yellow.

Stems downy or hairless

Narrow, toothed leaves, broader at base of plant

Flower-head on short stalk, with 6-12 rays

Brown seed with parachute of hairs

Goldenrod

Solidago virgaurea

5-70cm

| J | F | M | A | M | **J** |
| **J** | **A** | **S** | O | N | D |

Widespread on mountains and in woods, hedgerows and grassland.

CANADIAN FLEABANE

This New World immigrant, here seen growing with rosebay willowherb, grows in pavement cracks and on building sites as readily as by country roads. It came to Britain in the 17th century, and its spread was helped by the development of the railways. Its seeds have a 'parachute' of hairs and the draughts caused by passing trains aided their dispersal. The small flower-heads grow in open, branched spikes.

Slightly hairy stems

Many narrow leaves

Canadian fleabane

Conyza canadensis

7.5-100cm

| J | F | M | A | M | J |
| **J** | **A** | **S** | O | N | **D** |

Common on roadsides, waste ground and embankments, particularly in south and south-east England.

Parachute of hairs on seed

Central disc florets yellow, ray florets whitish

CORN MARIGOLD

Now that modern herbicides have reduced the threat that this plant once posed to corn harvests, it can be admired where it survives on waste ground for its finer points, particularly its rich, golden-yellow flower-heads. These are too big to miss, usually about 50mm across, growing singly on stalks thickened at the top, with long rays. The greyish leaves are narrow, fleshy and jaggedly toothed. The middle and upper ones partly clasp the stem.

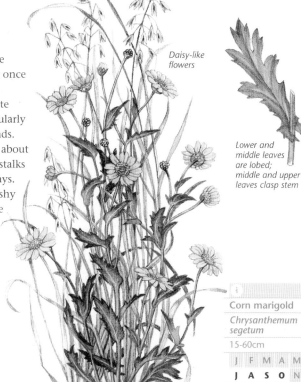

Daisy-like flowers

Lower and middle leaves are lobed; middle and upper leaves clasp stem

Single flower-head on each long stalk

Whole plant hairless

Corn marigold

Chrysanthemum segetum

15–60cm

| J | F | M | A | M | J |
| J | A | S | O | N | D |

Light, peaty or sandy soils throughout lowland areas.

HAWKWEED

The many different hawkweeds can only be identified by experts. In most cases the seed is produced without fertilisation, leading to the perpetuation of minor differences and to the creation in time of what amounts to new species. Botanists recognise over 250 hawkweeds in the British Isles alone. One of the commonest species is this tall, erect plant with numerous alternate leaves diminishing in length up the stem.

Dark green bracts

Wiry, unbranched hairy stem

Large flower-heads with many rays

Leaves lance-shaped, hairy, toothed

Hawkweed

Hieracium umbellatum

25-120cm

J F M A M J J A S O N D

Heathland and dunes in Britain; rare in Ireland.

SMOOTH SOW-THISTLE

It is not only the absence of prickles that differentiates this plant from the prickly sow-thistle. The leaves are dull, greyish-green and divided, with the terminal lobe much the largest. They are pointed at the base, loosely clasping the stem. The two plants' flower-heads are, however, very similar, though the flowers of smooth sow-thistle tend to be paler yellow. The leaves and stems produce a white milky juice.

Perennial sow-thistle has bigger flower-heads which, like its stems, are thickly covered in yellow glandular hairs.

Flower-heads in clusters

Rounded lobes clasp stem

Leaves shiny and bright green, with rounded bases

Perennial sow-thistle
Sonchus arvensis

Leaves toothed but spineless, with points at base, extending beyond stem

i		
Smooth sow-thistle		
Sonchus oleraceus		
20-150cm		

J	F	M	A	M	**J**
J	**A**	**S**	**O**	N	D

Common on waste and cultivated land and roadsides, often by walls, throughout most of British Isles.

PRICKLY SOW-THISTLE

The white, milky fluid contained in the leaves, stem and roots of this plant is attractive to animals – including sows, whose milk flow it is thought to improve. As a defence, the plant has armed itself with prickly, glossy green leaves. They are rounded at the base and wrap themselves flat against the stem. The white, fluffy fruiting head resembles a small dandelion 'clock'.

Spiny, toothed leaves clasp stem

Prickly sow-thistle

Sonchus asper

20-150cm

| J | F | M | A | M | J |
| J | A | S | O | N | D |

Widespread on waste and cultivated ground throughout British Isles.

Green triangular bracts

BRISTLY OX-TONGUE

With its leaves covered in what at first glance look like white blisters, and the whole bristling with stiff hairs, bristly ox-tongue can hardly be described as a pretty plant. But it can fairly claim to be one of the most distinctive of the dandelion-like flowers. It is a relative of the sow-thistle, but less common. The pale yellow flower-heads grow in irregular clusters.

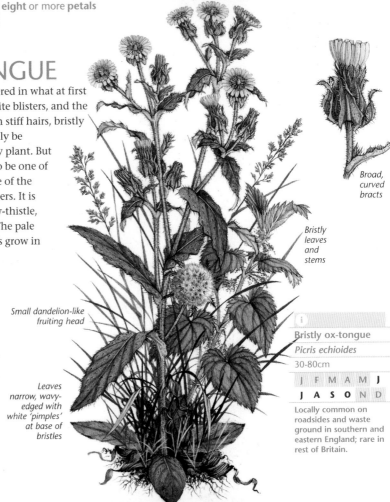

Broad, curved bracts

Bristly leaves and stems

Small dandelion-like fruiting head

Leaves narrow, wavy-edged with white 'pimples' at base of bristles

i

Bristly ox-tongue

Picris echioides

30-80cm

| J | F | M | A | M | **J** |
| **J** | **A** | **S** | O | N | D |

Locally common on roadsides and waste ground in southern and eastern England; rare in rest of Britain.

GREAT LETTUCE

There is nothing in the appearance of this wild lettuce to link it with the garden variety. The stem is usually red-tinged and very tall, sometimes reaching a height of 2m. The dark green, prickly leaves are gathered mainly on the lower half of the stem, below clusters of flower-heads. Prickly lettuce is a 'compass' plant; when fully exposed to the sun, its saw-edged leaves lie in a north-south plane. More widespread than both of these plants is wall lettuce, a hairless plant usually tinged red, with lobed leaves and clusters of small yellow flowers. As its name suggests, it grows on shady walls and limestone rocks.

Leaves clasp stem at base

Fruit has 'parachute' of hairs

i

Great lettuce

Lactuca virosa

60-200cm

J	F	M	A	M	J
J	**A**	**S**	O	N	D

Roadside verges and disturbed chalky ground, mainly in south and eastern England.

Leaves have bristles below on midrib, which is reddish

Saw-edged leaves

Prickly lettuce
Lactuca serriola

Stem and midrib of leaf whitish

CAT'S EAR

Small, dark, scale-like bracts grow spirally up the flower stems of this plant, like miniature cat's ears. The brilliant yellow flower does much to brighten grassy places – including, without invitation, garden lawns. The leaves are broadly toothed.

Mouse-ear hawkweed has creeping, rooting runners and woolly white hairs on the underside of its leaves, which form a rosette. The ray florets are lemon yellow and the outer rays are reddish beneath.

Unbranched, or little-branched, leafless stems

Flowers borne singly

Unbranched stems

Toothless leaves

Rooting runners

Mouse-ear hawkweed
Pilosella officinarum

Outer ray florets greenish or greyish beneath

Bracts may be bristly

Broad teeth

Hairy leaves in rosette

Cat's ear

Hypochoeris radicata

20-60cm

| J | F | M | A | M | J |
| J | A | S | O | N | D |

Pastures, grassy places and waysides throughout British Isles.

AUTUMN HAWKBIT

This plant does for roadsides in August and September what the dandelion does in May, turning the verge into a glowing border of golden-yellow flowers. Its leaves are similar in shape to the dandelion's – long, slender and deeply lobed. The stems are branched and leafless, with small scale-like bracts. Rough hawkbit is very hairy, usually with much less deeply lobed leaves.

Outer ray florets often reddish beneath

Scale-like bracts

Stems leafless, usually branched

Deeply lobed leaves in rosette at base

Autumn hawkbit
Leontodon autumnalis
5-60cm

J F M A M J
J A S O N D

Roadsides and grassy places throughout British Isles.

Leaves hairy, usually less deeply lobed

Rough hawkbit
Leontodon hispidus

GOAT'S BEARD

Also called Jack-go-to-bed-at-noon,
this plant attracts attention on
sunny mornings when its large,
dandelion-like flowers are out. They
quickly disappear about midday,
hidden within long, pointed
finger-like bracts. In
mid afternoon, with no flowers in
sight, the long, narrow leaves look
much like grass and can easily go
unnoticed. They sheathe the
stem in an unusual manner for
dandelion-like plants. The plant
has white milky juice.

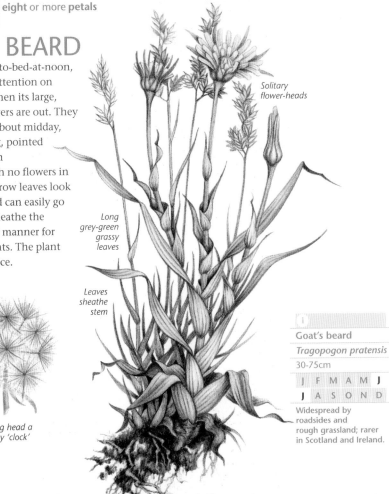

Solitary
flower-heads

Long
grey-green
grassy
leaves

Leaves
sheathe
stem

*Fruiting head a
downy 'clock'*

i						
Goat's beard

Tragopogon pratensis

30-75cm

J	F	M	A	M	**J**
J	**A**	**S**	**O**	**N**	D

Widespread by
roadsides and
rough grassland; rarer
in Scotland and Ireland.

NIPPLEWORT

This plant is readily identified by its clusters of flower-heads, resembling tiny dandelions, on long, slender, many-branched stalks. They close in the early afternoon, and do not open at all in bad weather. Each flower-head is enclosed by two rows of bracts, the outer bracts being few and tiny. The lower leaves have a large, toothed, terminal lobe with, below it, smaller, wing-shaped lobes.

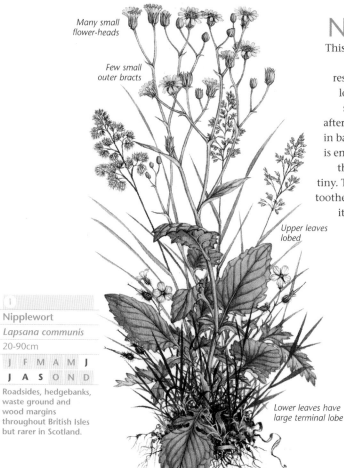

Many small flower-heads

Few small outer bracts

Upper leaves lobed

Lower leaves have large terminal lobe

Nipplewort

Lapsana communis

20-90cm

J F M A M J
J A S O N D

Roadsides, hedgebanks, waste ground and wood margins throughout British Isles but rarer in Scotland.

SMOOTH HAWK'S-BEARD

This plant has the smallest flowers of all the hawk's-beards – up to 15mm across. In bud they are often reddish in appearance, the outer florets being tinted underneath. They grow in branched clusters, each flower-head surrounded by two rows of bracts. The upper leaves are narrow, while the lower ones are broader and lobed, several forming a rosette at the base of the stem.

Two rows of bracts

Stem leaves narrow

Tiny flower-heads

Shiny leaves

Rosette leaves lobed

Lower leaves in rosette

Smooth hawk's-beard

Crepis capillaris

20-75cm

J F M A M **J**

J A S O N D

Common in pastures and waste places throughout British Isles.

DANDELION

Away from the garden, where its reputation is decidedly low, the dandelion can be appreciated as a flower full of character, filling roadsides and fields with a golden blaze of colour in spring. The large flower-heads are made up of some 200 ray florets, which close at night or in dull weather. The stalk produces a milky juice. Its leaves give the dandelion its name – a corruption of the French *dent de lion*, 'lion's tooth'.

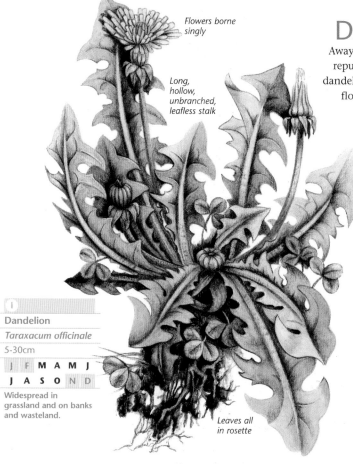

Flowers borne singly

Long, hollow, unbranched, leafless stalk

i

Dandelion

Taraxacum officinale

5-30cm

| J | F | **M** | **A** | **M** | **J** |
| **J** | **A** | **S** | **O** | N | D |

Widespread in grassland and on banks and wasteland.

Leaves all in rosette

White-haired fruits form dandelion 'clock'

TANSY

The sturdy, upright stems of tansy are surmounted by flat-topped clusters of golden button-like flowers, made up of tightly packed disc florets. Unlike most members of the daisy family, it has no ray florets. Both the flowers and the fernlike leaves are strongly aromatic, and once were used as an alternative to expensive imported spices. The chopped leaves were used to flavour omelettes and tansy oil to treat worms.

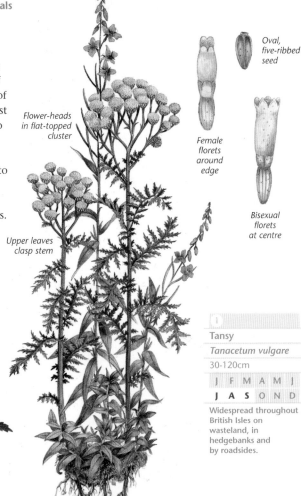

Flower-heads in flat-topped cluster

Oval, five-ribbed seed

Female florets around edge

Bisexual florets at centre

Upper leaves clasp stem

Bracts ring disc-shaped flower-head

Leaves made up of deeply toothed leaflets

Tansy

Tanacetum vulgare

30-120cm

J F M A M J
J A S O N D

Widespread throughout British Isles on wasteland, in hedgebanks and by roadsides.

SEA WORMWOOD

A silvery down covers the stems and both sides of the leaves of sea wormwood. Its feathery-looking leaves are finely divided and, when crushed, strongly but pleasantly aromatic. The flower-heads resemble those of mugwort (page 404), but they are brighter orange in colour and arranged in clusters that often droop. The florets are all bisexual.

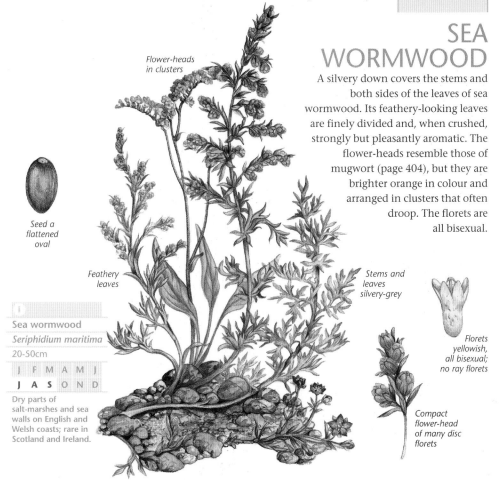

Flower-heads in clusters

Seed a flattened oval

Feathery leaves

Stems and leaves silvery-grey

Florets yellowish, all bisexual; no ray florets

Compact flower-head of many disc florets

Sea wormwood

Seriphidium maritima

20-50cm

J F M A M **J**
J A S O N D

Dry parts of salt-marshes and sea walls on English and Welsh coasts; rare in Scotland and Ireland.

COMMON RAGWORT

The deeply divided leaves give the plant a ragged look, which accounts for its name, but this is nevertheless a handsome plant, with fine daisy-like flowers. The outer florets spread out from the centre disc like the rays of a symbolic sun, often curling at the ends. Growing in flat-topped clusters, the flower-heads make an attractive sight. The inner bracts surrounding the flower-heads are dark-tipped. The leaves are highly poisonous to horses and cattle, but are the favourite food of the black-and-yellow striped caterpillar of the cinnabar moth.

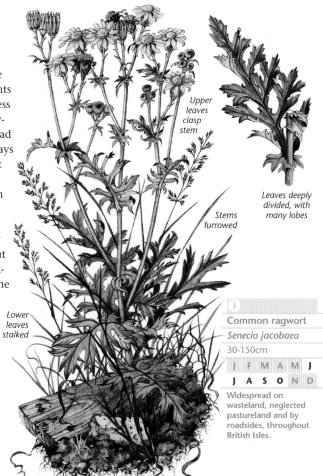

Upper leaves clasp stem

Leaves deeply divided, with many lobes

Stems furrowed

Lower leaves stalked

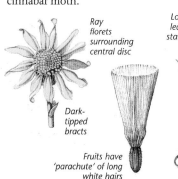

Ray florets surrounding central disc

Dark-tipped bracts

Fruits have 'parachute' of long white hairs

Common ragwort

Senecio jacobaea

30-150cm

J	F	M	A	M	**J**
J	**A**	**S**	**O**	N	D

Widespread on wasteland, neglected pastureland and by roadsides, throughout British Isles.

OXFORD RAGWORT

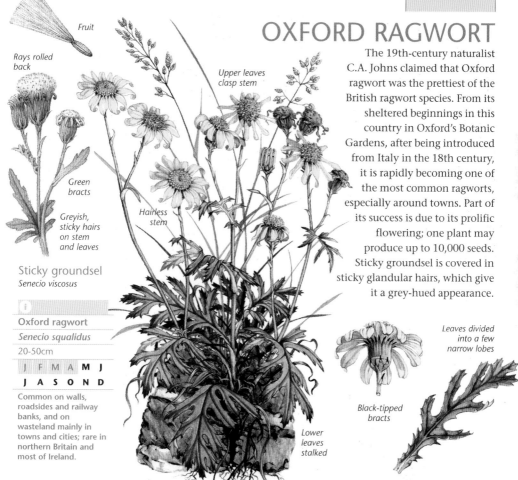

The 19th-century naturalist C.A. Johns claimed that Oxford ragwort was the prettiest of the British ragwort species. From its sheltered beginnings in this country in Oxford's Botanic Gardens, after being introduced from Italy in the 18th century, it is rapidly becoming one of the most common ragworts, especially around towns. Part of its success is due to its prolific flowering; one plant may produce up to 10,000 seeds. Sticky groundsel is covered in sticky glandular hairs, which give it a grey-hued appearance.

Fruit

Rays rolled back

Green bracts

Greyish, sticky hairs on stem and leaves

Hairless stem

Upper leaves clasp stem

Sticky groundsel
Senecio viscosus

Oxford ragwort
Senecio squalidus
20-50cm

J F M A **M J**
J A S O N D

Common on walls, roadsides and railway banks, and on wasteland mainly in towns and cities; rare in northern Britain and most of Ireland.

Leaves divided into a few narrow lobes

Black-tipped bracts

Lower leaves stalked

GROUNDSEL

After flowering, the tiny, yellow cylindrical flower-heads turn into fluffy balls of white hair. This feature is the origin of the plant's scientific name, from the Latin *senex*, 'old man'. Until this transformation occurs the flower-heads, which grow in loose clusters, are inconspicuous. Usually there are only disc florets but sometimes small, narrow ray florets are present. The bracts have black, pointed tips.

   Heath groundsel is a taller, bushier plant, often stickily hairy, growing on heaths and sandy ground. The flower heads have rolled-back rays around the edge, and are only produced from July to September.

White fruiting heads

Ray florets sometimes present

Black-pointed bracts

Leaves have toothed lobes

Leaves more deeply toothed

Heath groundsel
Senecio sylvaticus

---

i

Groundsel

Senecio vulgaris

7.5-30cm

| J | F | M | A | M | J |
| J | A | S | O | N | D |

Widespread on cultivated ground and in waste places throughout the British Isles.

CARLINE THISTLE

A curious feature of this plant is the way straw-coloured bracts surround the flower-heads like petals. They are usually seen spread out flat, but in wet weather they curl over; country people once used them as a simple barometer. The name 'carline' refers to the 8th-century Frankish king, Charlemagne. It is said that under divine guidance he chose this plant to cure his army of plague.

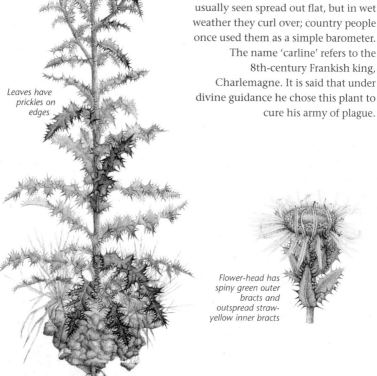

Old flowers remain after seed dispersed

Leaves have prickles on edges

Flower-head has spiny green outer bracts and outspread straw-yellow inner bracts

Carline thistle

Carlina vulgaris

10-60cm

J F M A M J **J A S O** N D

Widespread on grassland and scrub; absent from much of Scotland and northern Ireland.

Blue
FLOWERS

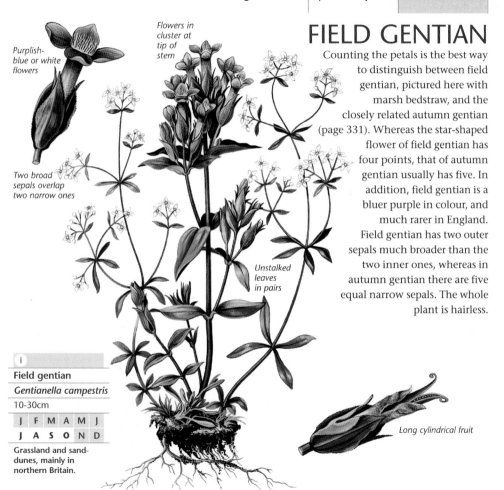

Purplish-blue or white flowers

Flowers in cluster at tip of stem

Two broad sepals overlap two narrow ones

Unstalked leaves in pairs

FIELD GENTIAN

Counting the petals is the best way to distinguish between field gentian, pictured here with marsh bedstraw, and the closely related autumn gentian (page 331). Whereas the star-shaped flower of field gentian has four points, that of autumn gentian usually has five. In addition, field gentian is a bluer purple in colour, and much rarer in England. Field gentian has two outer sepals much broader than the two inner ones, whereas in autumn gentian there are five equal narrow sepals. The whole plant is hairless.

i

Field gentian

Gentianella campestris

10-30cm

J	F	M	A	M	J
J	**A**	**S**	**O**	**N**	D

Grassland and sand-dunes, mainly in northern Britain.

Long cylindrical fruit

DEVIL'S-BIT SCABIOUS

The button-like heads of Britain's three scabious species consist of as many as 50 individual flowers. Devil's-bit scabious has violet-blue flowers and undivided leaves up the stem. Its flower-heads have equal sized individual flowers, unlike those of field scabious. Devil's-bit scabious is particularly at home in wet places such as marshes and damp grassland, though it may also grow on the drier grasslands favoured by field scabious. The plant's name is associated with its short root: legend has it that the Devil, jealous of its reputed skin-healing power, bit off part of the root.

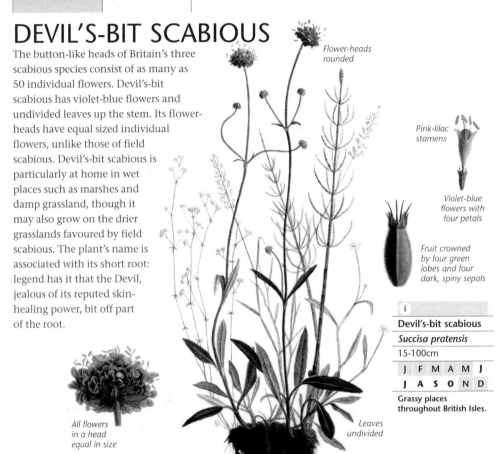

Flower-heads rounded

Pink-lilac stamens

Violet-blue flowers with four petals

Fruit crowned by four green lobes and four dark, spiny sepals

All flowers in a head equal in size

Leaves undivided

i
Devil's-bit scabious
Succisa pratensis
15-100cm

J	F	M	A	M	J
J	A	S	O	N	D

Grassy places throughout British Isles.

COMMON MILKWORT

A flower's sepals are normally green and insignificant, but the two inner sepals of the milkwort's are much larger than the three outer ones and brightly coloured – usually blue, but sometimes pink or white. These two inner sepals, called wings, all but conceal the flower's actual petals, which are joined together in a tube extending just beyond the sepals. Heath milkwort is a smaller plant, different also in having some pairs of opposite leaves at the base of the stem. Milkworts were believed to increase the milk yield of cows that fed on them.

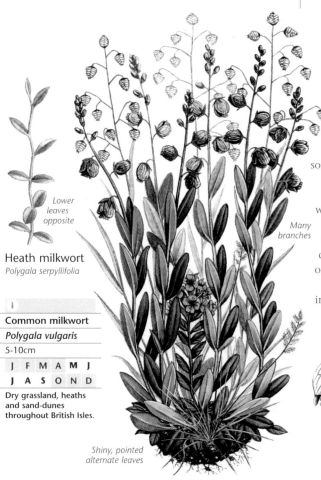

Lower leaves opposite

Heath milkwort
Polygala serpyllifolia

Many branches

i

Common milkwort

Polygala vulgaris

5-10cm

| J | F | M | A | M | J |
| J | A | S | O | N | D |

Dry grassland, heaths and sand-dunes throughout British Isles.

Shiny, pointed alternate leaves

Two large blue sepals enclose petals

Petals longer than sepals

BROOKLIME

The banks of streams and ponds in summer are often brightened by the blue splashes of brooklime and blue water speedwell. The flowers of both species grow in spikes; the individual flowers of blue water speedwell are smaller than those of brooklime, but they are grouped in longer spikes.

The round, fleshy, stalked leaves of brooklime are quite different from the leaves of blue water speedwell, which are lance-shaped and stalkless. Blue water speedwell is commonest in southern and eastern England, but is scattered elsewhere.

One narrower petal

Flowers in oppposite stalked spikes growing from base of leaves

Fruit roughly heart-shaped and flattened

Leaves stalked, oval, fleshy

Longer flower spikes

Upper leaves narrow and pointed, without stalks

Blue water speedwell
Veronica anagallis-aquatica

i

Brooklime

Veronica beccabunga

20-60cm

J	F	M	A	M	J
J	A	S	O	N	D

Wet places throughout British Isles, except far north.

GERMANDER SPEEDWELL

This is the familiar speedwell of grassland, hedge banks and roadsides. It has bright blue flowers, and the eye-like white ring at the centre of each flower has given the plant the alternative name of bird's-eye speedwell. Though many speedwells are superficially similar, germander speedwell has one unique feature: a sharply defined line of hairs down each side of the stem. The fruit is heart-shaped. Wood speedwell has hairs all around the stem and slightly smaller flowers than germander speedwell. It favours damp woodlands but is rare in northern Scotland.

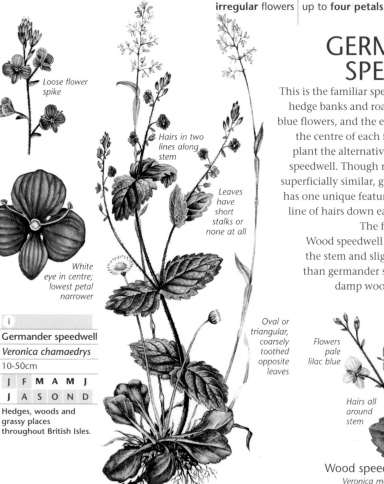

Loose flower spike

Hairs in two lines along stem

Leaves have short stalks or none at all

White eye in centre; lowest petal narrower

Oval or triangular, coarsely toothed opposite leaves

ⓘ
Germander speedwell
Veronica chamaedrys
10-50cm

J	F	M	A	M	J
J	A	S	O	N	D

Hedges, woods and grassy places throughout British Isles.

Flowers pale lilac blue

Hairs all around stem

Round fruits

Stalked leaves

Wood speedwell
Veronica montana

COMMON FIELD-SPEEDWELL

Introduced from western Asia early in the 19th century, the common field-speedwell grows on cultivated ground all over Britain. It flowers all year round. The flower, up to 12mm across, is borne on a long stalk arising from the angle of leaf and stem; it has a white lower petal.

Slender speedwell has thread-like creeping stems which take root and form a mat over river banks, verges and lawns. It flowers in April and May. Introduced from the Caucasus, it has spread throughout most of the British Isles since the 1920s.

Solitary long-stalked flowers

Shiny green leaves

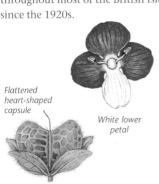

Flattened heart-shaped capsule

White lower petal

Flowers pale lilac blue

Tiny roundish leaves

Thin, creeping stems

Slender speedwell
Veronica filiformis

ℹ️		
Common field-speedwell		
Veronica persica		
10-50cm		
J F M A M J		
J A S O N D		
Cultivated ground all over the British Isles.		

WALL SPEEDWELL

As its name suggests, this plant grows in crevices in garden walls and rocks and on scree slopes from which it sends up tall straight stems bearing leafy spikes of tiny blue flowers, 2–3mm across. This hairy plant also grows in cultivated fields and dry grassland, when it can be identified by its very short flower stalk. Green field-speedwell has a single flower on a stalk rather than a spike of flowers, and the flower has white lower petals. It is commoner in the south than the north, but is decreasing everywhere.

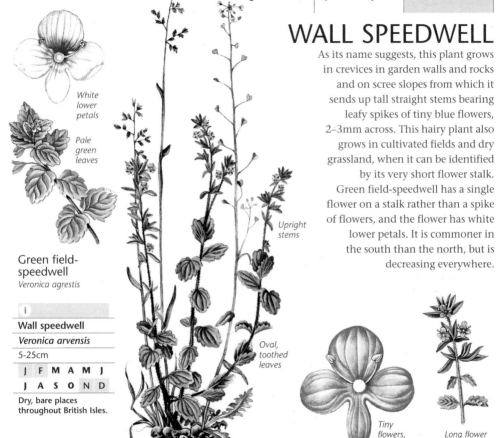

White lower petals

Pale green leaves

Green field-speedwell
Veronica agrestis

| i |

Wall speedwell

Veronica arvensis

5-25cm

| J | F | M | A | M | J |
| J | A | S | O | N | D |

Dry, bare places throughout British Isles.

Upright stems

Oval, toothed leaves

Tiny flowers, almost stalkless

Long flower spikes

IVY-LEAVED SPEEDWELL

The name indicates this speedwell's main distinguishing feature. The leaves have from three to seven lobes or teeth. The small flowers, borne singly on long stalks, are lilac or a pale Cambridge blue – or sometimes almost white – and the sepals are hairy and heart shaped. Ivy-leaved speedwell flowers early in the year and dies down in summer.

Thyme-leaved speedwell has oval toothless leaves, without hairs. Its flowers are pale blue or white with blue veins and are borne in a spike at the top of the stem.

Lilac to pale blue flowers

Hairy, heart-shaped sepals

Ivy-shaped leaves

Plant hairy

Very pale blue flowers

Rounded, almost toothless leaves

Thyme-leaved speedwell
Veronica serpyllifolia

> **ⓘ**
> **Ivy-leaved speedwell**
> *Veronica hederifolia*
> 10-50cm
>
> | J | F | **M** | **A** | **M** | J |
> |---|---|---|---|---|---|
> | **J** | **A** | **S** | **O** | **N** | **D** |
>
> Arable fields, gardens and bare ground throughout British Isles; rarer in north and west.

GROUND-IVY

Despite its name, ground-ivy is neither related to ivy, nor does it look like it, although it remains green in winter and spreads by long, creeping runners. Its blue or violet blue flowers bloom in whorls of two to four up the square stem in spring. Its alternative name of 'alehoof' derives from the fact that before the introduction of hops the leaves of ground-ivy were used to flavour beer.

Leaves heart-shaped, with rounded teeth

Darker marks on lower lip

Flowers in whorls on same side of stem

Long rooting runners

i

Ground-ivy

Glechoma hederacea

10-30cm

J	F	M	A	M	J
J	A	S	O	N	D

Open woods, grassland and hedgebanks all over Britain and Ireland; rarer in far north.

WILD CLARY

Two sizes of flower often appear on the same wild clary plant. The smaller flowers never fully open and are self-pollinating. The more conspicuous ones, up to 15mm long, are in whorls making up a long spike characteristic of the mint family to which it belongs. Wild clary can claim garden sage as a relative, though its greyish leaves have no culinary use.

Meadow clary, a rare plant of limestone grassland, has green rather than greyish leaves and bigger flowers, which are never self-pollinating.

Hood-shaped upper lip

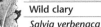

Flower spike a series of whorls

Greyish leaves large and wrinkled, with coarse teeth

ⓘ		
Wild clary		
Salvia verbenaca		
30–80cm		

J	F	M	A	M	J
J	A	S	O	N	D

Roadsides and dry grassland; commonest in southern England. Very rare in Scotland, Wales and Ireland.

BUGLE

Small spikes of blue flowers on short, stiff stems colour damp woods and grassland over most of Britain in late spring. Bugle spreads quickly by long runners and often forms large patches. It prefers shade, and is often found deep in oak woods. The opposite pairs of leaves, typical of the mint family, form a rosette at the base, and are often so glossy and dark as to appear almost purple. These lower leaves have stalks, whereas the smaller leaves higher up the stem are stalkless.

Flowers in whorled-spike

Leaves glossy green

i

Bugle

Ajuga reptans

10-30cm

| J | F | M | A | M | J |
| J | A | S | O | N | D |

Widespread in woods and damp grassland. Absent from far north of Scotland.

Leafy rooting runners

Very short upper lip

Rosette of leaves at base

SKULLCAP

This plant is unusual among members of the mint family in that most of its flowers grow in pairs facing the same way. Each pair sprouts from the angle between the stem and the leaves. The plant's common name is derived from the calyx or sepal tube surrounding the base of the flower; a projection on the top of this was thought to give it the appearance of a *galerum*, the leather skull helmet worn by Roman soldiers.

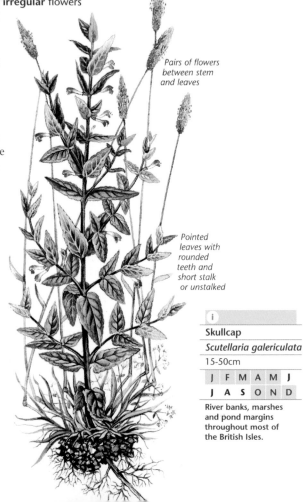

Pairs of flowers between stem and leaves

Pointed leaves with rounded teeth and short stalk or unstalked

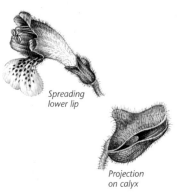

Spreading lower lip

Projection on calyx

Skullcap

Scutellaria galericulata

15-50cm

J	F	M	A	M	J
J	A	S	O	N	D

River banks, marshes and pond margins throughout most of the British Isles.

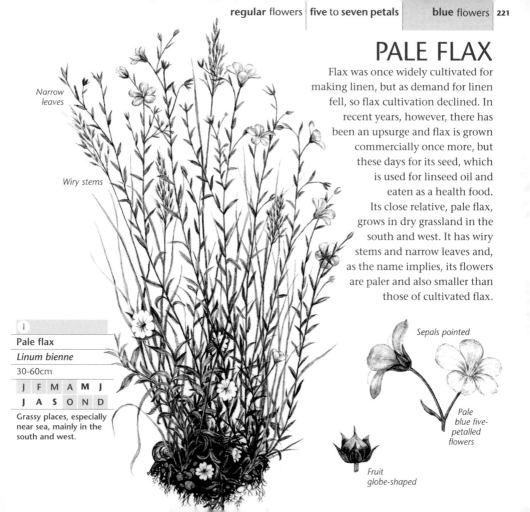

PALE FLAX

Flax was once widely cultivated for making linen, but as demand for linen fell, so flax cultivation declined. In recent years, however, there has been an upsurge and flax is grown commercially once more, but these days for its seed, which is used for linseed oil and eaten as a health food.

Its close relative, pale flax, grows in dry grassland in the south and west. It has wiry stems and narrow leaves and, as the name implies, its flowers are paler and also smaller than those of cultivated flax.

Narrow leaves

Wiry stems

Pale flax

Linum bienne

30-60cm

| J | F | M | A | M | J |
| J | A | S | O | N | D |

Grassy places, especially near sea, mainly in the south and west.

Sepals pointed

Pale blue five-petalled flowers

Fruit globe-shaped

MEADOW CRANE'S-BILL

The 'bill' of the plant's name is the long central beak of the fruit. Round the base of this beak are clustered five seeds, which are ejected as the outer wall of the lobes containing them springs upwards. There are many crane's-bills, most of which are pink-flowered. Meadow crane's-bill is distinguished by its large blue or violet-blue flowers, with radiating crimson veins on its petals to guide bees to the nectar. In bud and flower the hairy flower-stalks are upright, but bend down when the fruit ripens. Cultivated forms are often planted in gardens.

Wood crane's-bill is mainly northern and has pink-violet flowers.

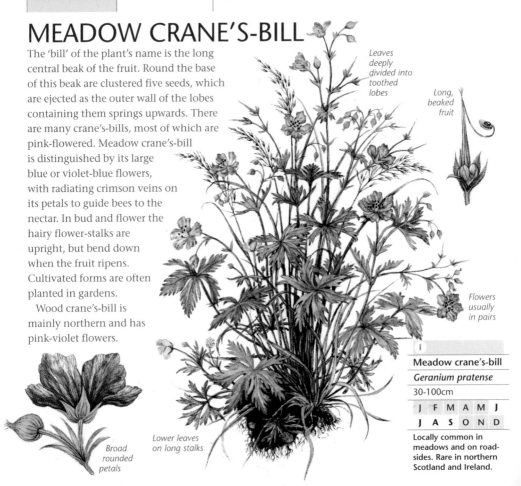

Leaves deeply divided into toothed lobes

Long, beaked fruit

Flowers usually in pairs

Broad rounded petals

Lower leaves on long stalks

Meadow crane's-bill

Geranium pratense

30-100cm

J	F	M	A	M	J
J	**A**	**S**	O	N	D

Locally common in meadows and on roadsides. Rare in northern Scotland and Ireland.

SEA HOLLY

The spiny leaves of sea holly have inflicted painful stabs on the bare feet of many a bather. It is cultivated in gardens for its showy display of metallic blue flowers and waxy leaves. The prickly heads are dried and used in flower arrangements. The greyish or bluish waxy covering on stalks and leaves represents an adaptation to seashore life, diminishing loss of moisture and protecting the plant against salt spray. The fruit has a covering of hooked bristles. For centuries the fleshy roots of sea holly were candied and sold as a delicacy known as 'eringoes'. The Elizabethans believed them to be a powerful aphrodisiac.

Flowers clustered in rounded flower-head

i					

Sea holly

Eryngium maritimum

30-60cm

J	F	M	A	M	J
J	**A**	**S**	**O**	**N**	D

Sand-dunes and shingle by the sea. Absent from north-eastern England and Scotland.

Spiny leaves, with white edge

Spiny bracts on flower

GREEN ALKANET

This plant's bright blue flowers with white centres resemble those of the garden forget-me-not, which belongs to the same family. It has sprays of flowers, which rise from the tip of a long stalk growing from the angle between the stem and an upper leaf. Alkanet was brought to Britain in the Middle Ages for the red dye yielded by its roots.

Borage has narrower petals, giving the flower a star-like appearance. Its leaves taste of cucumber and can be used in salad or infused to make a refreshing drink. Cultivated herbs have escaped to waste ground in the south.

Flowers in dense sprays

Stamens do not project beyond petals

White centre

Fruits hidden by sepals

Large bristly leaves at base, smaller leaves higher up

Star-like flowers

Dark bue stamens

Borage
Borago officinalis

Green alkanet	
Pentaglottis sempervirens	
30-100cm	

J	F	M	A	M	J
J	A	S	O	N	D

Hedges and wood margins; widely naturalised.

BUGLOSS

The bright blue flowers of bugloss, which dot cultivated fields throughout Britain in summer, are characteristic of the forget-me-not family to which it belongs – though the plant stands taller than many of its relatives. The modern use of weedkillers means that the plant is rarer than it used to be. It is a very hairy and bristly plant, the stiff hairs having distinct swollen bases. The bristly leaf surface is reflected in the plant's common name, which is derived from two Greek words meaning 'ox tongue'.

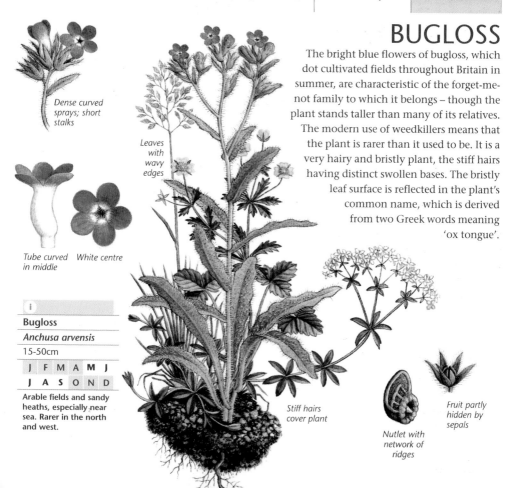

Dense curved sprays; short stalks

Leaves with wavy edges

Tube curved in middle *White centre*

ⓘ

Bugloss

Anchusa arvensis

15-50cm

J	F	M	A	M	J
J	A	S	O	N	D

Arable fields and sandy heaths, especially near sea. Rarer in the north and west.

Stiff hairs cover plant

Nutlet with network of ridges

Fruit partly hidden by sepals

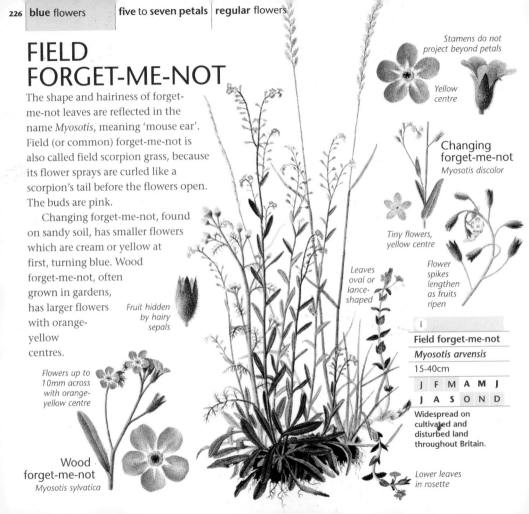

FIELD FORGET-ME-NOT

The shape and hairiness of forget-me-not leaves are reflected in the name *Myosotis*, meaning 'mouse ear'. Field (or common) forget-me-not is also called field scorpion grass, because its flower sprays are curled like a scorpion's tail before the flowers open. The buds are pink.

Changing forget-me-not, found on sandy soil, has smaller flowers which are cream or yellow at first, turning blue. Wood forget-me-not, often grown in gardens, has larger flowers with orange-yellow centres.

Fruit hidden by hairy sepals

Flowers up to 10mm across with orange-yellow centre

Wood forget-me-not
Myosotis sylvatica

Stamens do not project beyond petals

Yellow centre

Changing forget-me-not
Myosotis discolor

Tiny flowers, yellow centre

Flower spikes lengthen as fruits ripen

Leaves oval or lance-shaped

i

Field forget-me-not

Myosotis arvensis

15–40cm

J	F	M	A	M	J
J	A	S	O	N	D

Widespread on cultivated and disturbed land throughout Britain.

Lower leaves in rosette

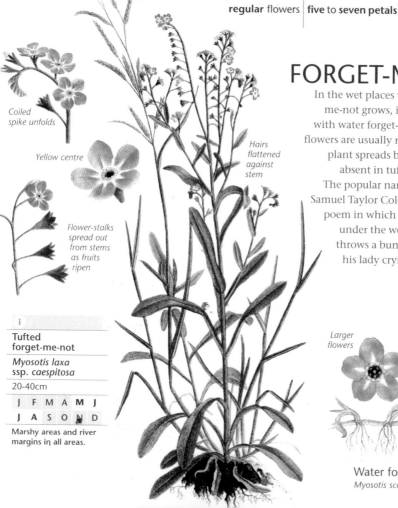

Coiled spike unfolds

Yellow centre

Hairs flattened against stem

Flower-stalks spread out from stems as fruits ripen

TUFTED FORGET-ME-NOT

In the wet places where tufted forget-me-not grows, it could be confused with water forget-me-not. The latter's flowers are usually much larger and the plant spreads by creeping runners, absent in tufted forget-me-nots. The popular name was provided by Samuel Taylor Coleridge, who wrote a poem in which a knight, drowning under the weight of his armour, throws a bunch of the flowers to his lady crying 'Forget me not!'

i

Tufted forget-me-not

Myosotis laxa ssp. *caespitosa*

20-40cm

| J | F | M | A | M | J |
| J | A | S | O | N | D |

Marshy areas and river margins in all areas.

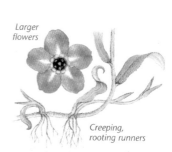

Larger flowers

Creeping, rooting runners

Water forget-me-not
Myosotis scorpioides

OYSTERPLANT

Although a member of the forget-me-not family, oysterplant has distinctive fleshy leaves which conserve water – an essential requirement on the seashore where plants quickly lose moisture to keen winds. Its flowers are bell-shaped rather than star-like, but like some other forget-me-nots they are pinkish when they open and only turn blue with age.

The sprawling stems creep to form blue-grey patches on shingle in northern areas. The plant's name is derived from the tangy flavour of its leaves, which were once eaten raw or cooked as greens.

Plant hairless and sprawling

Blue-grey leaves

Flowers pink, then blue

Fleshy stems and leaves

Bell-shaped flowers

Oysterplant

Mertensia maritima

To 60cm

| J | F | M | A | M | J |
| J | A | S | O | N | D |

Northern and western coasts, especially Scotland; rare and decreasing.

VIPER'S-BUGLOSS

Bristly leaves and short curved sprays of flowers are features which viper's-bugloss shares with other members of the forget-me-not family. But it is a tall plant, bearing its flowers in hairy spikes, and the long leaves come to a point. The pink buds open to bright blue flowers with pink stamens, making viper's-bugloss a decorative plant, especially noticeable on cliffs and sand-dunes. Bees and butterflies are attracted by its sugary nectar.

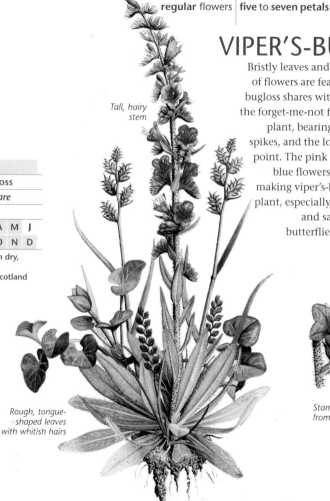

Tall, hairy stem

Rough, tongue-shaped leaves with whitish hairs

i
Viper's-bugloss
Echium vulgare
30-100cm

| J | F | M | A | M | J |
| J | A | S | O | N | D |

Widespread on dry, sandy or limy soils. Rare in Scotland and Ireland.

Stamens protrude from mouth of flower

SHEEP'S-BIT

The button-like flower-heads of sheep's-bit look more like those of daisies and scabious than those of the bellflower family to which it belongs. The heads are formed from a cluster of many separate tiny flowers, surrounded by a ring of green bracts, giving the alternative country names of 'blue bonnets' and 'blue buttons'. Sheep's-bit is cropped, or 'bit', by sheep in the rough grassland where it frequently grows.

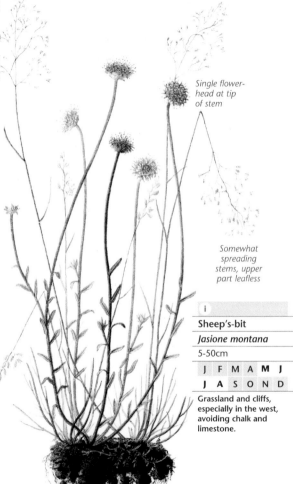

Single flower-head at tip of stem

Somewhat spreading stems, upper part leafless

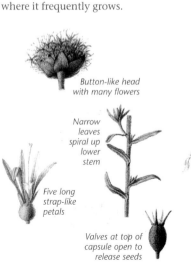

Button-like head with many flowers

Narrow leaves spiral up lower stem

Five long strap-like petals

Valves at top of capsule open to release seeds

i

Sheep's-bit

Jasione montana

5-50cm

J	F	M	A	M	J
J	A	S	O	N	D

Grassland and cliffs, especially in the west, avoiding chalk and limestone.

HAREBELL

The flowers of harebell – or bluebell to the Scots – hang on fine stems and nod in the slightest breeze, their delicate blue bells often half veiled by the grasses around them. Very rarely the flowers may be white or pinkish. Harebell has narrow, stalkless stem leaves. The rounded leaves at the base of the plant have often withered by the time the plant is in flower.

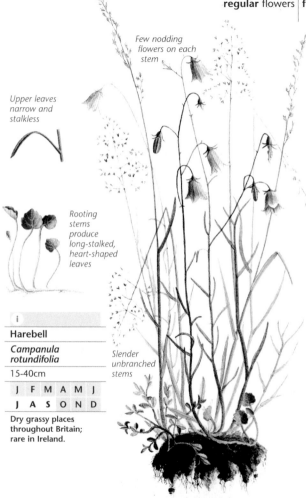

Few nodding flowers on each stem

Upper leaves narrow and stalkless

Rooting stems produce long-stalked, heart-shaped leaves

Slender unbranched stems

i
Harebell
Campanula rotundifolia
15-40cm

| J | F | M | A | M | J |
| J | A | S | O | N | D |

Dry grassy places throughout Britain; rare in Ireland.

Light blue style in centre of flower

Bell-shaped flower hangs down

Capsule releases seed through pores at base

NETTLE-LEAVED BELLFLOWER

Toothed, heart-shaped leaves like those of stinging nettles give this bellflower its name. The lower leaves are on long stalks, while the upper leaves are smaller and have short stalks. The flowers open from the top of the spike downwards, unlike those of the related giant bellflower, *Campanula latifolia*, which open from the base upwards. This tall woodland plant, most often seen in northern England and southern Scotland, has larger, paler blue, or sometimes white, flowers.

Stalked bell-shaped flowers in twos or threes

Plant roughly hairy

Broad, toothed leaves

Flowers open from top of spike

Nettle-leaved bellflower

Campanula trachelium

50-80cm

J	F	M	A	M	J
J	A	S	O	N	D

Woodland clearings and hedgebanks mainly in south.

BLUEBELL

The carpet of bluebells that covers our woodland floors in spring is a typically British spectacle, made even more memorable by the sweet fragrance of the flowers. Nowhere does the bluebell grow in such profusion as in Britain. In Scotland the flower is known as wild hyacinth. Brightly coloured bell-shaped flowers hang from the lower side of a tall, drooping stem. The long strap-like leaves all grow from the base and appear before the flowers.

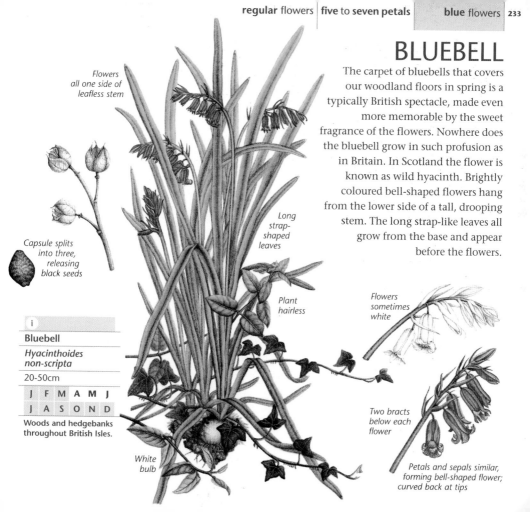

Flowers all one side of leafless stem

Capsule splits into three, releasing black seeds

Long strap-shaped leaves

Plant hairless

Flowers sometimes white

Two bracts below each flower

Petals and sepals similar, forming bell-shaped flower; curved back at tips

White bulb

ⓘ

Bluebell

Hyacinthoides non-scripta

20-50cm

J	F	M	A	M	J
J	A	S	O	N	D

Woods and hedgebanks throughout British Isles.

SPRING SQUILL

Like the bluebell, spring squill is a member of the lily family, but it is a much smaller plant, with star-shaped flowers on either side of its short stem, and a single bract below each flower. Its long, narrow, dark green leaves appear before the flowers and survive after them.

Autumn squill, a similar plant of south and south-west England, has dull purple flowers that appear without the leaves in August and September.

Stalks leafless

Fruit globe-shaped

One long bract below each flower

Star-shaped flowers in spike

Narrow leaves from bulb

i
Spring squill
Scilla verna
5-15cm

J	F	M	A	M	J
J	A	S	O	N	D

Grassy places near sea in west and north.

CHICORY

In late autumn, long after most summer flowers have faded, chicory still blooms in fields and on verges. The bright blue flowers open with the sun in the morning and close at about midday; in dull weather they stay closed. The lower leaves are long and lobed; the upper leaves are lance-shaped. The blanched shoots have long been eaten as a vegetable and the roots used as a coffee substitute.

Stiff, grooved stem

Lower leaves lobed

Chicory

Cichorium intybus

30-100cm

J	F	M	A	M	J
J	A	S	O	N	D

Grassland, especially on lime-rich soils; most common in south and east; rare in Scotland, Wales and Ireland.

Flowers tight against stem

Bright blue florets

Purple
FLOWERS

OPIUM POPPY

The flowers of the opium poppy are large – up to 18cm across – and its lilac colouring is distinctive. It is cultivated in the Far East for its white juice, the source of opium, and used to be widely grown in Britain to provide a sedative known as syrup of poppies, extracted from the round, hairless seed capsules in their immature form. The ripe seeds are not narcotic, and are baked into bread and cakes and crushed for oil.

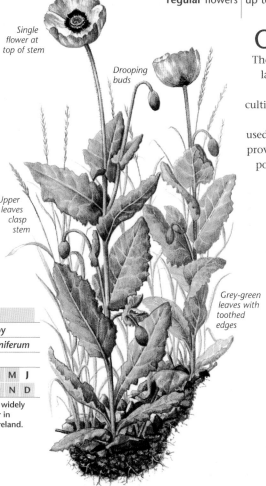

Single flower at top of stem

Drooping buds

Upper leaves clasp stem

Grey-green leaves with toothed edges

i
Opium poppy
Papaver somniferum
30-90cm

| J | F | M | A | M | J |
| J | A | S | O | N | D |

Waste ground, widely scattered; rarer in Scotland and Ireland.

Purple blotch at base of petals

HEATHER

The most common evergreen heath to brighten moors with its purple blooms in late summer is true heather, or ling. Some plants with white blooms are found. Ling's flowers and leaves differ from those of bell heather and cross-leaved heath. Petals are shorter than the sepals – similar in colour and texture – that surround them; and the unstalked leaves are in opposite pairs, overlapping one another. Heather shoots are a main food for grouse, while flowers produce heather ale and honey. In the past, the plant was used for thatching, fencing and making brooms, baskets and ropes.

ⓘ
Heather
Calluna vulgaris
To 60cm

| J | F | M | A | M | J |
| J | A | S | O | N | D |

Heaths and moors on peaty or sandy ground; most parts of Britain and Ireland.

Flowers in long, loose spikes

Straggling branches

Tiny overlapping evergreen leaves in pairs

Sepals longer than petals, same colour

WATER MINT

This wild form of mint, found growing in wet places, was used as a kitchen herb by the Romans 2000 years ago. Though its place in the kitchen garden has now been taken by other species, water mint is today the commonest of all wild mints, and the pungent smell of its leaves crushed underfoot perfumes many a walk beside marshes and streams. Peppermint is a hybrid, with the reddish stem of water mint and the flower spike of its other parent, spearmint. Its stamens do not protrude from the flowers. It grows wild in damp places and is cultivated for the oil in its leaves, used to flavour sweets and medicines.

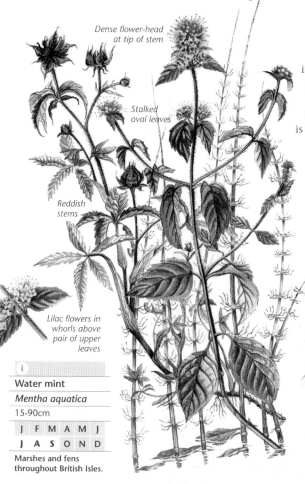

Dense flower-head at tip of stem

Stalked oval leaves

Reddish stems

Lilac flowers in whorls above pair of upper leaves

Water mint

Mentha aquatica

15-90cm

| J | F | M | A | M | J |
| J | A | S | O | N | D |

Marshes and fens throughout British Isles.

Protruding stamens

Sepals and flower-stalk hairy

Long flower spike

Reddish stems

Peppermint
Mentha × piperita

SPEARMINT

The mint cultivated in gardens for the aroma of its leaves is spearmint, introduced from central Europe as a kitchen herb and much used for mint sauce. It has escaped and become established widely on roadsides and other waste places. The stems are smooth and the leaves hairless and shiny. Additional flowering stems grow in the angle between unstalked leaf and main stem, and end in a long spike of pale lilac flowers in tight whorls.

Another mint cultivated as a herb is apple mint, a cross between spearmint and the rarer round-leaved mint.

Whorls of flowers in long spike

Long protruding stamens

Leaves narrow and hairless, prominent teeth

Stalkless leaves

Denser flower spike

Apple mint
Mentha x villosa

Leaves broad and usually hairy

i	
Spearmint	
Mentha spicata	
To 90cm	

J	F	M	A	M	J
J	A	S	O	N	D

Naturalised on roadsides and waste ground. Widespread, but very scarce in Ireland.

CORN MINT

One mint which lacks the normal minty smell is the wild corn mint. Instead it has a strong acrid smell like overripe cheese, often described as 'sickly'. Corn mint spreads mainly by creeping roots and grows widely in woodland clearings and on arable fields, where it can become a pest. It is usually found in drier places than water mint – the other common wild species. Corn mint's whorls of flowers are less conspicuous than those of most mints, being half hidden at the base of the broad hairy leaves. Corn mint is also unusual among mints in having no known medicinal or culinary properties.

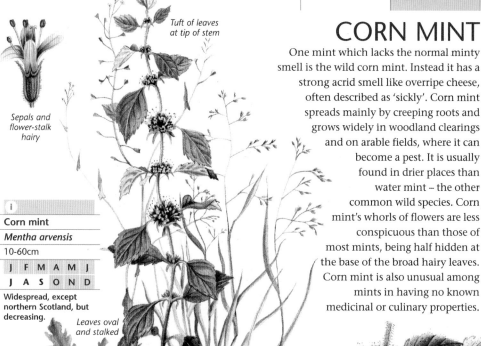

Tuft of leaves at tip of stem

Sepals and flower-stalk hairy

i
Corn mint
Mentha arvensis
10–60cm

| J | F | M | A | M | J |
| J | A | S | O | N | D |

Widespread, except northern Scotland, but decreasing.

Leaves oval and stalked

Flower whorls spaced out along stem

Stems green and hairy

FIELD MADDER

Long tangled stems of field madder sprawl over waste ground, unnoticed until sprays of tiny lilac flowers burst from the tips of the shoots. As if to compensate for their small size, the flowers keep on appearing through most of summer and into autumn. A red dye extracted from the roots of field madder was once used to colour cloth, while another species of madder yielded an even brighter dye used as long ago as Anglo-Saxon times. But these vegetable dyes have been largely superseded by synthetic products.

Long petal tube

Flowers cluster at tip of stem

Prickles on edges and lower surface of leaf

Trailing stems

Whorls of four to six leaves

Field madder

Sherardia arvensis

5-40cm

J	F	M	A	M	J
J	A	S	O	N	D

Widespread on arable and waste ground; rare in Scotland.

SEA ROCKET

Amid the line of driftwood and litter at the top of a sandy beach, the delicate purple, lilac or white flowers of sea rocket provide a contrasting splash of colour. It also grows higher up the shore, where it can help to stabilise young sand-dunes, though it is an annual plant and relies on the tides to disperse its buoyant seed-pods. The fleshy leaves conserve every drop of fresh water that the roots can find, and help the plant to survive salt spray and even burial by sand.

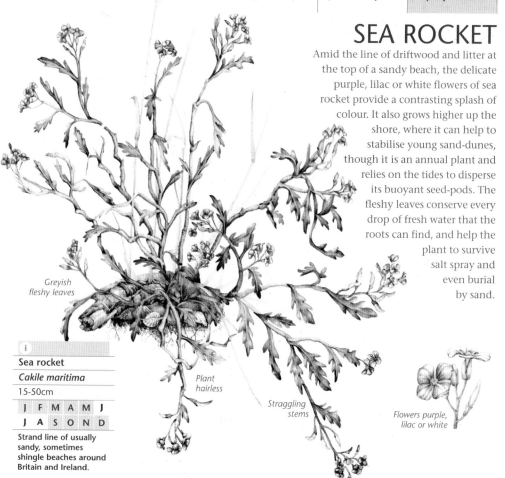

Greyish fleshy leaves

Plant hairless

Straggling stems

Flowers purple, lilac or white

Sea rocket

Cakile maritima

15-50cm

J	F	M	A	M	J
J	A	S	O	N	D

Strand line of usually sandy, sometimes shingle beaches around Britain and Ireland.

CUCKOO FLOWER

The large lilac petals of cuckoo flower often peep above the grass on fragile, criss-crossing stems in unmown pastures in spring. Its lower leaves look like those of watercress. The flowering time of cuckoo flower coincides with the arrival of the cuckoo, while its alternative name of lady's smock may derive from the associations of the rare white-flowered form with milkmaids' smocks.

Flowers cluster at tip of stem

Stems leaves have narrow leaflets

Flowers pale to deep lilac or white

Base leaves have oval leaflets

i						

Cuckoo flower

Cardamine pratensis

15–60cm

J	F	**M**	**A**	**M**	**J**
J	**A**	S	O	N	D

Widespread in damp pastures and meadows throughout the British Isles.

FOXGLOVE

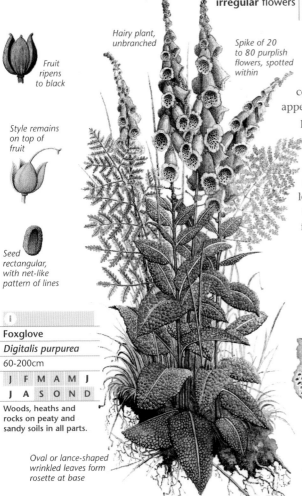

Fruit ripens to black

Style remains on top of fruit

Seed rectangular, with net-like pattern of lines

i

Foxglove

Digitalis purpurea

60–200cm

| J | F | M | A | M | J |
| J | A | S | O | N | D |

Woods, heaths and rocks on peaty and sandy soils in all parts.

Hairy plant, unbranched

Spike of 20 to 80 purplish flowers, spotted within

Oval or lance-shaped wrinkled leaves form rosette at base

As many as 80 separate flowers on a single tall stem make the foxglove conspicuous in woodland clearings. Its appearance belies its deadly quality: every part of the plant is poisonous, though digitalis from its leaves is used in small doses to treat heart disease. In its first year the foxglove produces only a rosette of softly hairy wrinkled leaves. In the second year it sends up a tall stem, and clusters of flowers open from the bottom upwards on one side only. The flowers are usually pinkish purple but sometimes white.

Flowers all on same side of stem

Flowers technically two-lipped with five indistinct lobes

Leaf-stalk winged where it joins stem

HEATH SPEEDWELL

The creeping roots of heath speedwell spread to form dense mats on the dry soils of heaths or woodland regions. The flowers are grouped in long, loose spikes. The individual flowers are on very short stalks, and their upper petals are larger than the lower ones. The leaves are toothed, and hairy on both sides. The name of speedwell may refer to the plant's supposed curative powers in respect of a wide range of ailments.

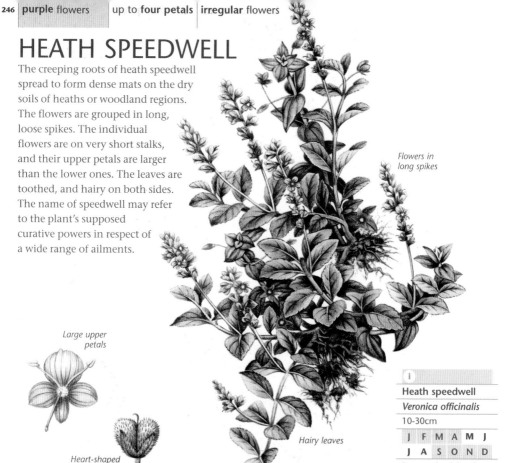

Flowers in long spikes

Large upper petals

Heart-shaped fruit

Hairy leaves

i					
Heath speedwell					
Veronica officinalis					
10-30cm					
J	F	M	A	M	J
J	A	S	O	N	D

Dry grassland, heaths and open woodlands throughout British Isles.

SELFHEAL

There is some resemblance to bugle in the way the closely packed purple flower-heads of selfheal rise above the short grass of meadows and woodland clearings in summer. Like bugle, selfheal also spreads quickly by runners to form a mat along dry, grassy banks. But, while the flowers of bugle have a very short upper lip, those of selfheal have a long hood-shaped upper lip, and the flower spikes of bugle are longer and less dense.

Flowers in dense oblong heads

Long, hood-shaped upper lip

ⓘ

Selfheal

Prunella vulgaris

5-30cm

| J | F | M | A | M | J |
| J | A | S | O | N | D |

Grasslands and waste ground everywhere.

Flat oval leaves, with stalks

MARSH LOUSEWORT

The rarer of Britain's two louseworts is also called red rattle because of the pinkish-purple colouring of its flowers, stem and leaves and the noise made when the ripe seeds are shaken inside the pods.

Marsh lousewort lives partly off other plants, attaching its roots to those of neighbouring grasses to tap their supply of water and mineral salts, without harming the host plant.

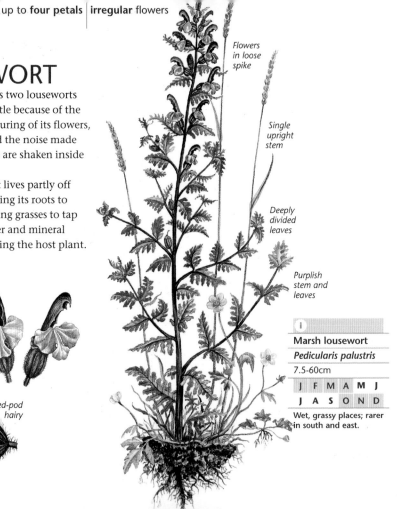

Flowers in loose spike

Single upright stem

Deeply divided leaves

Purplish stem and leaves

Narrow upper lip, broad lower lip

Seed-pod hairy

i						
Marsh lousewort						
Pedicularis palustris						
7.5-60cm						
J	F	M	A	**M**	**J**	
J	**A**	**S**	**O**	N	D	

Wet, grassy places; rarer in south and east.

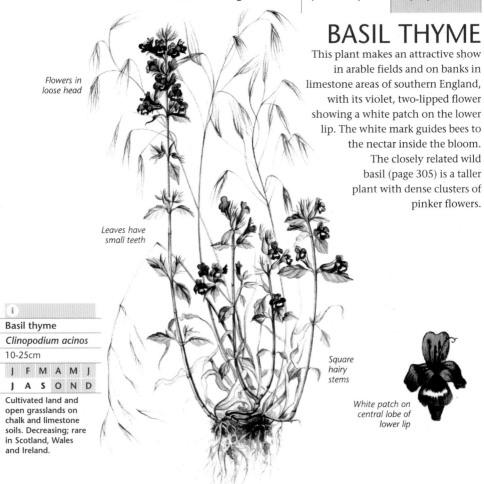

BASIL THYME

This plant makes an attractive show
in arable fields and on banks in
limestone areas of southern England,
with its violet, two-lipped flower
showing a white patch on the lower
lip. The white mark guides bees to
the nectar inside the bloom.
The closely related wild
basil (page 305) is a taller
plant with dense clusters of
pinker flowers.

*Flowers in
loose head*

*Leaves have
small teeth*

i

Basil thyme

Clinopodium acinos

10-25cm

| J | F | M | A | M | J |
| J | A | S | O | N | D |

Cultivated land and
open grasslands on
chalk and limestone
soils. Decreasing; rare
in Scotland, Wales
and Ireland.

*Square
hairy
stems*

*White patch on
central lobe of
lower lip*

SMALL TOADFLAX

This small purple-flowered annual has spread widely since the growth of the railways in the 19th century, as it has adapted itself to growing in the ballast along railway tracks. Related to the snapdragon, its flower tube is partially closed by the 'palate' or fold of the lower lip, and has a short curved spur at the lower end. The narrow greyish leaves mostly grow on alternate sides up the stem.

Flowers pale purple and pale yellow

Upright hairy stems, sometimes branched

Seed elongated and ridged

Narrow lance-shaped leaves

Two-lipped flower with narrow sepals and short spur

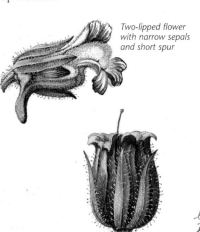

Fruit oval, with teeth

Small toadflax

Chaenorhinum minus

7.5–25cm

| J | F | M | A | M | J |
| J | A | S | O | N | D |

Waste places and arable land; rarer in Scotland and Ireland.

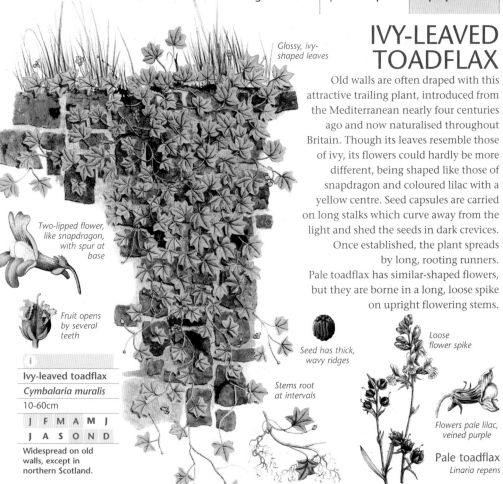

Glossy, ivy-shaped leaves

IVY-LEAVED TOADFLAX

Old walls are often draped with this attractive trailing plant, introduced from the Mediterranean nearly four centuries ago and now naturalised throughout Britain. Though its leaves resemble those of ivy, its flowers could hardly be more different, being shaped like those of snapdragon and coloured lilac with a yellow centre. Seed capsules are carried on long stalks which curve away from the light and shed the seeds in dark crevices. Once established, the plant spreads by long, rooting runners. Pale toadflax has similar-shaped flowers, but they are borne in a long, loose spike on upright flowering stems.

Two-lipped flower, like snapdragon, with spur at base

Fruit opens by several teeth

i

Ivy-leaved toadflax

Cymbalaria muralis

10-60cm

| J | F | M | A | M | J |
| J | A | S | O | N | D |

Widespread on old walls, except in northern Scotland.

Seed has thick, wavy ridges

Stems root at intervals

Loose flower spike

Flowers pale lilac, veined purple

Pale toadflax

Linaria repens

COMMON BUTTERWORT

An insect landing on the slimy leaf of common butterwort quickly finds itself trapped as the leaf curls round it like a clutching hand. The plant engulfs its prey and extracts mineral salts from the body, before the leaf reopens and the dried remains of the insect are blown away. The deadly leaves spread out in a rosette at the base of the stems like a yellow-green starfish. Above, the stems are tall and leafless, bearing at their tops delicate two-lipped violet coloured flowers. Butterwort is also known as bog violet from its favoured habitat of wet heaths and moors.

Single flower on leafless stem

Flowers two-lipped with long spur

Leaf curls up to trap insect

White patch in throat of flowers

Slimy leaves in rosette

i

Common butterwort

Pinguicula vulgaris

5-15cm

J	F	M	A	**M**	**J**
J	**A**	**S**	O	N	D

Wet, peaty ground, mainly in north and west. Rare in south.

BLACK HOREHOUND

Cattle avoid black horehound because of its offensive smell, noticeable to humans when the leaves are crushed between the fingers. As a result the plant flourishes unchecked on waste ground, its tall leafy stems ringed towards the top by whorls of dull red-purple flowers. Black horehound is a larger, coarser plant than red dead-nettle (page 307).

Stalked leaves

Whorls of flowers on upper stem

Black horehound

Ballota nigra

40-100cm

| J | F | M | A | M | J |
| J | A | S | O | N | D |

Hedgerows in England and Wales; rare in Scotland and Ireland.

Hairy stems, not swollen below leaves

White markings on lower lip of flowers

FIELD SCABIOUS

The tallest of the native British species, field scabious has hairy leaves, which are undivided at the base of the plant but become progressively more divided towards the top. Flower-heads are lilac, and the outer flowers are larger than the inner ones. The plants were once used to cure skin diseases such as scabies, hence the name scabious.

Small scabious is rarer, lower-growing and has much more finely segmented leaves on the upper part of its stem. Each individual flower has five petals and the bracts beneath the flower-head are very narrow.

Button-like flower-head

Four petals in each flower

Numerous lilac flowers in flower-head

Inner flower

Outer flower

Leaves divided towards top of stem

Bracts cup flower-head

Upper leaves finely divided

Small scabious
Scabiosa columbaria

ⓘ

Field scabious

Knautia arvensis

25-100cm

| J | F | M | A | M | J |
| J | A | S | O | N | D |

Dry fields throughout British Isles, but rare in northern and western Scotland and northern Ireland.

COMMON COMFREY

Along a river bank on a warm summer day the sight of tall, sturdy, common comfrey is a familiar one. Tight, curved sprays of flowers, purple or cream, rise above bristly stems and leaves. White comfrey has only white flowers, and differs also in having leaves which do not run down the stem. It is an introduced plant of grassy places, mainly in eastern England.

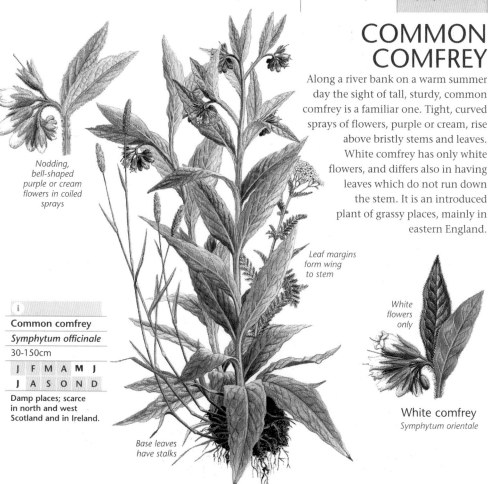

Nodding, bell-shaped purple or cream flowers in coiled sprays

Leaf margins form wing to stem

Base leaves have stalks

White flowers only

White comfrey
Symphytum orientale

i
Common comfrey
Symphytum officinale
30-150cm

J F M A M J
J A S O N D

Damp places; scarce in north and west Scotland and in Ireland.

LESSER PERIWINKLE

The evergreen leaves of periwinkle form a carpet which lasts throughout winter, and their violet flowers arrive early in spring. Rooting stems enable the plant to spread quickly, even though the fruits rarely ripen in Britain. Lesser periwinkle was probably introduced from the Continent in the 16th century.

Greater periwinkle has larger flowers, and longer stems. It is often naturalised, but rare in northern Britain.

Hairless leaves in pairs

White ring around centre

Single flowers on short stems

Stems take root

Sepals form tube with lance-shaped lobes

i					
Lesser periwinkle					
Vinca minor					
30-100cm					
J	F	**M**	**A**	**M**	J
J	**A**	S	O	N	D

Woods and hedges throughout Britain, except far north; very rare in Ireland.

HENBANE

Nobody would want to linger over this evil-looking plant unless, like Dr Crippen, he had murder in mind. All parts of the plant are packed with poison, including the chemical hyoscine, which was used by Crippen to murder his wife in 1910. Sticky white hairs cover the plant, which also emits a disagreeable smell.

The flowers, yellow with purple veins, grow in a leafy one-sided spike. The fruit is a capsule packed with seeds, which opens by a cap at the top. Although once common on waste ground, henbane is today quite rare.

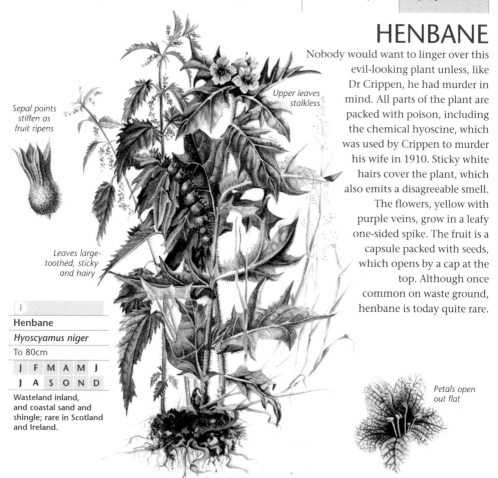

Sepal points stiffen as fruit ripens

Upper leaves stalkless

Leaves large-toothed, sticky and hairy

Petals open out flat

i

Henbane

Hyoscyamus niger

To 80cm

J	F	M	A	M	J
J	A	S	O	N	D

Wasteland inland, and coastal sand and shingle; rare in Scotland and Ireland.

COMMON CORNSALAD

Large, green, leaf-like bracts almost enclose the small lilac flower-heads of common cornsalad, making it an easy plant to overlook. This small member of the valerian family soon dies after it has flowered. The brittle stem is angled and covered in bristles. The leaves are at their greenest and crispest at the end of winter, when lambs are born and, being rich in vitamins, may form an important ingredient of their diet – giving the plant its alternative name of lamb's lettuce.

Angled stems with short prickles, repeatedly branched

Dense flower-heads at tip of branch

Tiny tube-shaped flowers

ℹ					
Common cornsalad					
Valerianella locusta					
5-20cm					

J	F	M	A	M	J
J	A	S	O	N	D

Widespread on rocks, banks and dunes.

COMMON STORK'S-BILL

This sand-loving plant, related to the crane's-bills, has fruits shaped like a long beak. Each seed's corkscrew-like beak twists with changes in humidity, causing the seed to burrow into the ground. Flowers are usually rose-purple, but sometimes white; the upper two petals often have a black spot at the base. Sea stork's-bill is a much smaller plant, its tiny flowers shedding their pink petals early in the day.

Leaves have two rows of finely divided leaflets

Fruit splits from base, each segment carrying corkscrew-beaked seed

Petals longer than sepals

Sea stork's-bill
Erodium maritimum

All parts of plant smaller

Leaves undivided

Stems erect or prostrate, usually hairy

---

i

Common stork's-bill

Erodium cicutarium

To 60cm

| J | F | M | A | M | J |
| J | A | S | O | N | D |

Heaths, dry grassland and sandy seaside areas all over British Isles but mainly in south east.

DOVE'S-FOOT CRANE'S-BILL

This plant gets its common name from the shape of its leaves and its scientific name of *molle*, Latin for 'soft', from the soft downy hair that covers them. In autumn the leaves of plants growing in dry places often turn a brilliant red.

Dusky crane's-bill has dark purple, almost black flowers and is a taller, stouter plant. Cut-leaved crane's-bill has leaves deeply divided into five to seven lobes. Shining crane's-bill has hairless, glossy leaves and is common on limestone walls and banks. All these plants flower from May to August or September.

Petals deeply notched

Stems semi-erect

Sepals pointed and hairy

Petals not notched

Leaves glossy, often reddish

Shining crane's-bill
Geranium lucidum

Petals notched

Leaves deeply divided

Cut-leaved crane's-bill
Geranium dissectum

Soft, rounded leaves, deeply lobed

i

Dove's-foot crane's-bill

Geranium molle

10-40cm

J	F	M	A	M	J
J	A	S	O	N	D

Widespread in grassy and waste places.

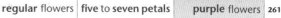

HEDGEROW CRANE'S-BILL

The crane's-bills get their name from the shape of their fruits, which end in a long pointed beak resembling that of a crane. In spite of their generic name they are quite distinct from garden geraniums, which belong to the genus *Pelargonium*. The various species of crane's-bills differ from each other in their colour, and in the way their petals are notched and their leaves divided. The small, pink-purple flowers of hedgerow (or mountain) crane's-bill make a delicate contrast with the tangle of leaves and stalks. The plant was not recorded in Britain until 1762.

Downy, upright stems

Rounded leaves, deeply lobed

i
Hedgerow crane's-bill
Geranium pyrenaicum
20-60cm

| J | F | M | A | M | J |
| J | A | S | O | N | D |

Hedgerows and grassy places, mainly in south and east.

Flowers in pairs, with deeply notched petals

WATER VIOLET

This graceful, aquatic member of the primrose family lives suspended in the water. Its leafless stems, crowned with delicate pinkish-lilac flowers with yellow throats, rise from the surface. Below the water are the green whorls of its finely divided leaves, and its long silvery roots.

Flowers in whorls above water

Fruit bends downwards to drop seeds into water

Water violet

Hottonia palustris

To 40cm above water

| J | F | M | A | **M** | **J** |
| **J** | **A** | S | O | N | D |

Clear water and ditches mainly in eastern and south-east England.

Finely divided leaves in whorls below water

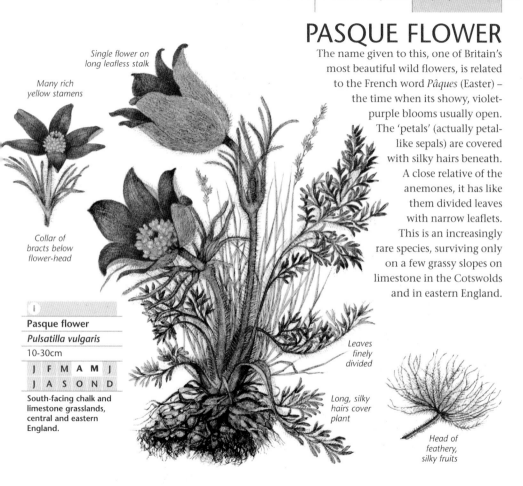

PASQUE FLOWER

The name given to this, one of Britain's most beautiful wild flowers, is related to the French word *Pâques* (Easter) – the time when its showy, violet-purple blooms usually open. The 'petals' (actually petal-like sepals) are covered with silky hairs beneath. A close relative of the anemones, it has like them divided leaves with narrow leaflets. This is an increasingly rare species, surviving only on a few grassy slopes on limestone in the Cotswolds and in eastern England.

Single flower on long leafless stalk

Many rich yellow stamens

Collar of bracts below flower-head

Pasque flower

Pulsatilla vulgaris

10-30cm

| J | F | M | A | M | J |
| J | A | S | O | N | D |

South-facing chalk and limestone grasslands, central and eastern England.

Leaves finely divided

Long, silky hairs cover plant

Head of feathery, silky fruits

BITTERSWEET

The slender stems of bittersweet (also known as woody nightshade) drape a colourful curtain over hedgerows in summer. The display starts with purple-and-yellow flowers in midsummer and continues with berries, green at first, ripening to yellow and finally red. (The related, but much less common, deadly nightshade, opposite, has black berries.) Bittersweet is not as poisonous as deadly nightshade, but all parts of the flower can cause sickness. An alkaloid in the plant is said to give its berries a bitter taste at first, then turning sweet – giving the plant its name.

Petals curve back against stem

Yellow stamens

Oval leaf blade, with shorter lobes beneath

Fruits yellow, then red

i		
Bittersweet		
Solanum dulcamara		
30-200cm		

| J | F | M | A | M | J |
| J | A | S | O | N | D |

Woods, hedges, ditches and shingle beaches throughout Britain, except far north.

DEADLY NIGHTSHADE

This plant has a unique notoriety among poisonous plants, which is perhaps due to the fact that it looks so benign. It is hard to believe that the tempting black, shiny berries could have such violent effects. Pheasants eat them with no ill results, but two or three berries are enough to kill a child. Unlike henbane, it is neither unpleasantly hairy, sticky nor evil smelling. It is a tall plant with dull green, pointed, oval leaves – looking large for the size of the plant – and dull brownish-purple flowers which grow singly in the angle of leaf and stem.

Bell-shaped flowers

Black, glossy berry

Leaves oval and untoothed, often in unequal-sized pairs

Single flower in angle of leaf and stem

i

Deadly nightshade

Atropa belladonna

To 200cm

| J | F | M | A | M | J |
| J | A | S | O | N | D |

Woodland, hedgerows and thickets in the south and east; rare elsewhere.

CLUSTERED BELLFLOWER

Usually a much smaller plant than nettle-leaved and giant bellflowers, clustered bellflower, as its name indicates, carries its flowers in stalkless clusters at the top of the stem. The flowers are rich violet coloured and bell shaped with five spreading lobes. The stems and leaves are hairy. Although the plant can be as much as 80cm tall, it is usually much shorter than this.

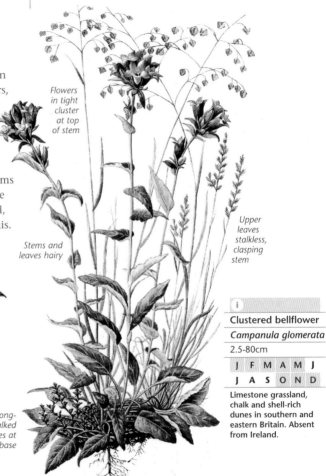

Flowers in tight cluster at top of stem

Stems and leaves hairy

Upper leaves stalkless, clasping stem

Stalkless violet flowers

Long-stalked leaves at base

Clustered bellflower

Campanula glomerata

2.5-80cm

| J | F | M | A | M | J |
| J | A | S | O | N | D |

Limestone grassland, chalk and shell-rich dunes in southern and eastern Britain. Absent from Ireland.

GOAT'S-RUE

Upright spikes of flowers make goat's-rue an attractive ornamental plant. It was introduced in the 16th century as a vegetable and medicinal herb but has now established itself on damp waste ground in the wild. A member of the pea family, goat's-rue is distinguished from the purple-flowered vetches by having a terminal leaflet instead of a tendril at the end of its leaves. White melilot, also found on waste ground, has only three leaflets to its leaves and its fruits contain a single seed compared with several in each pod of goat's-rue. It was introduced to Britain as a fodder plant.

Pods straight and smoothly rounded

Four to eight pairs of leaflets, with leaflet at tip

Flowers in upright spikes, lilac or white

i
Goat's-rue
Galega officinalis
60-150cm
J F M A M J J A S O N D
Naturalised in places on damp waste ground. Rare in Wales and Scotland; absent from Ireland.

Long upper petal

White melilot
Melilotus albus

LUCERNE

Introduced to Britain from the Mediterranean region in the 17th century, lucerne was, until quite recently, widely grown as a fodder crop. It is a member of the pea family and so has the ability to 'fix' nitrogen in the soil, enriching the ground for future cultivation. The violet flowers are carried in short spikes at the tips of branched stalks. Three leaflets, toothed towards the tip, make up the leaf, whose stalk has two narrow stipules at its base. The fruits are curved into spirals. Lucerne is also known as alfalfa.

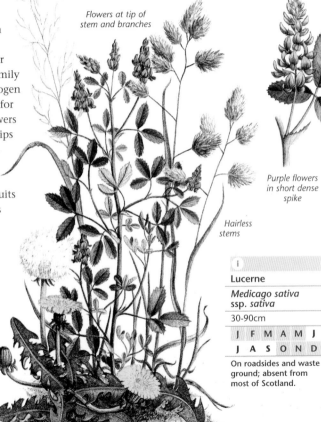

Flowers at tip of stem and branches

Purple flowers in short dense spike

Hairless stems

Three leaflets, toothed towards top; narrow stipules at base

i
Lucerne
Medicago sativa ssp. *sativa*
30-90cm
J F M A M J
J A S O N D
On roadsides and waste ground; absent from most of Scotland.

PURPLE MILK-VETCH

This creeping herb is inconspicuous until it comes into flower in May and produces heads of purple flowers on long stems. The flowers are very like those of clover, but the leaves are totally different, being divided into numerous leaflets covered with soft whitish hairs. The seed-pods, too, are covered with white hairs. Vast sweeps of purple milk-vetch bring rich colour to sandy hills in the Breckland region of Norfolk and Suffolk and other eastern areas; it is uncommon in the west. The plant's name derives from a belief that it increased the milk yield of goats.

Flower-heads on upright stems above leaves

Many hairy leaflets

i

Purple milk-vetch

Astragalus danicus

5-30cm

| J | F | M | A | M | J |
| J | A | S | O | N | D |

Chalk and limestone grassland, mainly in eastern Britain.

Short seed-pods covered with white hairs

Sepals joined into tube covered with short hairs

BUSH VETCH

Climbing by tendrils which grow from the tips of the leaves, bush vetch scrambles high over other plants, draping them with its long leaves and short spikes of dull purple flowers. The pods are black when ripe. This is one of the commonest British vetches, and its flowers appear throughout summer.

Wood vetch has larger flowers, delicately veined with lilac. It is most prolific on woodland borders, but grows also on cliffs and shingle by the sea. Hairy tare is also a vetch and has branched tendrils, rather than leaflets, at its leaf tips.

Up to six flowers in each flower-head

Each flower has five petals

Five to nine pairs of small leaflets

Stems climb by branched tendril at tip of leaf

Tendril at leaf tip

Tiny pale lilac flowers

Hairy tare
Vicia hirsuta

Larger flowers and leaflets

Wood vetch
Vicia sylvatica

i

Bush vetch

Vicia sepium

30-60cm

| J | F | M | A | M | J |
| J | A | S | O | N | D |

Rough, grassy places and hedges throughout British Isles.

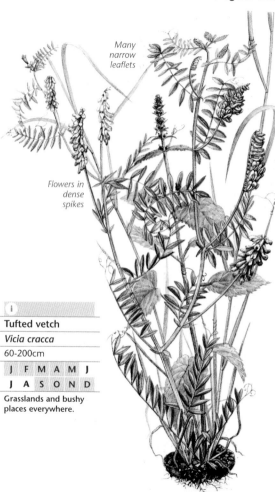

Many narrow leaflets

Flowers in dense spikes

TUFTED VETCH

As many as 30 attractive violet-purple flowers in a single spike make tufted vetch one of the most distinctive plants that scramble over grasslands and hedgerows. The pea-like flowers grow on only one side of the long stalk, and emerge continuously throughout summer. The leaves consist of up to 30 greyish leaflets. From the tip of the leaf emerges a branched tendril, which winds around neighbouring plants and enables tufted vetch to climb 180cm or more.

ⓘ

Tufted vetch

Vicia cracca

60–200cm

| J | F | M | A | M | J |
| J | A | S | O | N | D |

Grasslands and bushy places everywhere.

Branched tendril at leaf tip

Up to 30 flowers in each spike

COMMON VETCH

To distinguish common vetch from other British vetches, look first at the base of the leaf. Here, common vetch alone has a black blotch on each stipule. Despite its name, common vetch is very rare, apart from in south-east England, where it was introduced from the Continent for cattle food and subsequently spread on to waste ground. Like other vetches it climbs by branched tendrils sprouting from the tip of the leaf. At the end of summer the flowers develop into seed-pods 36–70mm long, which are slightly hairy, with depressions between the seeds.

Flowers usually in pairs

Four to eight pairs of leaflets

Branched tendrils

Stipules at base of stalk have dark blotch

Pods slightly hairy, with short beak

Common vetch

Vicia sativa ssp. *sativa*

15-150cm

| J | F | M | A | M | J |
| J | A | S | O | N | D |

Waste places, mainly in south-east England.

Tiny lilac flowers with five petals

Twines through other plants such as this knapweed

SMOOTH TARE

The name tare, originally applied to vetch seed, is today used for three small vetch species. In the Biblical parable, tare was the weed sown by the farmer's enemies to adulterate his wheat harvest. In 17th-century England, too, tare used to twine its way through crops of wheat, barley and oats – but this was mainly the pale lilac-flowered hairy tare (page 270). Smooth tare – with deep lilac flowers carried singly or in pairs, and smooth four-seeded pods rather than the hairy two-seeded pods of its relative – is a plant of grassy places. It has similar tendrilled leaves to other vetches.

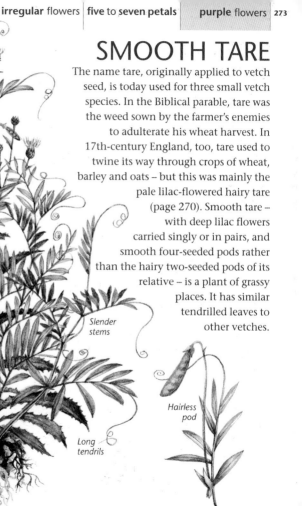

Slender stems

Hairless pod

i
Smooth tare
Vicia tetrasperma
15–60cm

| J | F | M | A | M | J |
| J | A | S | O | N | D |

Grassy places, mainly on clay soils in lowland Britain. Rare in Scotland and Ireland.

Long tendrils

SWEET VIOLET

Of around ten species of violets growing wild in Britain, only sweet violet has the scent which gives the family its reputation for fragrance. The plant flowers as early as February, long before most spring flowers have peeped above the wintry earth. The flowers rise on long stalks straight from the rosette of leaves at the base. White-flowered forms occasionally occur.

In addition to the showy flowers, the plant later bears small inconspicuous flowers at the base, which remain closed and produce seed capsules.

Flower-stalks leafless

Blunt sepals

Flowers rich violet with violet spur

Round, hairy capsule produced from inconspicuous closed flowers

Creeping runners grow from rosette and roots

i	
Sweet violet	
Viola odorata	
To 10cm	

J	F	M	A	M	J
J	A	S	O	N	D

Woods and hedgerows, mostly in England.

Hairy heart-shaped leaves which enlarge after flowering

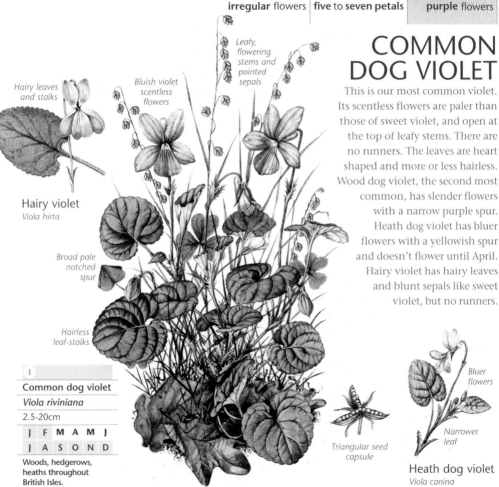

COMMON DOG VIOLET

This is our most common violet. Its scentless flowers are paler than those of sweet violet, and open at the top of leafy stems. There are no runners. The leaves are heart shaped and more or less hairless. Wood dog violet, the second most common, has slender flowers with a narrow purple spur. Heath dog violet has bluer flowers with a yellowish spur and doesn't flower until April. Hairy violet has hairy leaves and blunt sepals like sweet violet, but no runners.

Hairy leaves and stalks

Hairy violet
Viola hirta

Bluish violet scentless flowers

Leafy, flowering stems and pointed sepals

Broad pale notched spur

Hairless leaf-stalks

Common dog violet

Viola riviniana

2.5-20cm

| J | F | M | A | M | J |
| J | A | S | O | N | D |

Woods, hedgerows, heaths throughout British Isles.

Triangular seed capsule

Bluer flowers

Narrower leaf

Heath dog violet
Viola canina

EARLY PURPLE ORCHID

The flowers of this orchid brighten woodland in spring. The flower has a three-lobed lip, on which insects land, and a stout blunt-ended spur which holds nectar. Most of the glossy leaves are arranged in a rosette at the base of the stem, and they usually have purplish blotches on the upper surface.

The green-winged orchid is smaller, has no blotches on the leaves and green veins on the three upper petal-like sepals. It grows on grassland but is decreasing dramatically.

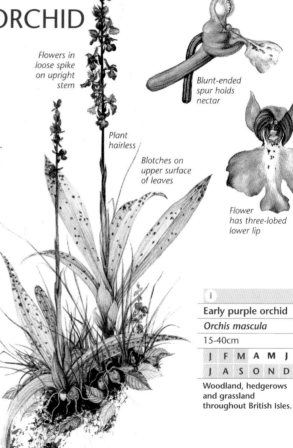

Flowers in loose spike on upright stem

Plant hairless

Blunt-ended spur holds nectar

Blotches on upper surface of leaves

Flower has three-lobed lower lip

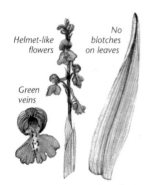

Helmet-like flowers

No blotches on leaves

Green veins

Green-winged orchid
Anacamptis morio

Early purple orchid

Orchis mascula

15–40cm

| J | F | M | A | M | J |
| J | A | S | O | N | D |

Woodland, hedgerows and grassland throughout British Isles.

SEA ASTER

Fleshy leaves enable the sea aster to retain as much fresh water as possible on the salt-marshes and sea cliffs where it grows. In August whole areas of salt-marsh take on a lilac tinge as the flower-heads open. Each flower- head is a tight cluster of small florets, yellow disc florets at the centre and bluish-lilac ray florets around the edge. Sometimes the outer florets are lacking. Sea aster was a popular garden plant in Elizabethan times. It is a close relative of garden Michaelmas daisies.

Plant hairless

Narrow fleshy leaves

i
Sea aster
Aster tripolium
15-100cm

J F M A M J
J A S O N D

Salt-marshes around most of coast.

Lilac and yellow florets

BLUE FLEABANE

Because its outer rings of petal-like purple florets remain upright rather than spreading, blue fleabane looks as though it is perpetually in bud instead of opening into full flower. It is a plant of chalk and limestone grassland, dunes and walls. The dull purple outer florets enclose an inner core of pale yellow, tube-shaped florets. White hairs on the flowers act as parachutes to disperse the seeds, which can lie dormant for years until the soil is turned.

Flower-heads remain tight

Narrow, unstalked leaves

Reddish hairy stems

Yellow at centre, dull purple at edge

i
Blue fleabane
Erigeron acer
10-60cm

| J | F | M | A | M | J |
| J | A | S | O | N | D |

Dry grassy places and walls, mainly in southern Britain; rare in Scotland and Ireland.

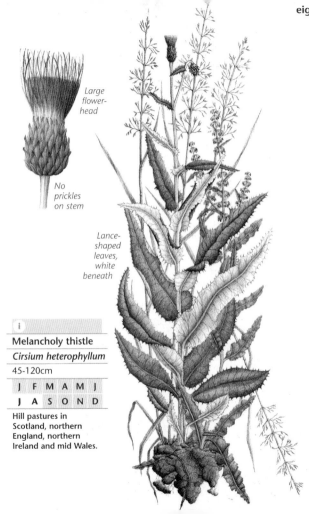

Large flower-head

No prickles on stem

Lance-shaped leaves, white beneath

Melancholy thistle
Cirsium heterophyllum
45-120cm

| J | F | M | A | M | J |
| J | A | S | O | N | D |

Hill pastures in Scotland, northern England, northern Ireland and mid Wales.

MELANCHOLY THISTLE

The large red-purple flower-heads of melancholy thistle – up to 50mm across – usually grow singly, though sometimes there are two or three together. The leaves are green above and white beneath, edged with soft prickles, and the lower ones may be lobed.

Dwarf thistle is the most unobtrusive of all thistles. Its low rosettes of spiny leaves, with up to four flower-heads (but usually just one) at the centre of each rosette, grow on short turf on dry, shallow, lime-rich soils.

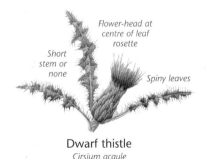

Flower-head at centre of leaf rosette

Short stem or none

Spiny leaves

Dwarf thistle
Cirsium acaule

COTTON THISTLE

This tall, sturdy thistle gets its name from the white cottony hairs that cover its stem and strongly spined leaves. Though popularly known as the Scotch thistle, this is a misnomer, as it is a rare plant in Scotland – in fact the thistle of Scottish heraldry is believed to be the spear thistle (opposite). The flower-head is large and usually solitary, and the florets are purple or, rarely, white.

Stalkless cottony leaves

Flower-head large, bracts spiny

Hairy stem with spiny wings

i

Cotton thistle

Onopordum acanthium

45-250cm

J	F	M	A	M	J
J	**A**	**S**	**O**	**N**	**D**

Roadsides and field edges in England and Wales; commonest in eastern England. Possibly native in East Anglia; introduced elsewhere.

CREEPING THISTLE

The sweetly scented lilac flowers of creeping thistle attract butterflies, but its invasive root system makes the plant unpopular with gardeners and farmers. Hairy 'parachutes' carry the seeds long distances. Spear thistle has larger flower-heads, spiny stems and spear-like leaf tips. Marsh thistle is a tall, often purple-tinged plant with spiny-winged stems and clustered flowers, dark red-purple or, quite often, white.

Bracts weakly spined, often purplish

Spineless stem with clusters of flowers at top

Spiny leaves, usually lobed

Creeping thistle

Cirsium arvense

30-120cm

| J | F | M | A | M | J |
| J | A | S | O | N | D |

Fields, roadsides and waste places throughout British Isles.

Long, narrow terminal lobe to leaf

Spear thistle
Cirsium vulgare

Clustered flower-heads

Spiny wings along stems

Marsh thistle
Cirsium palustre

WELTED THISTLE

Spine-covered wings, or welts, run up the length of the stem, stopping just short of the flower-heads. The leaves are lobed and very spiny. Spreading bracts surround the purple flower-heads, which grow in clusters. Butterflies, hoverflies and bees pollinate this tall prickly plant.

The musk thistle is distinguished by its nodding, red-purple flowers, which are scented. It normally grows on drier ground than the welted thistle.

Spiny wings or welts along stem

Bracts spreading

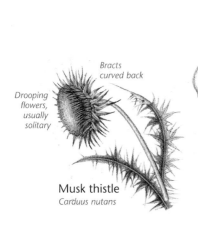

Bracts curved back

Drooping flowers, usually solitary

Musk thistle
Carduus nutans

i

Welted thistle

Carduus crispus

30-150cm

| J | F | M | A | M | J |
| J | A | S | O | N | D |

Damp grassy areas, scarcer in north and west.

SAW-WORT

The word *serratula* in saw-wort's scientific name is Latin for 'little saw', after the saw-like edge of the leaves, which were once believed to heal wounds; *tinctoria*, means 'pertaining to dyers', and shows that the plant was used in dyeing cloth. Saw-wort is often confused with knapweed, but it differs in having no feathery rim on the overlapping bracts round the flower-heads. The bracts are purplish and the small purple flower-heads are in clusters.

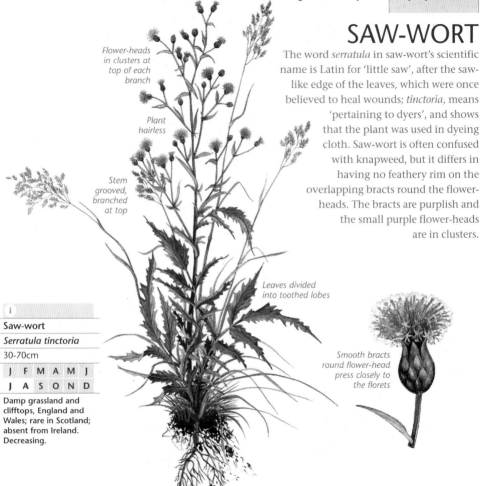

Flower-heads in clusters at top of each branch

Plant hairless

Stem grooved, branched at top

Leaves divided into toothed lobes

Smooth bracts round flower-head press closely to the florets

Saw-wort

Serratula tinctoria

30-70cm

J F M A M J
J A S O N D

Damp grassland and clifftops, England and Wales; rare in Scotland; absent from Ireland. Decreasing.

COMMON KNAPWEED

This tall grassland plant, rather like a thistle with no prickles, gets its alternative name of hardheads from its knob-like flower-buds; it is also known as black knapweed. The heads owe their hardness to the rows of overlapping blackish bracts, which surround the reddish-purple florets. The flower-heads usually have only disc florets but sometimes rayed florets are present.

Stalkless upper leaves

Hairy grooved stem

Bracts with blackish-brown tips

Lower leaves sometimes lobed

Feathery-tipped bracts cover base of flower-head

i
Common knapweed
Centaurea nigra
30-100cm

J	F	M	A	M	J
J	**A**	**S**	**O**	**N**	**D**

Widespread on grassland, roadsides and rough ground.

GREATER KNAPWEED

Though greater knapweed is larger than common knapweed, the easiest way to distinguish the two is to compare the flower-heads. Greater knapweed always has enlarged spreading florets, whereas common knapweed usually has only smaller disc florets. On common knapweed, the dark brown appendages at the top of the bracts are triangular or circular; on greater knapweed they are horseshoe shaped.

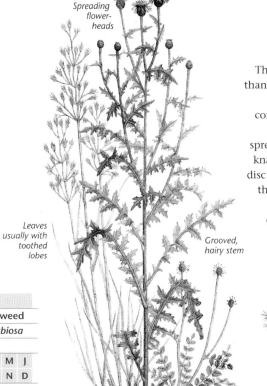

Spreading flower-heads

Leaves usually with toothed lobes

Grooved, hairy stem

Enlarged florets, dark brown edges to bracts

i
Greater knapweed
Centaurea scabiosa
30-120cm

J	F	M	A	M	J
J	A	S	O	N	D

Roadsides and dry, lime-rich grassland, rarer in north and west.

Red
AND pink
FLOWERS

BELL HEATHER

*Bell-shaped
flowers in spikes*

The plant's name highlights its most
easily recognised feature – the elegantly
shaped, deep crimson bells. These are
larger than the flowers of true heather,
and hang in loose spikes near the top
of the stem. When the plant is not
in bloom it can be recognised by the
dark green, hairless evergreen leaves
which grow on very short stalks in
whorls, usually of three. The habitat
of bell heather helps to distinguish
it from its relative
cross-leaved heath.
Bell heather grows
on the driest tussocks
of a moor, while cross-
leaved heath grows in the
wetter parts. The latter has
rose-pink flowers.

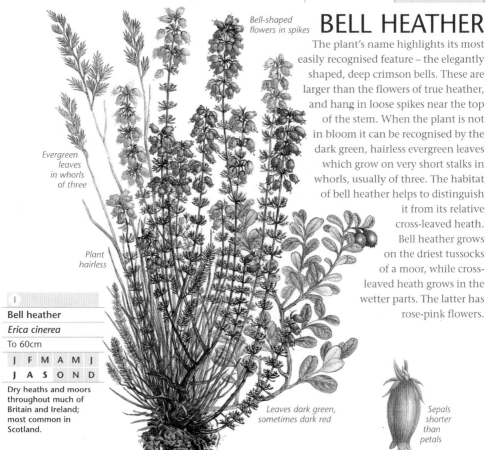

*Evergreen
leaves
in whorls
of three*

*Plant
hairless*

i
Bell heather
Erica cinerea
To 60cm

J	F	M	A	M	J
J	A	S	O	N	D

Dry heaths and moors
throughout much of
Britain and Ireland;
most common in
Scotland.

*Leaves dark green,
sometimes dark red*

*Sepals
shorter
than
petals*

CROSS-LEAVED HEATH

Whorls of four narrow leaves form a cross when looked at from above, giving this plant its name. The leaves are very hairy and have long bristles, each tipped with a round gland. The soft rose-pink flowers are rounder than those of bell heather and grouped in more compact, rounded heads at the top of the stem. The dense hairs on stems, leaves and sepals give the plant a greyish appearance. Like all heathers, cross-leaved heath is a sprawling plant, with central branches which tend to become bare as it ages.

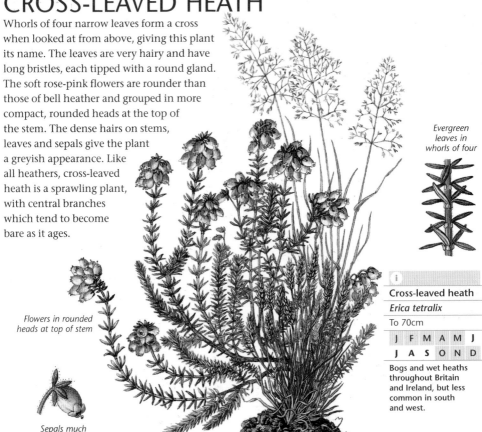

Evergreen leaves in whorls of four

Flowers in rounded heads at top of stem

Sepals much shorter than petals

Cross-leaved heath

Erica tetralix

To 70cm

| J | F | M | A | M | J |
| J | A | S | O | N | D |

Bogs and wet heaths throughout Britain and Ireland, but less common in south and west.

CRANBERRY

Flowers on long, thin stalks

Petals curl back

While the flowers of bilberry hide modestly among the leaves, those of cranberry rise proudly above the leaves on tall, thin stalks carried singly or in groups of up to four flowers. Perhaps the similarity of the shape of the stalk to that of a crane's neck gave the plant its name. The flowers of cranberry are also quite different in shape from those of other members of the heather family in having petals which curl back from the stamens. Cranberry is an evergreen plant of wet areas, especially bogs, and it spreads outwards by means of slender rooting stems. Its sharp red berries make tasty jam and sauce and a filling for pies.

Evergreen oval leaves, silvery beneath

Globular or pear-shaped berries

---

i

Cranberry

Vaccinium oxycoccos

To 30cm

| J | F | M | A | M | J |
| J | A | S | O | N | D |

Bogs and wet heaths in much of British Isles but absent from most of southern and eastern England and northern Scotland.

BILBERRY

The dainty bell-shaped flowers of bilberry mark the plant as a member of the heather family, but unlike its close relatives it sheds its leaves in winter. The flowers are often half concealed among the bright green leaves, which have conspicuous veins. Bilberry thrives on poor, acid soil and grows abundantly in high places such as mountain forests and moors. The berries turn black with a blue-grey bloom from July onwards and have an excellent flavour eaten raw or made into pies and jellies. They are also known as whortleberries or blaeberries.

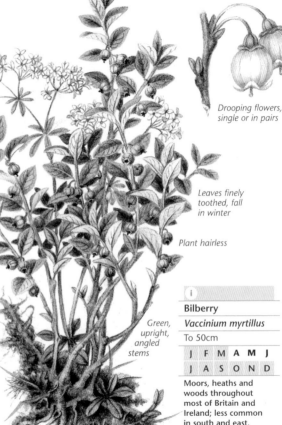

Drooping flowers, single or in pairs

Leaves finely toothed, fall in winter

Plant hairless

Green, upright, angled stems

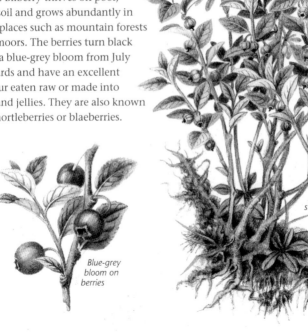

Blue-grey bloom on berries

i
Bilberry
Vaccinium myrtillus
To 50cm

J	F	M	A	M	J
J	A	S	O	N	D

Moors, heaths and woods throughout most of Britain and Ireland; less common in south and east.

CROWBERRY

The glossy evergreen leaves of crowberry are specially adapted to life on the dry rocky moors where it thrives. They curl inwards, almost meeting down the centre, to form a narrow tube that reduces the loss of moisture by evaporation through the pores on the leaf surface. Male and female flowers are borne on separate plants, the male flowers having three long red projecting stamens. Each flower has three petals and three sepals. The slender sprawling stems, often reddish when young, hug the ground and spread rapidly. The black fruits, acid to the taste, are eaten by grouse and ptarmigan.

Narrow, glossy, bright green leaves with edges rolled inwards

Crowberry

Empetrum nigrum

15-100cm

J F M A **M** J
J A S O N **D**

Moors and mountains; in Scotland, northern England, Wales and Ireland.

Slender sprawling stems

Tiny flower at base of leaf

Black, globe-shaped fruit

WILD THYME

The sprawling, low-growing stems of wild thyme are in sharp contrast with the upright spikes of the familiar garden herb, which comes from the Mediterranean and does not grow wild in Britain. Wild thyme forms a dense carpet on grassland and sand-dunes, often excluding other plants. Its short stems bear dense flower-heads which attract insects, especially honey-bees.

Large thyme, found mostly in southern England, is a more upright plant, differentiated from its more widespread relative by having hairs on the angles of its squarish stem instead of on two opposite faces and a stronger scent.

Hairs on all four angles of stem

Large thyme
Thymus pulegioides

Wild thyme
Thymus polytrichus
To 10cm

| J | F | M | A | M | J |
| J | A | S | O | N | D |

Widespread on dry grassland, heaths and dunes.

Many flowers in dense flower-head

Four-sided stem, hairy on two opposite sides

Sprawling stems and short upright flowering branches

FLOWERING-RUSH

Though it grows alongside rushes
beside rivers and ponds, flowering-
rush is not a rush at all but a much
more ornamental plant whose graceful
stance and brightly coloured flowers
have earned it a place in many gardens.
The greyish-green leaves all grow from
the base, and each leafless unbranched
stem supports a single cluster of
flowers, each with three petals
and three sepals.

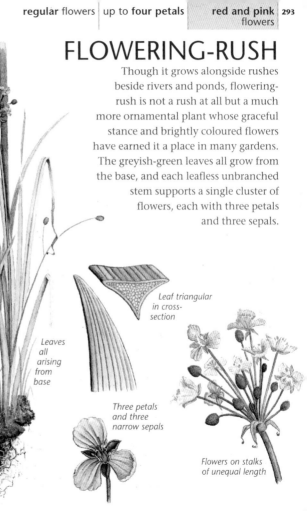

*Flowers in cluster
on leafless stem*

*Fruit in
six segments*

*Leaf triangular
in cross-
section*

*Leaves
all
arising
from
base*

*Three petals
and three
narrow sepals*

*Flowers on stalks
of unequal length*

Flowering-rush

Butomus umbellatus

To 150cm

| J | F | M | A | M | J |
| J | A | S | O | N | D |

Fresh water edges;
scattered in British Isles,
mainly in England, rare
in Scotland, Wales and
Ireland. Decreasing.

HOARY PLANTAIN

The hoary plantain's most obvious feature is its tall leafless spike rising from a flat rosette of leaves at the base. Pink stamens give the flower-head a pinkish appearance, unlike the green or brownish flowers of other plantains. These flowers are scented and attract insect pollinators; in this the hoary plantain differs from other plantains which are pollinated by the wind and do not need the attention of insects. The description 'hoary' refers to the whitish hairs covering the leaves, which also bear conspicuous veins.

Long pink stamens with whitish tips

Single flower-head on leafless stalk

Leaf has conspicuous veins and whitish hairs

Leaves with short stalks

Flat rosette of broad, oval leaves

i						
Hoary plantain						
Plantago media						
To 40cm						
J	F	M	A	**M**	**J**	
J	**A**	**S**	**O**	**N**	D	

Usually on chalk and limestone grassland, mostly in England.

GREAT WILLOWHERB

The height of great willowherb is as distinctive as the hairiness of its stem and leaves which gives the species its scientific name of *hirsutum*. The upright stems bear solitary rosy flowers, which form bright patches of colour by the edge of rivers and in field-side ditches. The plant's seeds are plumed to ensure wide dispersal, but the plant also spreads by fleshy stems just below ground. These give rise to dense clumps, which exclude other plants.

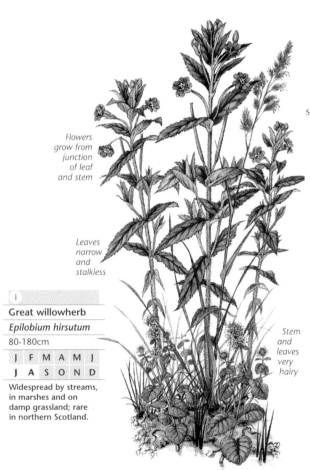

Flowers grow from junction of leaf and stem

Leaves narrow and stalkless

Stem and leaves very hairy

> **Great willowherb**
>
> *Epilobium hirsutum*
>
> 80-180cm
>
> | J | F | M | A | M | J |
> | J | A | S | O | N | D |
>
> Widespread by streams, in marshes and on damp grassland; rare in northern Scotland.

Cream stigma four-lobed and cross-shaped

Sepals green

Petals slightly notched

BROAD-LEAVED WILLOWHERB

Willowherbs are named after their narrow willow-like leaves, but the leaves of this species are slightly broader than those of its relatives. They are in opposite pairs, growing out horizontally from the stem on short stalks. The long ripe seed-capsule splits into four from the top to release the plumed seeds.

American willowherb, first recorded in Britain in 1891, is now common on old railway lines and waste places. Its upper stem is covered in glistening hairs. It has a club-shaped stigma.

Flower has four-lobed, cross-shaped stigma

Narrow sepals reddish-green

Petals deeply notched

Leaves broad and very short-stalked

Stems almost hairless

Petals notched and horizontal

Upper stem has glistening hairs

American willowherb
Epilobium ciliatum

i
Broad-leaved willowherb
Epilobium montanum
To 75cm

J	F	M	A	M	J
J	A	S	O	N	D

Widespread in shady places, hedgerows throughout the British Isles.

ROSEBAY WILLOWHERB

Tall stems bright with purplish red flowers in summer and white with fluffy seed heads in autumn make this one of the most easily recognised flowers of waste ground. It thrives especially on bonfire sites in cleared woodland – hence its alternative name of 'fireweed'. The Victorians often grew rosebay willowherb in gardens. Left to itself in such surroundings, however, it would quickly drive out other flowers.

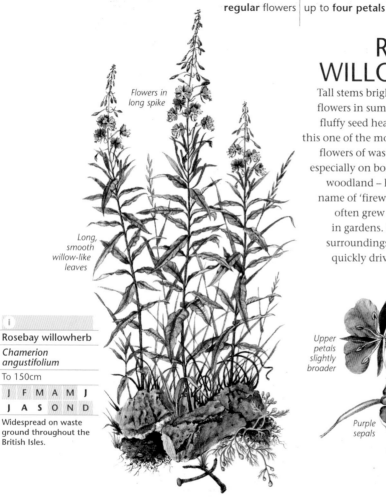

Flowers in long spike

Long, smooth willow-like leaves

ⓘ
Rosebay willowherb
Chamerion angustifolium
To 150cm
J F M A M **J**
J **A S O** N **D**
Widespread on waste ground throughout the British Isles.

Upper petals slightly broader

Purple sepals

Four-lobed stigma

WILD TEASEL

The spiny oval heads of teasel tower above surrounding vegetation. The spikiness of teasel is not confined to the heads. The rest of the plant is also prickly – there are toothed bracts below the heads, prickles along the stem and pointed, saw-toothed leaves. Flowers in the middle area of the flower-head open before those above and below. The dead stems and flower-heads remain throughout winter. The name 'teasel' comes from its former use for teasing out wool fibres in preparation for spinning.

Long pointed leaves, joined at base to form cup

Four lilac-pink petals per flower and many flowers per flower-head

Prickly flower-head surrounded by curved, spiny bracts

Spiny prickles on angled stem

Wild teasel

Dipsacus fullonum

45-200cm

| J | F | M | A | M | J |
| J | A | S | O | N | D |

Rough pastures and roadsides in England, Wales and southern Scotland; rare elsewhere.

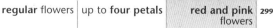

COMMON POPPY

Weedkillers have largely eradicated the poppies which used to blaze scarlet among the growing corn – but the poppy is making a fighting comeback in hedgerows and along the banks of new roads. A single plant may produce more than 400 flowers in succession during summer, and seeds are scattered like pepper from a pot. The shape of the seed-pod distinguishes the common poppy from its more northerly relative, the long-headed poppy, which has paler flowers.

Rounded seed-pod

Petals overlap

Stamen tips bluish-black

Large solitary flowers

Blotch at base of petal

Upper leaves stalkless, with oblong lobes

Hairs at right angle to stem

Common poppy

Papaver rhoeas

20-60cm

| J | F | M | A | M | J |
| J | A | S | O | N | D |

Lowland, field edges and roadsides; rarer in north and west.

Hairs flat

Long, narrow seed-pod

Long-headed poppy
Papaver dubium

GREAT BURNET

Damp old meadows provide a haven for the great burnet, which in many areas has lost ground to intensive farming. It is an upright perennial, with many hairless branches. The leaves are composed of paired rows of toothed leaflets, and the tiny crimson flowers are closely packed in an oblong head 10-13mm long. The flowers have no petals, the colour coming from the dark red sepals and stamens.

The related salad burnet (page 374) is a smaller, green-flowered plant.

Dark green, toothed leaflets

Flowers have no petals

Hairless stems

Flowers in dense head

Great burnet

Sanguisorba officinalis

30-120cm

J	F	M	A	M	J
J	A	S	O	N	D

Old meadows, central and northern England and Wales.

RED BARTSIA

A less conspicuous relative of the foxglove, red bartsia has small purplish-pink flowers which are almost lost among the leaf-like bracts below them. The stems and bracts are often reddish coloured. Hairs growing all over the plant give it a dusty appearance. Red bartsia is a partial parasite, its roots fastening on to those of nearby plants and obtaining nutrients from them.

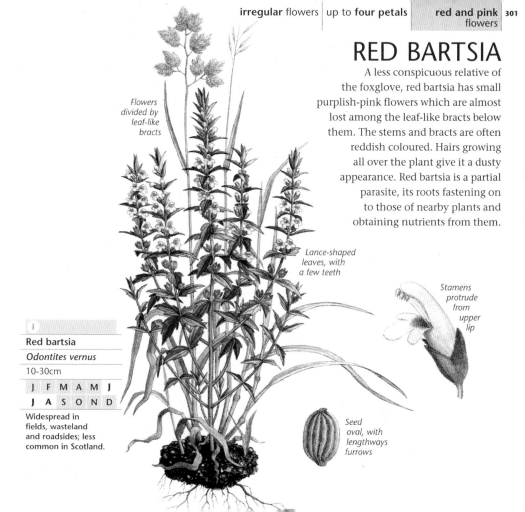

Flowers divided by leaf-like bracts

Lance-shaped leaves, with a few teeth

Stamens protrude from upper lip

i

Red bartsia

Odontites vernus

10-30cm

| J | F | M | A | M | J |
| J | A | S | O | N | D |

Widespread in fields, wasteland and roadsides; less common in Scotland.

Seed oval, with lengthways furrows

LOUSEWORT

The commoner of Britain's two
louseworts is a creeping plant
with many short trailing or upright
stems. The leaves of both species are
divided into many toothed leaflets.
Lousewort is, however, a paler plant
than red rattle, or marsh lousewort.
The sepal tube becomes inflated
around the seed-pod. Lousewort
obtains nutrients from the roots
of plants growing around it.

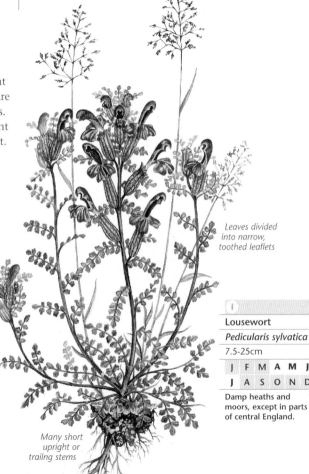

*Leaves divided
into narrow,
toothed leaflets*

*Lower lip has
three lobes*

*Sepal tube
inflated
around
seed-pod*

*Many short
upright or
trailng stems*

i
Lousewort
Pedicularis sylvatica
7.5-25cm

J	F	M	A	M	J
J	A	S	O	N	D

Damp heaths and
moors, except in parts
of central England.

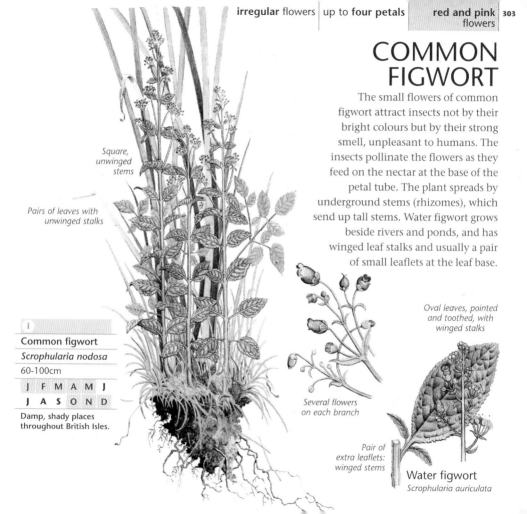

COMMON FIGWORT

The small flowers of common figwort attract insects not by their bright colours but by their strong smell, unpleasant to humans. The insects pollinate the flowers as they feed on the nectar at the base of the petal tube. The plant spreads by underground stems (rhizomes), which send up tall stems. Water figwort grows beside rivers and ponds, and has winged leaf stalks and usually a pair of small leaflets at the leaf base.

Square, unwinged stems

Pairs of leaves with unwinged stalks

i

Common figwort

Scrophularia nodosa

60-100cm

J F M A M J J A S O N D

Damp, shady places throughout British Isles.

Several flowers on each branch

Oval leaves, pointed and toothed, with winged stalks

Pair of extra leaflets: winged stems

Water figwort
Scrophularia auriculata

WILD MARJORAM

The cultivated marjoram used as a herb in the kitchen comes from the Mediterranean, but the wild variety growing on chalk and limestone grassland in Britain is grown as the herb oregano. The leaves, which exude a scent, can be used to make a herb tea and herb sachets. Like those of other members of the mint family, wild marjoram's flowers are tube-shaped, with two lips. The tiny flowers are pink, but the leaf-shaped bracts beneath them give a purplish tinge to the flower-heads. These are carried at the top of the tall, upright stem, which has leaves in opposite pairs.

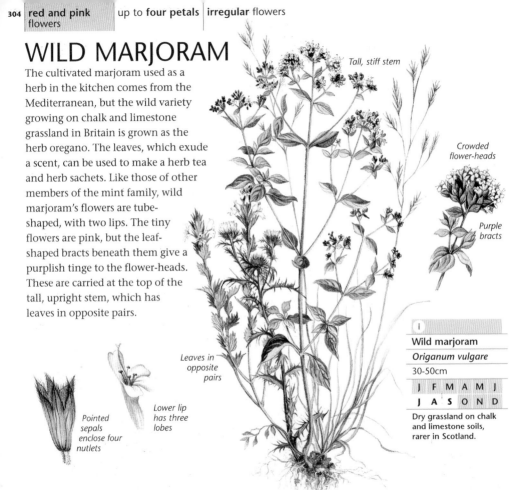

Tall, stiff stem

Crowded flower-heads

Purple bracts

Leaves in opposite pairs

Lower lip has three lobes

Pointed sepals enclose four nutlets

Wild marjoram	
Origanum vulgare	
30-50cm	

J F M A M J
J A S O N D

Dry grassland on chalk and limestone soils, rarer in Scotland.

WILD BASIL

Though less strongly scented than thyme or marjoram, wild basil is another member of the mint family which has been used in medicine and cookery over the centuries. Wild basil is a different plant from the basil grown in herb gardens. Its name, derived from the Greek *basilikon*, 'kingly', reflects the esteem in which it was once held. Its leaves smell faintly like those of thyme when crushed. The little two-lipped pink flowers of wild basil are grouped in dense whorls, each whorl being immediately above a pair of leaves. The stems are tallish and often rather straggly, with few side branches, and hairs covering the leaves make them appear dull.

Upper sepals broader than lower sepals

Unbranched stem

Oval, hairy leaves

Middle lobe wide and notched

Flowers in dense whorls above pair of leaves

Wild basil

Clinopodium vulgare

30-80cm

J	F	M	A	M	J
J	**A**	**S**	**O**	**N**	**D**

Hedgerows and wood edges; absent from northern and western Scotland.

COMMON HEMP-NETTLE

The most easily detected difference between common hemp-nettle and the similar-looking red dead-nettle and black horehound is the way in which the hairy stems of hemp-nettle are swollen below each pair of nettle-like leaves and covered in downward-pointing, red-tipped hairs. The flowers are often creamy white instead of the usual purplish pink. The name 'hemp' was applied to the plant because of the apparent similarity of its leaves to those of Indian hemp – but there is no cannabis to be extracted from our innocent British hemp-nettle. Indeed, unlike many other members of the mint family, it has no herbal or medicinal value, though it shares their square stems and tube-shaped flowers.

Whorls of flowers

Stems swollen below leaves

Branching hairy stem

Dark red and yellow markings on lower lip

Long sharp teeth on sepal tube

Fruit has four nutlets

i

Common hemp-nettle

Galeopsis tetrahit

10-100cm

| J | F | M | A | M | J |
| J | A | S | O | N | D |

Widespread on roadsides, cultivated land and in woodland clearings.

RED DEAD-NETTLE

The name dead-nettle is given to convey the information that these plants do not sting. The leaves of white dead-nettle (page 38) are quite similar in appearance to those of common nettle (page 366), but those of red dead-nettle are rather different, being shorter and less sharply toothed. The flowers of red dead-nettle are purple-pink and two-lipped, totally unlike the green flowers of nettles, which hang in catkins. Stems and upper leaves are often tinged purplish. Henbit dead-nettle has stalkless upper leaves fused together to form a disc below each whorl of flowers.

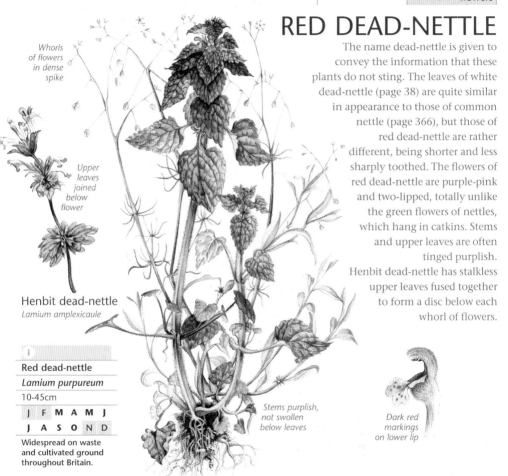

Whorls of flowers in dense spike

Upper leaves joined below flower

Henbit dead-nettle
Lamium amplexicaule

Red dead-nettle

Lamium purpureum

10-45cm

| J | F | M | A | M | J |
| J | A | S | O | N | D |

Widespread on waste and cultivated ground throughout Britain.

Stems purplish, not swollen below leaves

Dark red markings on lower lip

MARSH WOUNDWORT

Even if woundworts are no longer used in medicine, modern experiments have shown that the oil that some of them yield does have antiseptic qualities. Like other woundworts, marsh woundwort has the two-lipped flowers arranged in a spike. The sepals are often tinged with purple. The main difference between this damp-loving plant and its drier-soil relative, hedge woundwort (opposite), is its narrow, short-stalked leaves.

The much smaller field woundwort is a low-growing farmland weed that became rarer with the burning of corn stubble and earlier ploughing.

Plant hairy

Narrow leaves with fine teeth, on short stalks

White markings on lower lip

Whorls of flowers in loose spike

Heart-shaped leaves

Field woundwort
Stachys arvensis

i						

Marsh woundwort

Stachys palustris

40-100cm

J	F	M	A	M	J
J	A	S	O	N	D

Widespread in ditches, swamps and fens throughout the British Isles.

Whorls of flowers in loose spike

White markings on lower lip

HEDGE WOUNDWORT

The offensive smell of its crushed leaves belies the usefulness of hedge woundwort to man since the days of the ancient Greeks, as a poultice to treat wounds and to stem bleeding. It is easily recognised by its hairy, heart-shaped leaves and by its whorls of long, claret-coloured flowers, borne in loose spikes on the top of purplish stems. Betony has also been used as a remedy for many ills, including headaches and digestive ailments. It can be distinguished from hedge woundwort by its oblong leaves, with rounded teeth, mostly in a rosette at the stem base, and by its shorter flower spike.

Hedge woundwort
Stachys sylvatica
30-100cm

J F M A M J
J A S O N D

Widespread in woods, hedgerows and shady places throughout the British Isles.

Purplish stems, not swollen below leaves

Oblong leaves

No white markings on lower lip

Betony
Stachys officinalis

LESSER SKULLCAP

Unusually among members of the mint family, skullcap (pictured here with bog pimpernel) has flowers in pairs, each pair facing the same way and growing from the base of the light green leaves. What gives the plant its name, however, is the shape of its sepal tube, said to resemble the leather helmet worn by Roman soldiers. The common skullcap (page 220) has blue flowers; the lesser is a smaller plant, usually only 20cm tall, with small lilac-pink flowers, the lower lip spotted purple.

Flowers usually in pairs

Leaves almost toothless

Helmet-shaped sepal tube

i
Lesser skullcap
Scutellaria minor
20-25cm

| J | F | M | A | M | J |
| J | A | S | O | N | D |

Wet heaths in southern and western Britain and southern Ireland; rare in central and eastern England.

COMMON FUMITORY

Seen in a mass across a distant field, the common fumitory is a grey, smoky haze. The name fumitory derives from Latin words meaning 'smoke of the earth', and the plant's smoky-grey, feathery leaves certainly give that impression. In summer the colour of the leaves is offset by the soft, dusky pink of the flowers which darken to a blackish-red at the tip. The colour of the flower distinguishes common fumitory from the related Climbing corydalis and white ramping fumitory (both on page 39).

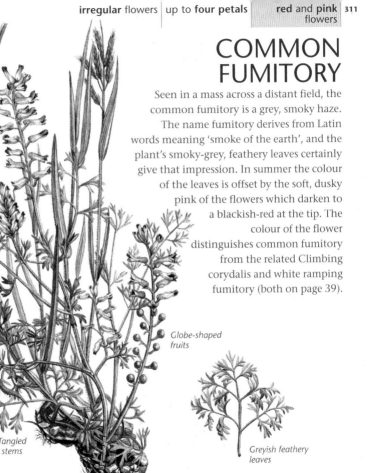

Flowers in loose spike

Dark tip

Blunt spur

Globe-shaped fruits

i
Common fumitory
Fumaria officinalis
To 20cm

| J | F | M | A | **M** | **J** |
| **J** | **A** | S | **O** | **N** | D |

Widespread on cultivated ground and by roads; less common in the west.

Tangled stems

Greyish feathery leaves

PINK WATER SPEEDWELL

Once a farmer has cleared his drainage ditches, the flower-spikes of water speedwell are often among the first to make an appearance. This pink-flowered species often grows together with blue water speedwell (page 212), with which it will hybridise. The two plants differ from most other speedwells in having narrow, pointed leaves. The leaves have tiny teeth and no stalks.

Flower-spikes grow from angle where leaves join the stem

Fruit stalk at right angles to stem

Two stamens in flower

Lowest petal smallest

Upright stems, often tinged purple

Lance-shaped, finely toothed leaves

Pink water speedwell

Veronica catenata

To 50cm

| J | F | M | A | M | J |
| J | A | S | O | N | D |

Wet and muddy places, especially ponds and streams, mainly in southern and eastern England.

INDIAN BALSAM

Touched at the base, the ripe pods of
the Indian balsam shower the passer-
by in autumn with a fusillade of seeds,
released by the spring action of the
opening sides of the pod. The
seeds float on water. The plant
was brought to Britain in 1839
and grown in greenhouses before
it escaped into the wild, where
damp river banks are its
commonest habitat. The
colour of the flowers is very
variable, ranging from dark to
pale purple-pink to white.

*Stout fleshy
ribbed stem*

*Toothed hairless,
lance-shaped leaves*

*Pear-
shaped
fruit*

*Spur at base
of flower*

Indian balsam

Impatiens glandulifera

100-200cm

| J | F | M | A | M | J |
| J | A | S | O | N | D |

Widespread on river
banks and waste places;
rarer in Scotland and
Ireland but increasing.

THRIFT

The leaves of this plant stay green throughout the year, and when dried the flowers are virtually everlasting. It has been a garden favourite for more than 400 years. The flowers are pale to bright pink or occasionally white. Thrift is also known as sea pink.

Sea-lavender is a plant of salt-marshes, colouring whole stretches lilac when in flower in late summer. It is rare in Scotland and absent from Ireland.

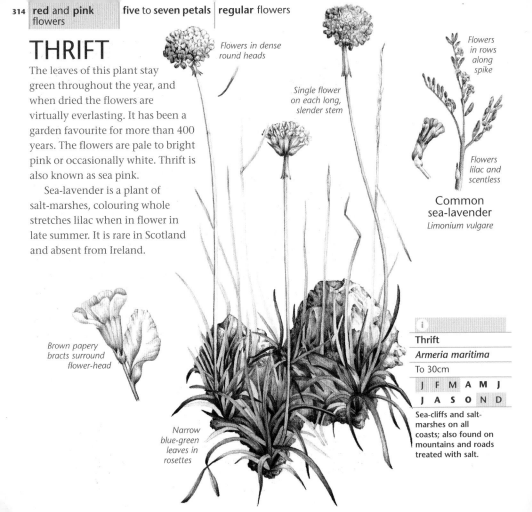

Flowers in dense round heads

Single flower on each long, slender stem

Flowers in rows along spike

Flowers lilac and scentless

Common sea-lavender
Limonium vulgare

Brown papery bracts surround flower-head

Narrow blue-green leaves in rosettes

Thrift					
Armeria maritima					
To 30cm					
J	F	M	A	M	J
J	A	S	O	N	D

Sea-cliffs and salt-marshes on all coasts; also found on mountains and roads treated with salt.

NIGHT-FLOWERING CATCHFLY

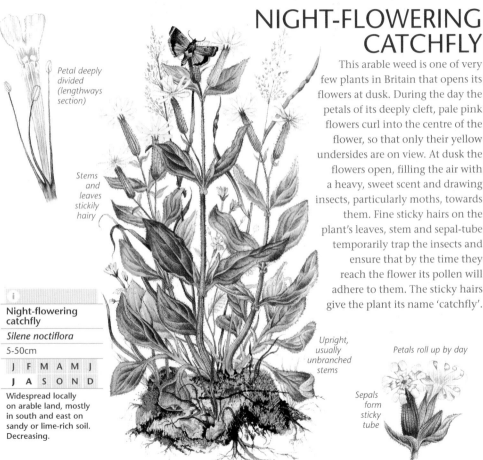

Petal deeply divided (lengthways section)

Stems and leaves stickily hairy

This arable weed is one of very few plants in Britain that opens its flowers at dusk. During the day the petals of its deeply cleft, pale pink flowers curl into the centre of the flower, so that only their yellow undersides are on view. At dusk the flowers open, filling the air with a heavy, sweet scent and drawing insects, particularly moths, towards them. Fine sticky hairs on the plant's leaves, stem and sepal-tube temporarily trap the insects and ensure that by the time they reach the flower its pollen will adhere to them. The sticky hairs give the plant its name 'catchfly'.

Upright, usually unbranched stems

---

i

Night-flowering catchfly

Silene noctiflora

5–50cm

| J | F | M | A | M | J |
| J | A | S | O | N | D |

Widespread locally on arable land, mostly in south and east on sandy or lime-rich soil. Decreasing.

Petals roll up by day

Sepals form sticky tube

SOAPWORT

This plant's flowers grow in pretty clusters and it is sometimes grown in borders but its ability to spread by means of rooting runners can cause problems for the gardener. The flowers are fragrant, with undivided pink petals which have two slender scales at the base. The green parts of soapwort were once boiled to produce a lathery liquid used for washing wool. Some of the wild soapwort seen today is growing near the places in which it was once grown commercially, but it is often a garden throw-out.

Upright, hairless stems

Leaf has three or five veins

Soapwort

Saponaria officinalis

30-90cm

J	F	M	A	M	J
J	A	S	O	N	D

Grassy places, especially roadsides and streamsides; rare in Scotland but fairly widespread elsewhere.

Flowers in compact clusters

Creeping rooting runners

RAGGED-ROBIN

The name suggests a somewhat unkempt flower, but this is far from the case. It is a delightful, exceptionally pretty plant, immediately recognisable by the long, finger-lobed petals from which it gets its common name. The flowers are more delicate than ragged. The seed capsule has five short teeth which bend back to open. Despite the appeal of the flowers, it has traditionally been considered unlucky to pick them and take them indoors.

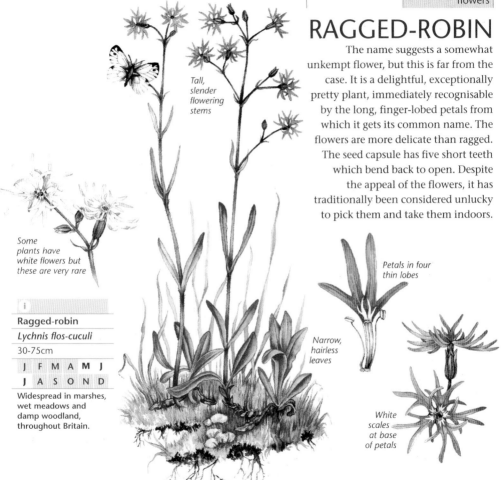

Tall, slender flowering stems

Some plants have white flowers but these are very rare

Petals in four thin lobes

Narrow, hairless leaves

White scales at base of petals

Ragged-robin

Lychnis flos-cuculi

30-75cm

| J | F | M | A | M | J |
| J | A | S | O | N | D |

Widespread in marshes, wet meadows and damp woodland, throughout Britain.

RED CAMPION

Unlike white campion (page 40) which has a faint scent, red campion is scentless. Whereas white campion is mainly a plant of open cultivated ground, red campion is more shade-loving and can be found in woods throughout the British Isles. It is a tall, handsome plant, with masses of red flowers, rarely white, which would look well in any garden. Male and female flowers grow on separate plants. When red and white campions grow together the two often hybridise, producing plants with flowers in a wide range of pinks. The seed capsules have short, curled back teeth.

Upright flowering stems

Petals deeply divided

Upper leaves unstalked

Lower leaves have long winged stalks

Hairy stems and leaves

Inner ring of white scales on petals

i
Red campion
Silene dioica
30-100cm

J	F	**M**	**A**	**M**	**J**
J	**A**	**S**	**O**	**N**	D

Hedgerows and woods on rich soils in most parts of Britain but rarer in Ireland.

MAIDEN PINK

This wild flower is well known to gardeners as a rockery plant. While it lacks scent, it is nevertheless an attractive plant, with its long, branching shoots which suddenly burst into deep pink flower. The flowers are freckled with spots, paler or darker than the rest of the petals. They close in dull weather. The leaves are long, slender and rough-edged. Maiden pink has a mixture of flowering and non-flowering shoots. By contrast, all the shoots of Deptford pink bear flowers. Like maiden pink, Deptford pink is increasingly rare, and confined to dry grassy places in parts of southern England and Wales.

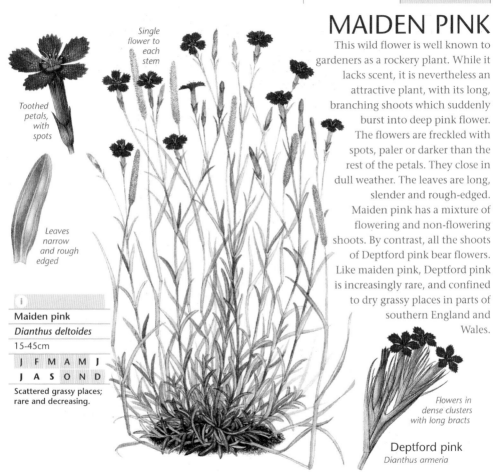

Single flower to each stem

Toothed petals, with spots

Leaves narrow and rough edged

Leaves narrow and rough edged

i
Maiden pink
Dianthus deltoides
15-45cm

J F M A M J
J A S O N D

Scattered grassy places; rare and decreasing.

Flowers in dense clusters with long bracts

Deptford pink
Dianthus armeria

SAND SPURREY

The five petals of sand spurrey's star-shaped flower are separated by five green sepals, usually slightly longer than the petals. The narrow, pointed leaves are greyish-green, in whorls, and tipped with a bristle-like point. At the base of the leaves are distinctive silvery stipules.

Greater and lesser sea spurrey grow on salt-marshes but they are increasingly found inland by roads that have been salted in winter. Rock sea spurrey grows on sea-cliffs and sea walls.

Large, silvery stipules

Whorls of greyish leaves

Many sprawling stems

Petals shorter than sepals

Sand spurrey

Spergularia rubra

5-25cm

J	F	M	A	**M**	**J**
J	**A**	**S**	**O**	**N**	D

On lime-free ground in most of Britain, but rarer in Scotland and in Ireland.

ORPINE

There is no mistaking this rose-red flower, even in the half light of shady woodland, where it is most often found. It has two striking features: the big, broad heads of little flowers, with their spreading petals; and the large, fleshy, oval leaves which grow alternately all the way up the unbranching stems. The leaves and stems store water, enabling the plant to survive prolonged drought and to remain fresh for some time after being picked. It has a carrot-like underground root tuber which also stores water.

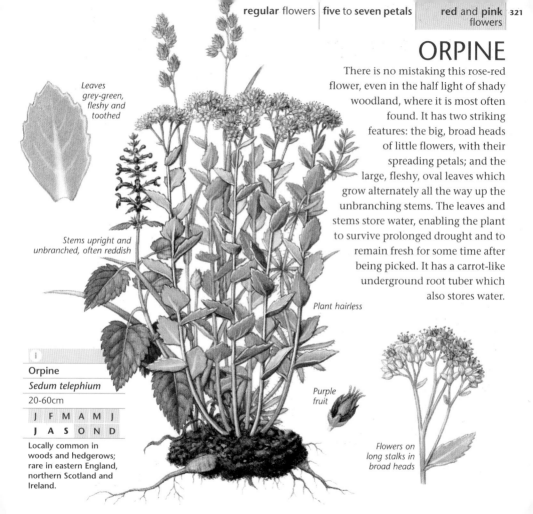

Leaves grey-green, fleshy and toothed

Stems upright and unbranched, often reddish

Plant hairless

Purple fruit

Flowers on long stalks in broad heads

i

Orpine

Sedum telephium

20-60cm

| J | F | M | A | M | J |
| J | A | S | O | N | D |

Locally common in woods and hedgerows; rare in eastern England, northern Scotland and Ireland.

COMMON MALLOW

A close relative of the old favourite of cottage gardeners, the hollyhock, common mallow's bright purple-pink flowers are veined with dark purple. The stamens are fused into a distinctive central whorl. The crinkly leaves usually have a dark spot where the leaf joins the stalk, and the fruit is a round disc of nutlets, which are edible and have a nutty taste.

Musk mallow has lighter, rose-pink, or sometimes white, scented flowers even bigger than those of common mallow. They grow in spikes and have broader petals than the petals of common mallow. Musk mallow is often grown in cottage gardens.

Stem leaves ivy-shaped

Basal leaves rounded

Stem leaves deeply divided

Musk mallow
Malva moschata

| i | | | | | | |

Common mallow

Malva sylvestris

30-100cm

J	F	M	A	M	J
J	A	S	O	N	D

Roadsides and waste ground throughout lowland areas; rare in northern Scotland.

Round, flattened fruit has many nutlets

Narrow, dark-veined petals

Basal leaves rounded and lobed

PINK PURSLANE

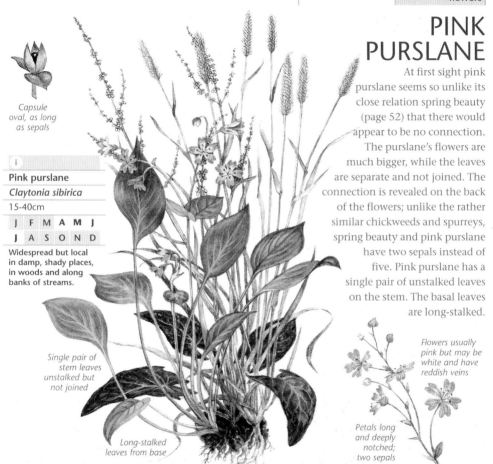

Capsule oval, as long as sepals

i	

Pink purslane

Claytonia sibirica

15-40cm

J	F	M	A	M	J
J	A	S	O	N	D

Widespread but local in damp, shady places, in woods and along banks of streams.

At first sight pink purslane seems so unlike its close relation spring beauty (page 52) that there would appear to be no connection. The purslane's flowers are much bigger, while the leaves are separate and not joined. The connection is revealed on the back of the flowers; unlike the rather similar chickweeds and spurreys, spring beauty and pink purslane have two sepals instead of five. Pink purslane has a single pair of unstalked leaves on the stem. The basal leaves are long-stalked.

Single pair of stem leaves unstalked but not joined

Long-stalked leaves from base

Flowers usually pink but may be white and have reddish veins

Petals long and deeply notched; two sepals

PURPLE LOOSESTRIFE

This tall, beautiful plant brings a touch of the tropics to the edge of still, inland waters in Britain, with its long spikes of vivid purple-red flowers. They cluster on the stout, square stems in whorls, and sometimes grow in such abundance by lakesides that the water, seen from a distance, seems edged with a purple mist. The leaves are untoothed and grow in opposite pairs on the upper parts of the stems and in whorls of three below. The upper leaves are usually much shorter.

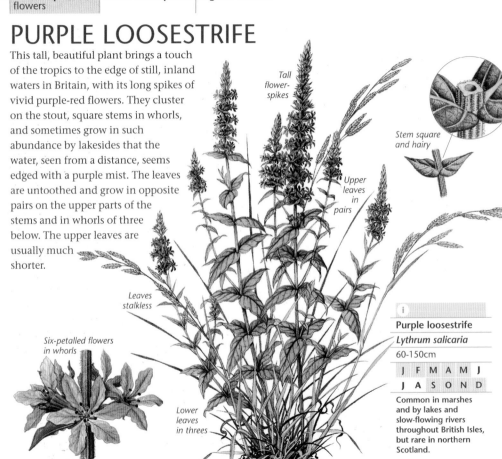

Tall flower-spikes

Stem square and hairy

Upper leaves in pairs

Leaves stalkless

Six-petalled flowers in whorls

Lower leaves in threes

Purple loosestrife

Lythrum salicaria

60-150cm

| J | F | M | A | M | J |
| J | A | S | O | N | D |

Common in marshes and by lakes and slow-flowing rivers throughout British Isles, but rare in northern Scotland.

WATER PURSLANE

A small creeping plant, water purslane has tiny leaves and minute pinkish flowers at their bases. Its stems, often reddish, send out roots at leaf junctions to form whole strings of connected plants. Dense creeping mats are created, and these often spread into water. The tiny, stalkless flowers normally have six pink petals surrounded by pointed sepals. Leaves are paired and are widest near the tip. They have short stalks. The flowers grow singly at the junction of leaf and stem. Its closest relative is purple loosestrife (opposite) although the plants are very different.

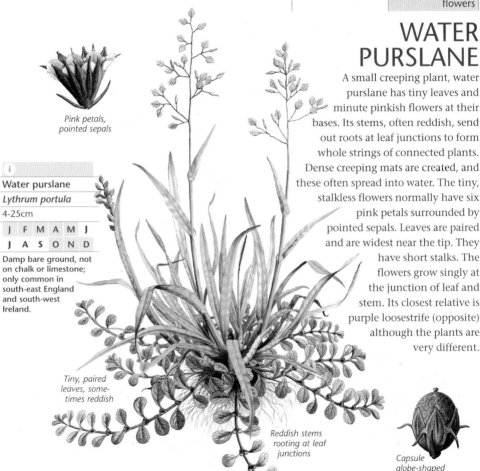

Pink petals, pointed sepals

---

i

Water purslane

Lythrum portula

4-25cm

| J | F | M | A | M | J |
| J | A | S | O | N | D |

Damp bare ground, not on chalk or limestone; only common in south-east England and south-west Ireland.

Tiny, paired leaves, sometimes reddish

Reddish stems rooting at leaf junctions

Capsule globe-shaped

COMMON SORREL

Once sorrel was widely eaten as a vegetable; now it is more appreciated for bringing a splash of colour to the grassy places where it grows. The flowers are green with red edgest and in late summer the leaves and stems often turn a lovely crimson. Sorrel is sturdy and upright, with branched spikes of tiny flowers. Male and female flowers grow on separate plants. The lance-shaped leaf has two backward-pointing lobes at the base.

Dense, branched flower spikes

Lance-shaped leaf with two lobes at base

Female flower has bent-back petal-like sepals

Male flower has yellow anthers

Three veined outer sepals enclose fruit

i					

Sorrel

Rumex acetosa

To 80cm

J	F	M	A	**M**	J
J	A	S	O	N	D

Common on grassland throughout British Isles.

Branched, leafless flower spikes

Spearhead-shaped leaf

SHEEP'S SORREL

The tiny red flowers of sheep's sorrel are not much to look at individually and have no noticeable scent. They do not have to be enticing to insects: they are not pollinated by them, but by the wind. Male and female flowers are on separate plants; the males produce abundant pollen which is blown to the females. The leaf, shaped like a spearhead, has lobes at its base and is often tinged red. Patches of the plant form rusty-coloured areas which are visible from a long distance. The plant spreads rapidly by means of rooting runners. The juice of the leaves was once used in the form of an extract to treat kidney and bladder ailments.

ⓘ

Sheep's sorrel

Rumex acetosella

To 30cm

J	F	M	A	M	J
J	A	S	O	N	D

Heaths and short grasslands, mainly on peaty or sandy soil.

Female flower has three feathery styles

Male flower has yellow anthers

REDSHANK

This plant gets its name from the colour of its stem. One of its more noticeable features is the dark grey patch which usually occurs on the leaf. Where this is present, it is a valuable aid to identification. The flowers are pink and arranged in short spikes. The sheath which surrounds the flower stem just above each leaf-stalk is fringed with hairs. The plant can be a troublesome weed in gardens and arable fields.

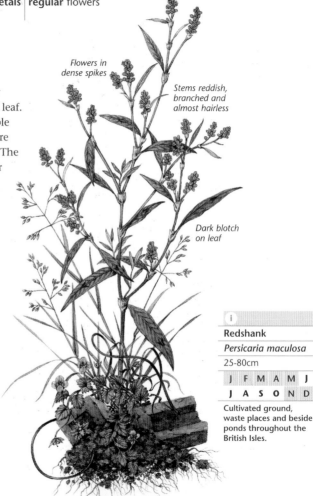

Flowers in dense spikes

Stems reddish, branched and almost hairless

Dark blotch on leaf

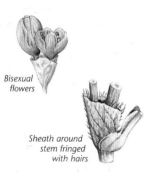

Bisexual flowers

Sheath around stem fringed with hairs

i
Redshank
Persicaria maculosa
25–80cm
J F M A M J
J A S O N D
Cultivated ground, waste places and beside ponds throughout the British Isles.

COMMON BISTORT

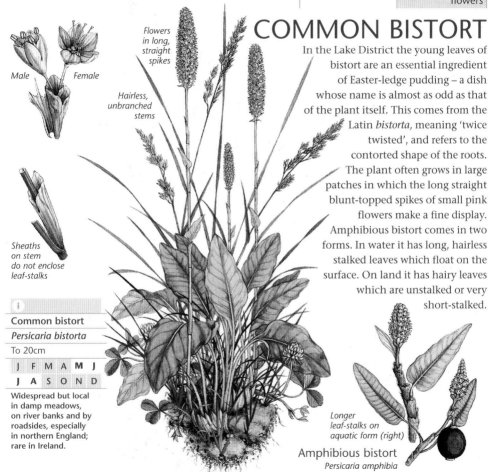

In the Lake District the young leaves of bistort are an essential ingredient of Easter-ledge pudding – a dish whose name is almost as odd as that of the plant itself. This comes from the Latin *bistorta*, meaning 'twice twisted', and refers to the contorted shape of the roots. The plant often grows in large patches in which the long straight blunt-topped spikes of small pink flowers make a fine display. Amphibious bistort comes in two forms. In water it has long, hairless stalked leaves which float on the surface. On land it has hairy leaves which are unstalked or very short-stalked.

Male *Female*

Flowers in long, straight spikes

Hairless, unbranched stems

Sheaths on stem do not enclose leaf-stalks

ⓘ

Common bistort

Persicaria bistorta

To 20cm

| J | F | M | A | **M** | **J** |
| **J** | **A** | S | O | N | D |

Widespread but local in damp meadows, on river banks and by roadsides, especially in northern England; rare in Ireland.

Longer leaf-stalks on aquatic form (right)

Amphibious bistort
Persicaria amphibia

COMMON CENTAURY

According to the conditions in which it grows, common centaury can be a single stem only 50mm high – or a plant with several stems and many branches 30cm or more tall. The plant has a rosette of leaves, with three to seven prominent veins, at the base of the stem. The flowers are unusually unstalked and grow in dense clusters.

Lesser centaury has no rosette of leaves and looser clusters of stalked flowers.

Flowers unstalked or very short-stalked

No leaf rosette at base

Lesser centaury
Centaurium pulchellum

Petal tube extends beyond sepals

Leaf rosette at base

ⓘ
Common centaury

Centaurium erythraea

5-50cm

| J | F | M | A | M | J |
| J | A | S | O | N | D |

Dunes and dry grassy places; rare in Scotland, widespread elsewhere.

AUTUMN GENTIAN

Flowering later than its four-petalled relative, field gentian (page 209), autumn gentian is usually dull reddish-purple rather than bluish-purple in colour, although in the north it is creamy-white with dull red outer parts. Its opposite pairs of leaves are set at right angles to each other up the stem. Autumn gentian is also known as felwort. Gentian roots yield a bitter liquid used in medicinal tonics. The rare early gentian is a smaller plant which flowers in May and June on some chalk and limestone grasslands in southern England.

Stem usually tinged purple

Oval leaves in pairs at right angles up stem

i
Autumn gentian
Gentianella amarella
5-30cm

J	F	M	A	M	J
J	**A**	**S**	**O**	**N**	**D**

Widespread on grassland and dunes in England; rarer elsewhere.

Pale hairs in throat of flower

Fruit cylindrical

FIELD BINDWEED

The speed at which bindweed wraps itself round the nearest convenient support has been timed. The ends of the thin but strong, thread-like stems twine themselves round anything they touch and complete a full circle, travelling anti-clockwise, in under 2 hours. Not only does bindweed strangle other plants, but it has a deep and extensive root system that makes it a pernicious weed. The trumpet-shaped flowers smell of almonds.

Sea bindweed has sprawling stems which do not climb. It is confined to the coast, and absent from the far north.

Flowers may be pink, white or pink and white

Trumpet-shaped flower with short, rounded sepals

Leaves shaped like arrowheads

i

Common bindweed

Convolvulus arvensis

20-100cm

| J | F | M | A | M | J |
| J | A | S | O | N | D |

Cultivated land and open grassland, especially road verges in lowlands; rarer in Scotland.

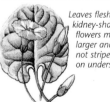

Leaves fleshy and kidney-shaped; flowers much larger and not striped on underside

Flowers have mauve stripes on underside

Sea bindweed
Calystegia soldanella

COMMON DODDER

This rootless parasite grows by twining
its red, wiry stem anti-clockwise
round other plants – usually gorse or
heather – and sending out suckers
which penetrate the stem of the host,
allowing the dodder to absorb
nutrients from it. The leaves are
reduced to tiny scales on the stems.
The plant has no green coloration. The
dodder has dense clusters of pretty pale
pink scented flowers. The flower
clusters are unstalked and spaced out
along the stems. Each individual flower
is bell-shaped, with five petals.

*Flowers in dense,
globe-shaped
heads*

*Bell-shaped
flower with
short, pointed
sepals*

i
Common dodder
Cuscuta epithymum

J	F	M	A	M	J
J	A	S	O	N	D

Heathland, usually
on gorse or heather,
mainly in southern
England.

*Wiry red
stems bind
host plant,
heather*

SCARLET PIMPERNEL

Although the bright, starry flowers of this pimpernel are usually scarlet, they can also be pink, white, lilac or blue. It has even been known for red and blue flowers to be found on the same plant. Nor is it so 'damned elusive' as the Pimpernel hero of Baroness Orczy's famous novel – it is found all over Europe. It is elusive in another sense, though, in that its flowers close in mid-afternoon and are always shut during dull or wet weather, giving it the alternative name 'poor man's weather glass'. The flowers grow on long, slender stalks and have purple-based petals tipped with glandular hairs.

Leaves in pairs, oval and stalkless

Square stem

Overlapping petals

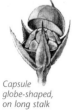

Capsule globe-shaped, on long stalk

Many sprawling branches

Scarlet pimpernel

Anagallis arvensis

5-40cm

| J | F | M | A | M | J |
| J | A | S | O | N | D |

Widespread on cultivated and waste land and dunes, but rare in Scotland.

BOG PIMPERNEL

This delicately coloured relative of the scarlet pimpernel has flowers of pale rose-pink with darker veins and tiny, pale green leaves. The combination creates an extremely pretty effect. Unlike the scarlet pimpernel, bog pimpernel is a creeping plant with rooting stems, often growing so densely that it forms a mat. The leaves are more rounded than those of scarlet pimpernel, and very small, growing in opposite pairs on short stalks. The elegant, bell-shaped flowers grow on long, slender, erect stalks. They open only when the sun is out. Bog pimpernel is illustrated growing with the deeper pink cranberry (page 289).

Bell-shaped flowers

Rooting stems

Leaves in pairs, rounded and on short stalks

Fruit globe-shaped, splitting around middle

i

Bog pimpernel

Anagallis tenella

5-15cm

| J | F | M | A | M | J |
| J | A | S | O | N | D |

Locally common in bogs and damp grasslands on peaty ground; widespread in western Britain, rare in Scotland.

SEA MILKWORT

This plant overcomes the saltiness of its environment by storing the limited fresh water it can obtain in its fleshy leaves. It is a pale green, hairless plant which usually grows in a thick, spreading mat, so reducing water loss by evaporation. The small, oblong leaves grow in crowded pairs along the creeping stems. The apparent petals of the pretty little pale pink flowers are, in fact, sepals. Sea milkwort is not related to common milkwort, but is a member of the primrose family.

Plant hairless

Fruit splits into five parts

Single flower at junction of leaf and stem

Creeping, rooting stems

Fleshy, stalkless leaves

Sea milkwort

Glaux maritima

10–30cm

| J | F | M | A | M | J |
| J | A | S | O | N | D |

Rocks, cliffs and salt-marshes round coasts; occasionally inland.

Flowers in loose spikes

Upper leaves stalkless

Greyish, hairy stems and leaves

Fruit has four spiny nutlets

HOUND'S-TONGUE

In the 17th century, a leaf of hound's-tongue placed under the big toe was said to deter dogs. The flowers are small, maroon-coloured and very pretty, with velvety scales at the centre, closing the mouth. They resemble those of its close relatives, the forget-me-nots, but have an unpleasant smell. The leaves and stem are covered with hairs, giving the plant a greyish appearance. Spines on the nutlets catch on to passing animals which disperse them, allowing them to germinate in new places.

Hound's-tongue

Cynoglossum officinale

30-60cm

| J | F | M | A | M | J |
| J | A | S | O | N | D |

Bare dry ground, sand and shingle; rare in Scotland and Ireland.

Lower leaves stalked

Sprays of five-petalled flowers

WILD ONION

Known also as crow garlic, wild onion was once a common weed of grassland; eaten by cattle, it gave milk and butter an unpleasant flavour. Modern methods of cultivation have almost eliminated it from arable land. It is a strange-looking plant, with a large, papery bract shielding each flower-head like a monk's cowl. It usually has only purple-red bulbils, but sometimes pinkish or reddish flowers are present. The whole plant smells of onion. The related field garlic is much less widespread. It always has flowers. These are white, tinged with pink or brown.

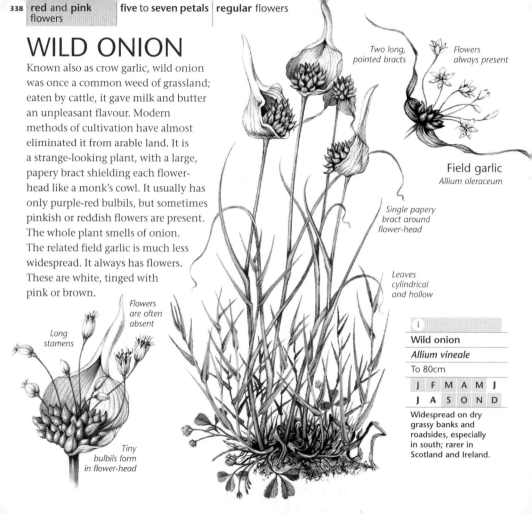

Two long, pointed bracts

Flowers always present

Field garlic
Allium oleraceum

Single papery bract around flower-head

Leaves cylindrical and hollow

Flowers are often absent

Long stamens

Tiny bulbils form in flower-head

i	
Wild onion	
Allium vineale	
To 80cm	

J	F	M	A	M	J
J	A	S	O	N	D

Widespread on dry grassy banks and roadsides, especially in south; rarer in Scotland and Ireland.

STINKING IRIS

When the flat, pointed leaves of this plant are crushed they give off a smell vaguely reminiscent of roast beef. It is shorter than the other species of wild iris native to Britain, the yellow iris (page 172), and has flowers of an unusual dull greyish-mauve colour, with darker veins. The three styles, or female parts, are yellow and petal-like and are situated above the petals and sepals. The flowers are short-lived, but the bright orange seeds cling to the split capsule for some time. Other names for stinking iris are 'gladdon' and 'roast-beef plant'.

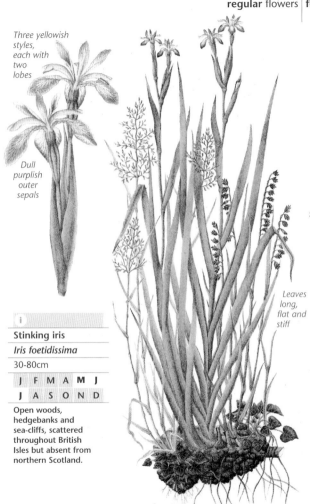

Three yellowish styles, each with two lobes

Dull purplish outer sepals

Leaves long, flat and stiff

i
Stinking iris
Iris foetidissima
30-80cm

| J | F | M | A | **M** | **J** |
| **J** | **A** | S | O | N | D |

Open woods, hedgebanks and sea-cliffs, scattered throughout British Isles but absent from northern Scotland.

Capsule green, turning brown, with orange seeds

HERB-ROBERT

A member of the crane's-bill family, herb-robert has the characteristic beaked fruit shaped like a bird's bill. The pink petals are unnotched, and contrast nicely with the orange pollen of the stamens. The deeply divided fern-like leaves and hairy stems of this crane's-bill turn a fiery red, When crushed, the leaves give off a smell, which has led to the plant's nickname of 'Stinking Bob'.

Leaves have three to five lobes

Stems branch from base

Rounded petals, not notched

i

Herb-robert

Geranium robertianum

10-50cm

| J | F | M | A | M | J |
| J | A | S | O | N | D |

Widespread in shade on hedge-banks and walls or in woods or on shingle throughout Britain.

MARSH CINQUEFOIL

The leaflets of this wet-loving plant are usually found in groups of five – hence the name cinquefoil, from the French for 'five leaves'. It can be found growing up to an altitude of 900m, spreading by means of creeping underground stems, or rhizomes. The narrow purplish-red petals are shorter than the broad dark red sepals. The red fruits are carried on spongy receptacles. In the Isle of Man the plant is called 'marsh strawberry'. Damp conditions also suit the water avens, which has nodding orange-pink flowers with purplish sepals and hooked, bur-like fruiting heads.

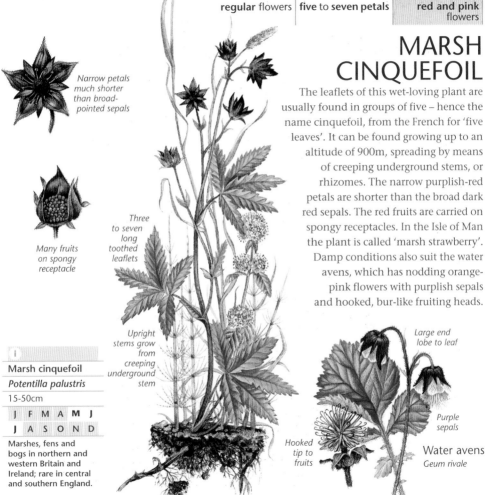

Narrow petals much shorter than broad-pointed sepals

Many fruits on spongy receptacle

Three to seven long toothed leaflets

Upright stems grow from creeping underground stem

Large end lobe to leaf

Purple sepals

Hooked tip to fruits

Water avens
Geum rivale

---

i

Marsh cinquefoil

Potentilla palustris

15-50cm

| J | F | M | A | **M** | **J** |
| **J** | **A** | **S** | **O** | **N** | D |

Marshes, fens and bogs in northern and western Britain and Ireland; rare in central and southern England.

COMMON VALERIAN

This handsome plant, with its sturdy, upright stem and clusters of pale pink flowers, is a common sight on uncultivated land. Each flower is composed of a tube with five spreading lobes at the top and has three protruding stamens. The leaf stalks carry leaflets arranged in opposite pairs. The fruits are carried through the air by feathery 'parachutes'.

Marsh valerian is smaller and has creeping, rooting stems. The lowest leaves are oval and long stalked. Male and female flowers are on separate plants.

Flower tube has pouch at base

Upper leaves stalkless, lower stalked

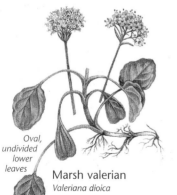

Oval, undivided lower leaves

Marsh valerian
Valeriana dioica

Fruit has 'parachute'

i

Common valerian

Valeriana officinalis

20-200cm

| J | F | M | A | M | J |
| J | A | S | O | N | D |

Rough, often damp grassland throughout British Isles.

RED VALERIAN

Dense clusters of little flowers bursting from the end of long slender tubes makes this fragrant herb easy to spot. The flowers are usually red or pink, but may be white: the plant is called red valerian and the Latin species name, *ruber*, means 'red'. The greyish-green leaves are sometimes slightly toothed. A feathery parachute develops at the top of the sepals, carrying the seed away on the wind. Sprouting vigorously from old walls and dry banks, valerian shows its Mediterranean origins. It was introduced into British gardens several hundred years ago.

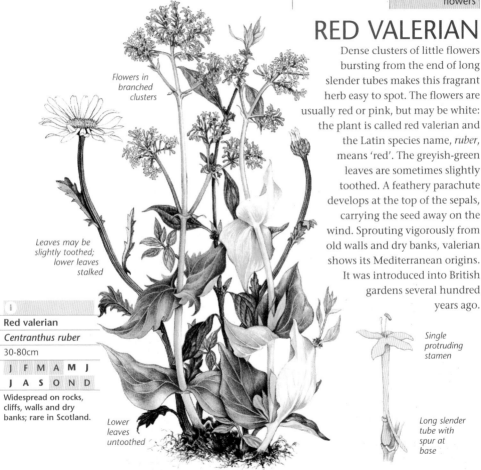

Flowers in branched clusters

Leaves may be slightly toothed; lower leaves stalked

Lower leaves untoothed

Single protruding stamen

Long slender tube with spur at base

Red valerian

Centranthus ruber

30-80cm

J F M A M J J A S O N D

Widespread on rocks, cliffs, walls and dry banks; rare in Scotland.

HARSH DOWNY ROSE

This rose is the scarcest of our downy roses, found mainly in southern England. It has tall arching stems armed with straight or slightly curved prickles. The flowers, usually a deeper pink than those of dog rose, have stalks covered with gland-tipped hairs. The egg-shaped fruits also have these hairs.

Our commonest downy rose – Sherard's – has deep pink flowers and heavy blue-green leaves. It is plentiful in Scotland. Also common in Scotland is the soft downy rose, which has straight thorns, deeper-coloured flowers and shorter stems.

Oval fruit with glandular hairs

Arching stems; undersides and often tops of leaves hairy

Straight stems with straight thorns

Flowers on hairy stalks

Fruit has glandular hairs

Soft downy rose
Rosa mollis

Dog rose
Rosa canina

Usually hairless leaves

Arching stems with straight or slightly curved thorns

ⓘ

Harsh downy rose

Rosa tomentosa

90-300cm

| J | F | M | A | M | J |
| J | A | S | O | N | D |

Woods and hedges in southern England and Wales, rare in northern England, Ireland and Scotland.

MARSH PENNYWORT

The leaf of the marsh pennywort is cup-like – *hydrocotyle* in its Latin name means 'water cup'. Its greenish-pink flowers are tiny and often hidden away at the base of the leaves. Marsh pennywort is a prostrate, creeping plant with rooting stems carpeting marshy and boggy areas. It sometimes grows on sphagnum moss. Once it was blamed for killing sheep – perhaps because it thrives in the same marshy places as the sheep parasite, liver fluke.

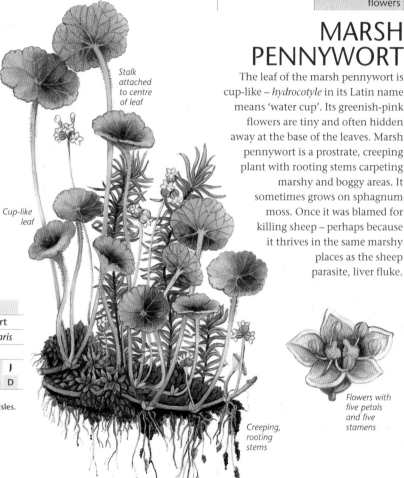

Stalk attached to centre of leaf

Cup-like leaf

Creeping, rooting stems

Flowers with five petals and five stamens

Marsh pennywort
Hydrocotyle vulgaris
1.3-25cm

J F M A M J
J A S O N D

In wet places throughout British Isles.

BITTER VETCH

The leaves of this member of the pea family end in a short point, not a branched tendril. There are two to four pairs of leaflets to each leaf. The flowers are purple-red, fading to blue, and the sepals bluish. The hairless stems are winged.

Narrow-leaved everlasting pea has branched tendrils and one pair of leaflets to each leaf.

Flowers crimson, fading to blue

Leaves end in short point, without tendril

Two to four pairs of leaflets

Spike of three to eight flowers

Narrow-leaved everlasting pea
Lathyrus sylvestris

i

Bitter vetch

Lathyrus linifolius

15-40cm

| J | F | M | A | M | J |
| J | A | S | O | N | D |

Woods, thickets, hedgerows and grassland, except in some east and central areas.

SAINFOIN

Spikes of magenta-pink flowers up to 60cm high make sainfoin one of our more spectacular grassland plants. It is probably native on limestone and chalk grassland, but was once widely grown as cattle fodder, a use reflected in its common name, which comes from French words for 'wholesome hay' but is pronounced 'sayn foyn'. From farmlands it has spread to roadside verges. The flowers are borne in a narrow cone-shaped spike on the top of long stems. Below them is a delicate tracery of feathery, grey-green leaves consisting of numerous pairs of leaflets with a single leaflet at the tip. Sainfoin is a member of the pea family.

6–14 pairs of leaflets, with one at tip

Sainfoin

Onobrychis viciifolia

10-60cm

| J | F | M | A | M | J |
| J | A | S | O | N | D |

Chalk and limestone grassland in southern England; occasionally on roadsides elsewhere.

Red-veined flowers in conical spike

RESTHARROW

The deep, tough roots and matted stems of restharrow used to be the bane of farmers in the days before tractors – 'arresting' the harrow. Now the plant can be admired for its more positive qualities, particularly its pretty pink flowers. The stems are hairy all round and root at the base. Some of the leaves have three leaflets, others only one. The plant usually lacks spines, but soft spines are sometimes present.

Spiny restharrow has more upright spiny stems, which do not root like those of common restharrow, and have two lines of hairs. It is limited to well-drained soils in England and south-west Scotland.

Hairy sepals at base of flower

Pod shorter than joined sepals

Stems hairy

Spiny stems

Spiny restharrow
Ononis spinosa

Trailing stems root at base

i					
Restharrow					
Ononis repens					
30-60cm					
J	F	M	A	M	J
J	A	S	O	N	D

Dry, grassy places and sand-dunes; rarer in Scotland and Ireland.

RED CLOVER

The purple-pink flowers of red clover look like Olympic torches, held aloft on hairy stems. The trefoil leaves are distinctive, too, with their pale, crescent-shaped bar in the middle of each leaflet. Occasionally a four-leaf clover is found – in folklore a supreme source of good fortune. Red clover nourishes the soil with nitrogen, provides fodder for animals and, being entirely pollinated by bees, produces superb honey. Zigzag clover has stalked heads of redder flowers and no obvious pale markings on the narrower leaves.

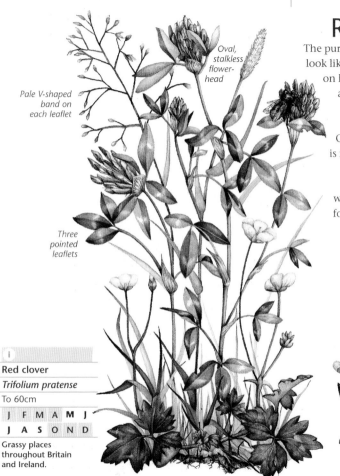

Pale V-shaped band on each leaflet

Oval, stalkless flower-head

Three pointed leaflets

Red clover

Trifolium pratense

To 60cm

| J | F | M | A | M | J |
| J | A | S | O | N | D |

Grassy places throughout Britain and Ireland.

Heads on stalks

Narrow leaves with no clear V-band

Zigzag stems

Zigzag clover
Trifolium medium

VERVAIN

The tiny lilac pink flowers of this wayside plant are carried in spikes on tough, upright stems, which are square in section. The flowers open from the bottom of the spike upwards. The hairy leaves are in pairs and are often divided into lobes with curved teeth. Vervain was prized as a medicinal herb from ancient times, even held to be a cure for the plague, and was believed to have magical properties.

Stems branch

Leaves in opposite pairs

Upper two petals slightly smaller than other three

Flowers in long, slender spikes

Vervain

Verbena officinalis

30-75cm

J	F	M	A	M	J
J	A	S	O	N	D

Roadsides and grassy places. Common in southern England; less common in the rest of England, Wales and Ireland; absent from Scotland.

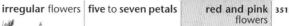

FRAGRANT ORCHID

A plant mainly of chalk and limestone grassland, this lilac-pink flowered orchid can fluctuate enormously in numbers from year to year. It gets its name from its clove-like scent, which is irresistibly attractive to moths and other long-tongued insects. The individual pollen grains are bound into tiny clusters or 'pollinia' which are carried by the insect from one flower to the next. The flowers form long spikes.

Leaf hooded at tip

Upright, hairless stem

Long, narrow leaves with prominent keel

Three-lobed lip

Long spur

Fragrant orchid

Gymnadenia conopsea

15-40cm

| J | F | M | A | M | J |
| J | A | S | O | N | D |

Grassland, fens and marshes, scattered throughout British Isles.

PYRAMIDAL ORCHID

A striking plant of chalk downland, the pyramidal orchid gets its name from its triangular spikes of pink flowers. This shape distinguishes it from the fragrant orchid, with which it might otherwise be confused. Its scent is also less strong than the clove-like scent of fragrant orchid, but is highly attractive to moths and butterflies. The nectar filled flower spurs are long and slender, and the flowers are various shades of pink, very often bright pink.

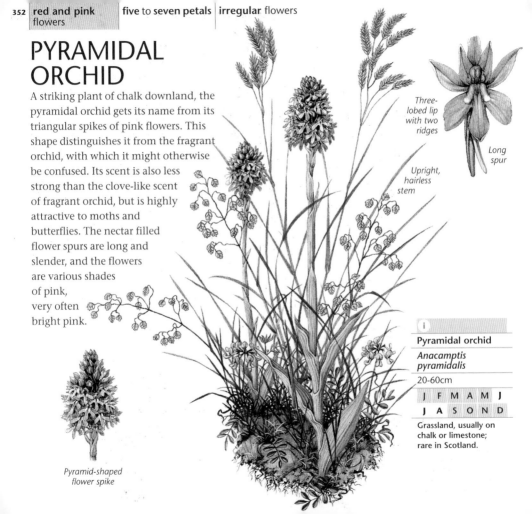

Three-lobed lip with two ridges

Long spur

Upright, hairless stem

Pyramid-shaped flower spike

Pyramidal orchid
Anacamptis pyramidalis
20-60cm

| J | F | M | A | M | J |
| J | A | S | O | N | D |

Grassland, usually on chalk or limestone; rare in Scotland.

BEE ORCHID

This fascinating and beautiful plant lives up to its name: each flower looks as though it has a bee resting on its rim. The purpose of the deception is to lure a real bee to mate with the false one; while this activity is taking place, pollen attaches itself to the bee's head, to be transferred to the stigma of the next orchid it visits. In fact, the plants are usually self-pollinating. The leaves are oval and unspotted, and decrease in size up the single stem of the plant. Like the fragrant orchid (page 351), bee orchid numbers vary enormously from year to year in any particular location.

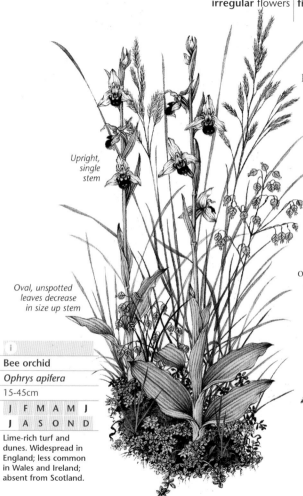

Upright, single stem

Oval, unspotted leaves decrease in size up stem

i
Bee orchid
Ophrys apifera
15-45cm

| J | F | M | A | M | J |
| J | A | S | O | N | D |

Lime-rich turf and dunes. Widespread in England; less common in Wales and Ireland; absent from Scotland.

Outer petal-like segments pink

Brown bee-like lip to flower

HEATH SPOTTED ORCHID

Unlike many other orchids, which flourish on chalky soils, the heath spotted orchid likes acid conditions and can be found growing on moorland and on bogs on top of sphagnum moss. The leaves, usually marked with small dark spots, vary from oblong to lance-shaped, folding upwards to a sharp tip. The flowers, carried in a dense cluster, may be lilac, pink or white, with small crimson blotches. The outer segments of the lip are larger than the middle one.

The closely related common spotted orchid prefers alkaline soils and may be found in damp meadows. The lip is three-lobed with the central lobe longest. The flower spike is long and narrow.

Broad flower spike

Outer petal-like segments spread horizontally

Leaves usually have dark spots

Flower spike more pointed

Common spotted orchid
Dactylorhiza fuchsii

Heath spotted orchid

Dactylorhiza maculata ssp. *ericetorum*

15-40cm

| J | F | M | A | M | J |
| J | A | S | O | N | D |

Damp acid soils throughout most of the British Isles.

BROAD-LEAVED HELLEBORINE

This woodland orchid bears an amazing number of flowers, sometimes as many as 100, down one side of its stem. The flowers are a subtle combination of greens and purples. The lowest segment forms a cup, deep brownish-red inside with a heart-shaped lip, which may be red, pink, purple or greenish. The ribbed leaves are much larger at the base.

The marsh helleborine is a smaller plant. The cup on the lowest flower segment is striped red on the inside, while the frilly-edged lip is white with a yellow base. It grows in fens, marshes and dune slacks.

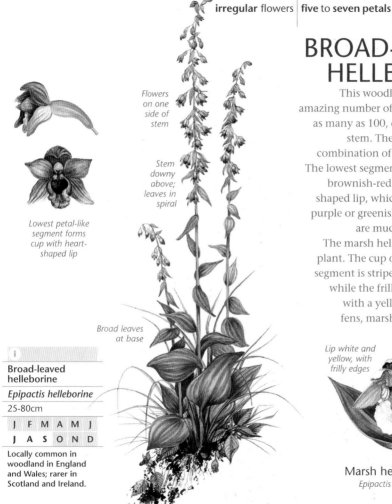

Flowers on one side of stem

Stem downy above; leaves in spiral

Broad leaves at base

Lowest petal-like segment forms cup with heart-shaped lip

Broad-leaved helleborine

Epipactis helleborine

25-80cm

| J | F | M | A | M | J |
| J | A | S | O | N | D |

Locally common in woodland in England and Wales; rarer in Scotland and Ireland.

Lip white and yellow, with frilly edges

Narrower leaves

Marsh helleborine
Epipactis palustris

HOTTENTOT FIG

The many-petalled magenta or sometimes yellow flowers of Hottentot fig festoon cliffs in the south west in summer. The plant was introduced to Britain from South Africa in about 1690 and has become fully naturalised from lengths of stem thrown out of gardens, where it soon becomes invasive. Trailing stems bear narrow, fleshy, upward-curving leaves, triangular in cross-section and turning reddish towards the tip in autumn. The plant gets its name from the fact that its fleshy fruits, looking rather like figs, were eaten by the nomadic Hottentot tribesmen of Africa.

Conservation bodies are having to remove the plants from cliffs where they are smothering and killing rare native plants.

Five sepals around fleshy fruit

Trailing stems

Curving, fleshy leaves

ⓘ

Hottentot fig

Carpobrotus edulis

7.5-spread of 300cm

J	F	M	A	M	J
J	A	S	O	N	D

Sea cliffs mainly in south-west England, but also some other coasts of England, Wales and Ireland; absent from Scotland.

BUTTERBUR

This creeping plant, with rhubarb-like leaves up to 90cm across, is often found by streams and ditches. The leaves, once used for wrapping butter, develop fully during summer, after the pink flowers have died. In spring, male and female flowers are carried on separate plants which are often visited by bees. Male plants are much more common than female ones. The cylindrical fruit is borne on the wind by a 'parachute' of whitish hairs, but the butterbur spreads to cover large areas by means of its underground roots. In the Middle Ages, these roots were used to remove skin blemishes, to treat heart conditions and even to combat the plague.

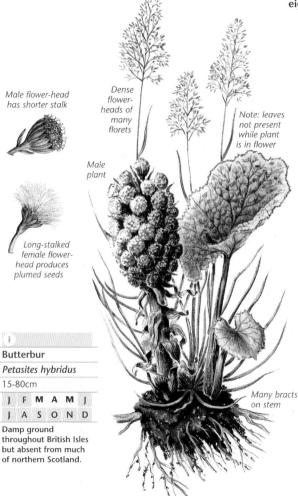

Male flower-head has shorter stalk

Dense flower-heads of many florets

Male plant

Note: leaves not present while plant is in flower

Long-stalked female flower-head produces plumed seeds

Many bracts on stem

Butterbur

Petasites hybridus

15-80cm

| J | F | M | A | M | J |
| J | A | S | O | N | D |

Damp ground throughout British Isles but absent from much of northern Scotland.

Leaves up to 90cm across, felted beneath

LESSER BURDOCK

The thistle-like flower-heads or burs of this common roadside plant often have to be picked off clothing or extracted from dogs' coats after a country walk, as the hooked spiny bracts surrounding the purple-red flower-heads attach the burs to anything that brushes against them. The furrowed stems are reddish and woolly, with stalked leaves. At one time the juice was used to soothe burns and sores, and the young stalks were eaten in salads.

Greater burdock has larger flower-heads on longer stalks, and broader leaves. It is mainly found in southern and central England.

Bracts with hooked spines

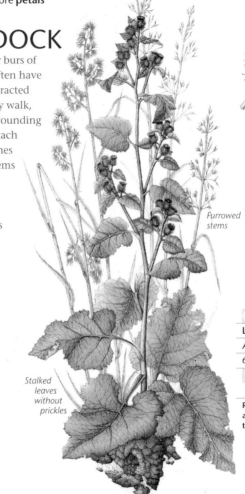
Furrowed stems

Stalked leaves without prickles

Oval, pointed leaves, cottony on underside

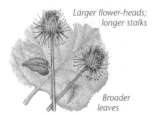
Larger flower-heads; longer stalks

Broader leaves

Greater burdock
Arctium lappa

i						

Lesser burdock

Arctium minus

60-200cm

J	F	M	A	M	J
J	A	S	O	N	D

Roadsides, woods and waste ground throughout British Isles.

HEMP-AGRIMONY

A dash of colour on many river banks is provided by hemp-agrimony's massed clusters of pink flowers on tall, hairy stems. The flowers are known in Dorset as 'raspberries and cream'; each flower-head consists of five or six florets, surrounded by purple-tipped bracts. In spite of its name, hemp-agrimony is related neither to hemp nor to agrimony, though the leaves somewhat resemble those of hemp. The downy leaves, which usually consist of three toothed leaflets, were once used to make a purgative and an emetic.

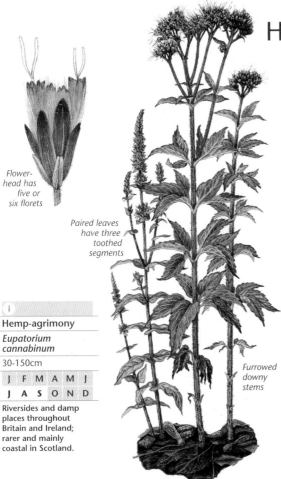

Flower-head has five or six florets

Paired leaves have three toothed segments

Furrowed downy stems

Flower-heads in dense clusters

ⓘ

Hemp-agrimony

Eupatorium cannabinum

30-150cm

| J | F | M | A | M | J |
| J | A | S | O | N | D |

Riversides and damp places throughout Britain and Ireland; rarer and mainly coastal in Scotland.

Green
FLOWERS

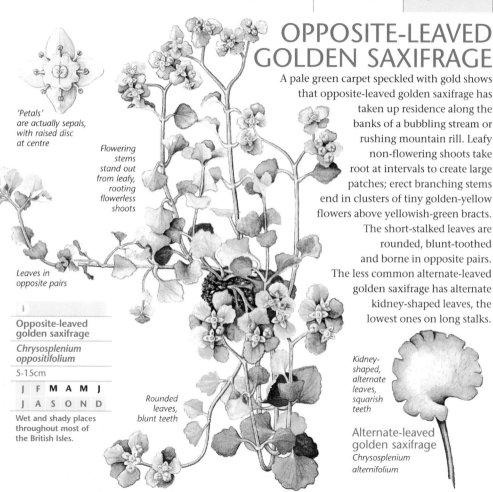

OPPOSITE-LEAVED GOLDEN SAXIFRAGE

A pale green carpet speckled with gold shows that opposite-leaved golden saxifrage has taken up residence along the banks of a bubbling stream or rushing mountain rill. Leafy non-flowering shoots take root at intervals to create large patches; erect branching stems end in clusters of tiny golden-yellow flowers above yellowish-green bracts. The short-stalked leaves are rounded, blunt-toothed and borne in opposite pairs. The less common alternate-leaved golden saxifrage has alternate kidney-shaped leaves, the lowest ones on long stalks.

*'Petals'
are actually sepals,
with raised disc
at centre*

*Flowering
stems
stand out
from leafy,
rooting
flowerless
shoots*

*Leaves in
opposite pairs*

**Opposite-leaved
golden saxifrage**

*Chrysosplenium
oppositifolium*

5-15cm

| J | F | **M** | **A** | **M** | **J** |
| **J** | **A** | **S** | **O** | **N** | **D** |

Wet and shady places
throughout most of
the British Isles.

*Rounded
leaves,
blunt teeth*

*Kidney-
shaped,
alternate
leaves,
squarish
teeth*

**Alternate-leaved
golden saxifrage**
*Chrysosplenium
alternifolium*

PERENNIAL GLASSWORT

This glasswort grows in the upper and middle areas of salt-marshes. The stems bear segmented flowering branches. Each segment is formed by a pair of fleshy leaves fused around a woody stem; it is dark green at first but later turns yellow or reddish. Each segment carries three equal-sized green flowers.

Purple glasswort often turns purplish-red. Each flower has only one stamen, and the central flower of each group of three is larger than those on either side.

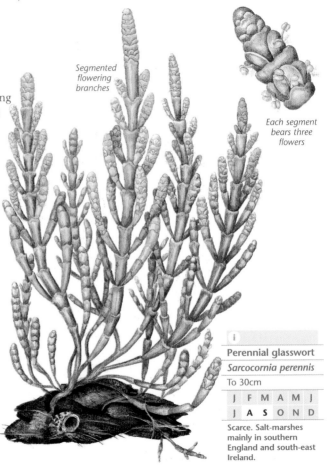

Segmented flowering branches

Each segment bears three flowers

Purplish-red stems

Purple glasswort
Salicornia ramosissima

i					
Perennial glasswort					
Sarcocornia perennis					
To 30cm					
J	F	M	A	M	J
J	A	S	O	N	D

Scarce. Salt-marshes mainly in southern England and south-east Ireland.

PROCUMBENT PEARLWORT

Look at a grassy bank, verge or footpath anywhere in Britain and procumbent pearlwort may well be found, its many stems sprawling outwards from a dense, mossy-looking rosette of leaves. They bear tiny flowers on long stalks. The flowers usually look green because often only sepals are present, not petals, but sometimes there are tiny greenish-white petals, too. The narrow, hairless leaves end in a short bristle. Annual pearlwort forms upright stalks, has no central rosette of leaves and is often somewhat hairy.

Tiny flower, on long stalk

Stems sprawl out from central rosette

Procumbent pearlwort

Sagina procumbens

To 20cm

J F M A M J
J A S O N D

Bare and grassy places throughout British Isles.

Flower has tiny petals or none

Stalks droop after flowering

Annual pearlwort
Sagina apetala

Stems upright

COMMON WATER STARWORT

Water starwort's upper leaves, almost round, form a floating rosette in ponds and ditches or on wet mud at their edges. Below the surface the leaves are paired and somewhat narrower. Plants are anchored to the bottom by roots from the lower part of the stem; the higher roots trail in the water. Of some half-dozen species of water starwort, hard to tell apart, common water starwort is distinguished from most of the others by its winged fruits and its more rounded leaves. The tiny green flowers are borne singly at the base of the leaves. They have no petals, and separate male and female flowers grow on the same plant. Pollen is blown by the wind or carried along the surface of the water.

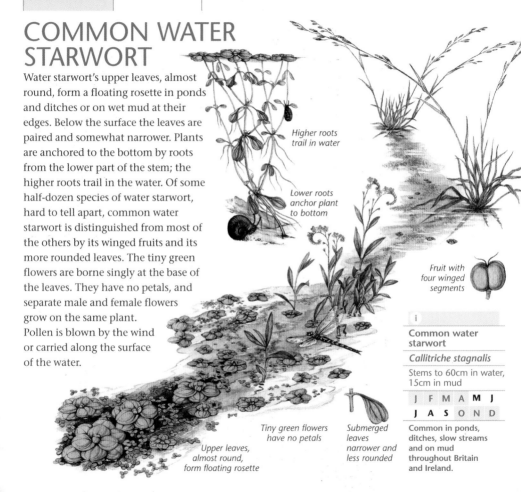

Higher roots trail in water

Lower roots anchor plant to bottom

Fruit with four winged segments

Tiny green flowers have no petals

Upper leaves, almost round, form floating rosette

Submerged leaves narrower and less rounded

i

Common water starwort

Callitriche stagnalis

Stems to 60cm in water, 15cm in mud

| J | F | M | A | **M** | **J** |
| **J** | **A** | S | O | N | D |

Common in ponds, ditches, slow streams and on mud throughout Britain and Ireland.

DOG'S MERCURY

Woodland floors are often carpeted by dog's mercury, adding splashes of green to the shadows. The plant is highly poisonous and gives off a strongly fetid smell. Male and female flowers are carried on separate plants. Annual mercury is a more or less hairless plant with branched stems and paler green leaves. It grows on waste ground, largely in the south, and flowers much later.

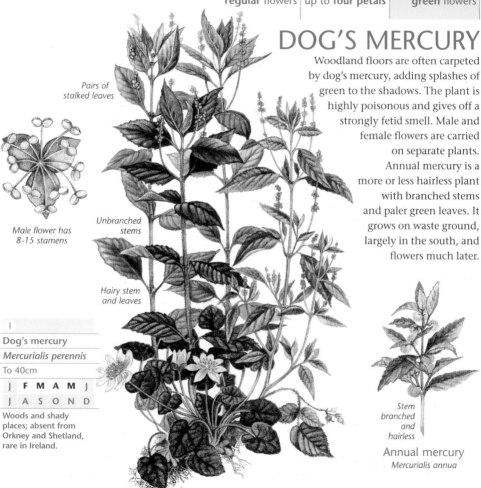

Pairs of stalked leaves

Male flower has 8-15 stamens

Unbranched stems

Hairy stem and leaves

Dog's mercury
Mercurialis perennis
To 40cm

| J | F | M | A | M | J |
| J | A | S | O | N | D |

Woods and shady places; absent from Orkney and Shetland, rare in Ireland.

Stem branched and hairless

Annual mercury
Mercurialis annua

STINGING NETTLE

The stinging or common nettle is one of Britain's most prolific growers. It is the curse of farmers and gardeners and the bane of bare legs. The nettle's creeping, rooting stems produce upright, leafy stems, and the whole plant bristles with stinging hairs. The stinging mechanism is simple: on being touched, the hair tip breaks off and releases an acid which causes a painful rash. The plant is, however, eaten by the caterpillars of small tortoiseshell and peacock butterflies.

The small nettle is smaller and less common. It has rounder leaves, and male and female flowers grow together on shorter catkins.

Plant bristles with stinging hairs

Male and female flowers grow together

Small nettle
Urtica urens

On male plant, catkins are usually erect

On female, flower catkins hang down

i						

Stinging or common nettle

Urtica dioica

To 150cm

J	F	M	A	M	J
J	A	S	O	N	D

Waste ground, especially near buildings, hedgerows and woods in all areas.

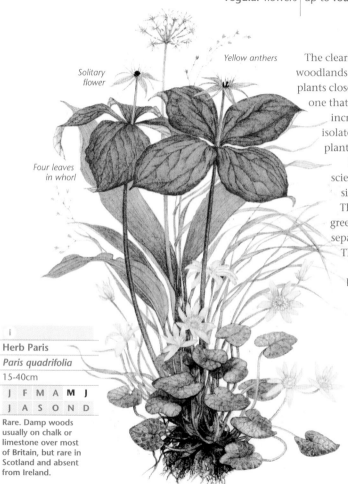

Solitary flower

Yellow anthers

Four leaves in whorl

HERB PARIS

The clearing of large areas of Britain's woodlands has driven many woodland plants close to extinction. Herb Paris is one that survives, but it is becoming increasingly rare, found only in isolated patches. It is a distinctive plant, with a single whorl of four leaves – the *quadrifolia* of its scientific name – just below the single large pale green flower. There are four narrow yellow-green petals, four broader green sepals and eight green stamens. The flower has an unpleasant smell, and the dark purple berry into which it develops is poisonous. The plant is difficult to spot when, as often, it grows with dog's mercury (page 365).

i

Herb Paris

Paris quadrifolia

15–40cm

J	F	M	**A**	**M**	**J**
J	**A**	S	O	N	D

Rare. Damp woods usually on chalk or limestone over most of Britain, but rare in Scotland and absent from Ireland.

Single round, black berry

BUCK'S-HORN PLANTAIN

The numerous, many-toothed leaves of buck's-horn plantain at first grow flat against the ground in a star-like rosette, then turn up at the ends to form a bowl shape. The cylindrical hairy stems also curve upwards.

Sea plantain grows near salt water and on mountains inland. Its leaves are fleshy and strap-shaped, sometimes with one or two teeth. The flowers are borne in long narrow spikes at the tops of the stems. Usually the plant is hairless.

Long yellow stamens

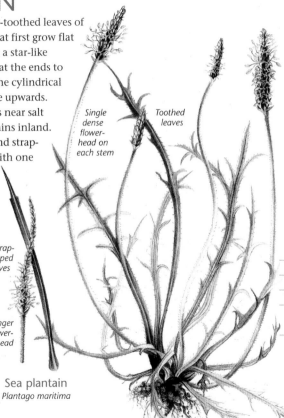

Single dense flower-head on each stem

Toothed leaves

Strap-shaped leaves

Longer flower-head

Sea plantain
Plantago maritima

i
Buck's-horn plantain
Plantago coronopus
To 20cm

J	F	M	A	**M**	J
J	**A**	S	O	N	D

Sand, gravel and rocks, especially near sea; most coasts of the British Isles.

RIBWORT PLANTAIN

The dark flower spike at the tip of a furrowed stem makes ribwort plantain distinctive. The flowers have four whitish sepals, each with a brown central keel and four brownish petals. The long stamens are creamy-white – unlike the purple stamens of hoary plantain (page 294) which give that plant a reddish appearance. Greater plantain, common in garden paths and lawns, has broad, almost hairless leaves. Its flower spikes are long and pale green at the top of unfurrowed stalks.

Dense, dark flower spike

Tall, grooved stem

Ribwort plantain

Plantago lanceolata

7.5-50cm

J F **M A M J**
J A S O N D

Pastures, lawns, waste ground and roadsides throughout the British Isles.

Long, hairy ribbed leaves in upright rosette

Broad hairless leaves

Greater plantain
Plantago major

CURLED PONDWEED

An adornment to still or slow-moving water, curled pondweed is easily recognised by its parallel-sided, wavy-edged, finely toothed leaves. The much branched stems bear only submerged leaves, which are a favourite food and hiding place for fish and crustaceans. Short and rather loose flower spikes emerge above the water, the petal-like segments of each flower being larger than in broad-leaved pondweed. Curled pondweed is rarely found in acidic water.

Fruiting spike above water

All leaves submerged

Long wavy-edged leaves with parallel veins

Flower with large petal-like segments

Plant often entwined with darker green Canadian pondweed

i
Curled pondweed
Potamogeton crispus
Stems 30-120cm long

J	F	M	A	**M**	**J**
J	**A**	**S**	**O**	N	D

Common in ponds, streams and canals; rarer in Scotland and Wales.

BROAD-LEAVED PONDWEED

A common plant of pond and river, broad-leaved pondweed has sparsely branched stems bearing submerged and floating leaves. The floating leaves are broad, coarse and leathery with many parallel veins, whereas the submerged leaves are narrow and parallel-sided. Rather than having separate petals and sepals, the flowers have four rounded segments around the stamens and styles. The pollen is carried by the wind – curiously, for a water plant, the pollen is quickly made sterile by contact with water. A fruiting spike rises above the surface and carries many olive-green, flattened fruits.

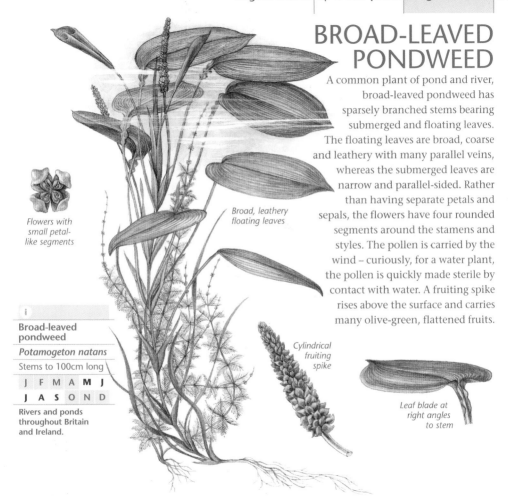

Flowers with small petal-like segments

Broad, leathery floating leaves

Cylindrical fruiting spike

Leaf blade at right angles to stem

Broad-leaved pondweed

Potamogeton natans

Stems to 100cm long

| J | F | M | A | M | J |
| J | A | S | O | N | D |

Rivers and ponds throughout Britain and Ireland.

LADY'S MANTLE

This plant is often found alongside hilly roads. It is not, in fact, a single species but a group of very similar species, some of which can only be separated by experts. Each of the leaves, which rise from the roots, has between 5 and 11 toothed lobes. There are four green sepals and four green outer sepals but no petals.

Alpine lady's mantle is smaller, with greyer, star-shaped leaves, deeply divided to the base. The leaves are densely covered with silky silver hairs below. It grows on mountains, mainly in central and northern Scotland.

Leaves deeply divided

Alpine lady's mantle
Alchemilla alpina

Leaf has 5-11 toothed lobes

Four sepals and four outer sepals

ℹ️

Lady's mantle

Alchemilla vulgaris agg.

5-60cm

J	F	M	A	M	J
J	A	S	O	N	D

Damp grassland, but rare in south-east of Britain.

PARSLEY-PIERT

A lover of shallow, stony soil, parsley-piert is a familiar sight in arable fields and bare ground. It has tiny green flowers with four sepals and no petals, and the stipules at the leaf bases form a cup that encloses the flowers. The short-stalked leaves have three toothed lobes. The fruit is oval. Because it often grows between stones, parsley-piert was once thought to be able to break rocks, a property which led to its use as a treatment for gallstones and kidney stones.

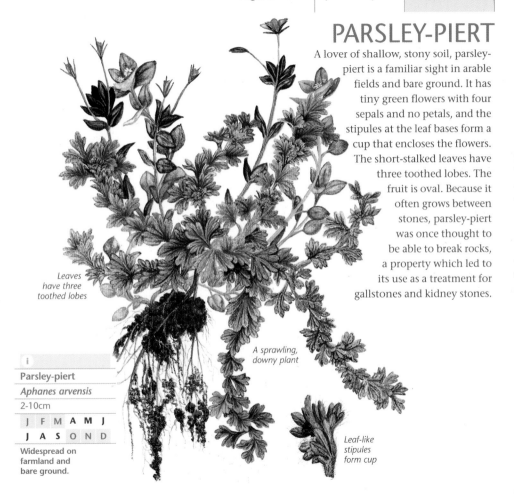

Leaves have three toothed lobes

A sprawling, downy plant

Leaf-like stipules form cup

i
Parsley-piert
Aphanes arvensis
2-10cm

J	F	M	A	M	J
J	A	S	O	N	D

Widespread on farmland and bare ground.

SALAD BURNET

Not only is salad burnet smaller than great burnet (page 300), it also has much less conspicuous flowers. There are no petals but each flower has four green sepals. The tiny flowers are grouped in ball-shaped heads, the upper female flowers with purple stigmas, the lower male ones with yellow stamens and also bisexual flowers with both stigmas and stamens. The leaves smell of cucumber when crushed, and, as the plant's name suggests, can be eaten in salads. They are composed of many pairs of small, toothed, short-stalked leaflets. The plant grows on chalk and limestone grassland.

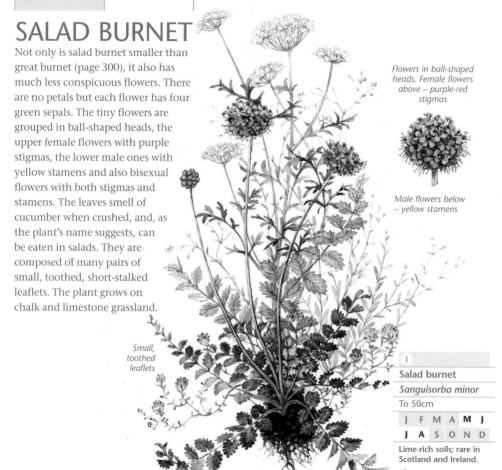

Flowers in ball-shaped heads. Female flowers above – purple-red stigmas

Male flowers below – yellow stamens

Small, toothed leaflets

i

Salad burnet

Sanguisorba minor

To 50cm

| J | F | M | A | **M** | **J** |
| **J** | **A** | S | O | N | D |

Lime-rich soils; rare in Scotland and Ireland.

SPIKED WATER-MILFOIL

Only the spikes of tiny flowers of spiked water-milfoil can be seen above the surface of the still or slow-moving water where it makes its home. The flowers have minute reddish petals and are arranged in whorls of four. Under water, the many feathery leaves are divided into many fine segments; the plant's common and botanical names come from Latin and French words for 'thousand leaves'. Mare's-tail has dark green undivided leaves above the water as well as beneath. The leaves are arranged in whorls of 6 to 12.

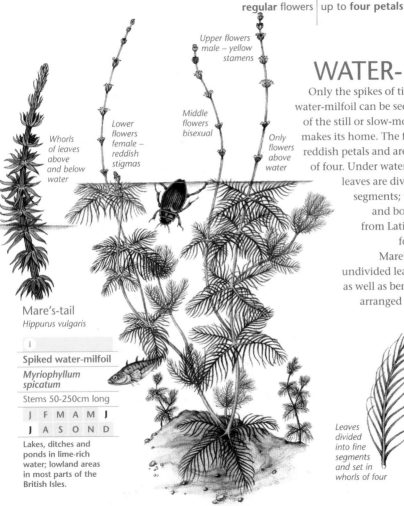

Whorls of leaves above and below water

Lower flowers female – reddish stigmas

Upper flowers male – yellow stamens

Middle flowers bisexual

Only flowers above water

Mare's-tail
Hippurus vulgaris

Spiked water-milfoil

Myriophyllum spicatum

Stems 50-250cm long

| J | F | M | A | M | J |
| J | A | S | O | N | D |

Lakes, ditches and ponds in lime-rich water; lowland areas in most parts of the British Isles.

Leaves divided into fine segments and set in whorls of four

WOOD SAGE

Spikes of yellow-green flowers and wrinkled, toothed leaves make the wood sage easily recognisable. The flowers are borne in pairs at the top of the upright stem, and below them the short-stalked leaves grow in opposite pairs. Each flower has a five-lobed lower lip with a large, spreading middle lobe; there is no upper lip, and the purplish stamens are exposed. The fruit consists of four smooth nutlets. This plant is not a true sage although, like the sages, it belongs to the mint family. The 19th-century gardener Gertrude Jekyll thought the wood sage worthy of a place in the garden. In taste and smell it resembles hops.

Flowers in leafless spikes

Lower lip has large, spreading middle lobe

Heart-shaped toothed leaves on square, hairy stem

Flowers in pairs, with leaf-like bracts below

i						
Wood sage						
Teucrium scorodonia						
15-50cm						
J	F	M	A	M	J	
J	A	S	O	N	D	

Dry, usually acid soils throughout British Isles.

PETTY SPURGE

Daintily decorative on patches of waste ground, petty spurge can become a pest on cultivated land. Like other spurges, the plant has milky-white juice, and its flowers have neither sepals nor petals. Instead the male and female flowers are contained in cup-like structures, surrounded by four horned glands. Wood spurge is tall and hairy with kidney-shaped upper bracts joined around the stem. The flower glands have converging horns. It is confined to southern Britain and flowers in spring.

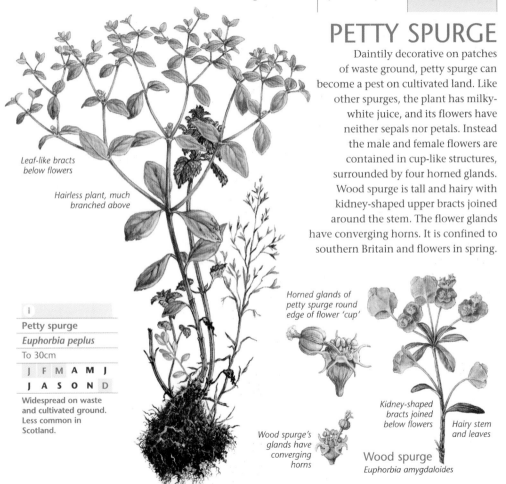

Leaf-like bracts below flowers

Hairless plant, much branched above

i

Petty spurge

Euphorbia peplus

To 30cm

J	F	M	A	M	J
J	A	S	O	N	D

Widespread on waste and cultivated ground. Less common in Scotland.

Horned glands of petty spurge round edge of flower 'cup'

Wood spurge's glands have converging horns

Kidney-shaped bracts joined below flowers

Hairy stem and leaves

Wood spurge
Euphorbia amygdaloides

SUN SPURGE

This plant has a single stem or is sometimes branched near the base. The bracts below the flowers resemble the oval, stalkless leaves, which are finely toothed. The flower clusters are bright yellowish-green, and each flower has four rounded yellow glands.

Dwarf spurge is bluish-green, with narrow leaves and bracts. Its flower glands have long slender horns. It is a decreasing arable weed, rare in Wales and Ireland and very rare in Scotland.

Stalkless, fine-toothed leaves

Bluish stem and leaves

Glands kidney-shaped and hornless

Dwarf spurge
Euphorbia exigua

i					

Sun spurge

Euphorbia helioscopia

To 50cm

J	F	**M**	**A**	**M**	**J**
J	**A**	**S**	**O**	**N**	D

Widespread on cultivated and waste ground; rarer in Scotland.

LORDS-AND-LADIES

The flowers of lords-and-ladies – also known as cuckoo pint – are hidden within a pale yellowish-green sheath-like hood called a spathe. A long purple finger called a spadix beckons insects towards the tiny flowers, which cluster around its base. The flowers are not visible unless the plant is cut open. The spadix is warm and gives off a slight smell attractive to insects. Its lower part has long backward-pointing hairs which trap the insect and ensure that it is well covered in pollen. The berries are highly poisonous.

Club-like spadix

Flowers hidden at base, male flowers above female

Ribbed spathe

Arrow-shaped, glossy leaves, usually spotted

Orange-red berries with pitted seeds

Lords-and-ladies

Arum maculatum

20-35cm

| J | F | M | **A** | **M** | J |
| J | **A** | **S** | **O** | **N** | D |

Woods and hedgerows; absent from far north.

ANNUAL KNAWEL

A wiry and bushy plant, annual knawel has narrow, pointed leaves and greenish, petal-less flowers little more than 4mm across. Its slender stems, bearing short hairs, give it the name knawel, which comes from the German and means 'a tangle of threads'. The flowers are in clusters. The fruit is a dry nut, hidden by five pointed sepals with narrow white borders.

Leaves in pairs

Each pair of leaves joined at base

Branching stems with short hairs

Pointed green sepals with narrow white border

i
Annual knawel
Scleranthus annuus
2.5-20cm

| J | F | M | A | M | J |
| J | A | S | O | N | D |

Sandy soils scattered over much of the British Isles; rarer in Wales, Scotland and Ireland.

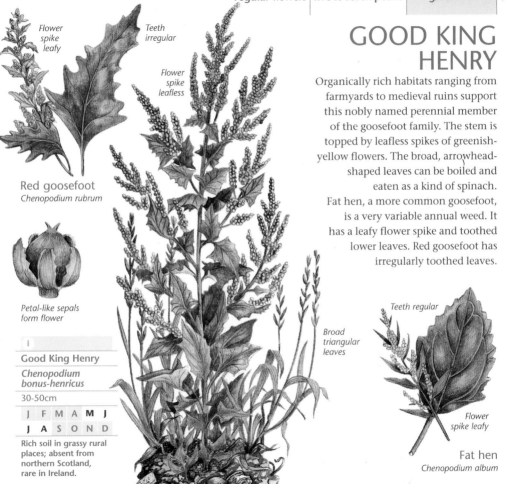

Flower
spike
leafy

Teeth
irregular

Flower
spike
leafless

Red goosefoot
Chenopodium rubrum

Petal-like sepals
form flower

i
Good King Henry
Chenopodium bonus-henricus
30-50cm

J	F	M	A	M	J
J	A	S	O	N	D

Rich soil in grassy rural
places; absent from
northern Scotland,
rare in Ireland.

GOOD KING HENRY

Organically rich habitats ranging from
farmyards to medieval ruins support
this nobly named perennial member
of the goosefoot family. The stem is
topped by leafless spikes of greenish-
yellow flowers. The broad, arrowhead-
shaped leaves can be boiled and
eaten as a kind of spinach.
Fat hen, a more common goosefoot,
is a very variable annual weed. It
has a leafy flower spike and toothed
lower leaves. Red goosefoot has
irregularly toothed leaves.

Broad
triangular
leaves

Teeth regular

Flower
spike leafy

Fat hen
Chenopodium album

SEA BEET

This sprawling plant, with small flowers and large glossy leaves, may not have a very striking appearance but it is a tough seaside dweller. Its leaves and flowering stems are sometimes tinged with red; the flowers – each with five greenish sepals – grow in clusters. Sea beet belongs to the goosefoot family – which includes beetroot, sugar beet and spinach – and was cultivated as food in the Middle East as long as 2000 years ago. Its leaves have been eaten in Britain as 'sea spinach'.

Greenish sepals contain stamens and styles

Glossy leaves

Flowers in clusters form long spike

Stems often reddish and sprawling

Sea beet

Beta vulgaris ssp. *maritima*

30-80cm

| J | F | M | A | M | J |
| J | A | S | O | N | D |

Most shores around the British Isles; rarer in Scotland.

COMMON ORACHE

The oraches and their close relatives the goosefoots are distinguished from one another by their flower structure. Goosefoot flowers are usually bisexual, while those of the orache are male or female. Each goosefoot flower is surrounded, but not enclosed, by five sepals; the female flower of the orache is enclosed by two green bracts. The lobes at the base of the lowest leaves point forwards. Spear-leaved orache often grows alongside the common species. The lowest leaves are broadly triangular with sideways pointing lobes at the base.

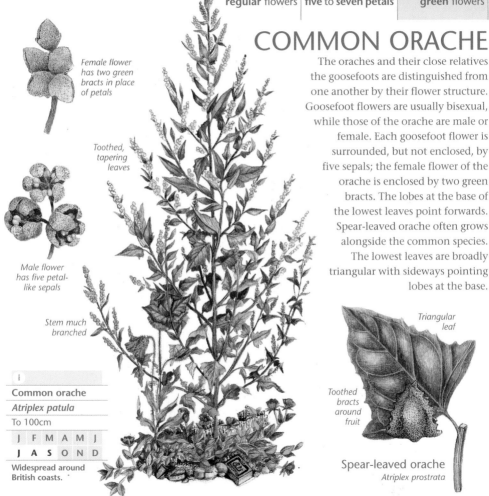

Female flower has two green bracts in place of petals

Toothed, tapering leaves

Male flower has five petal-like sepals

Stem much branched

Common orache

Atriplex patula

To 100cm

| J | F | M | A | M | J |
| J | A | S | O | N | D |

Widespread around British coasts.

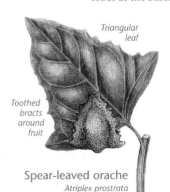

Triangular leaf

Toothed bracts around fruit

Spear-leaved orache
Atriplex prostrata

SEA-PURSLANE

The hardy, attractive sea-purslane often draws attention to itself by its silvery-grey leaves which can be seen from some distance. This silvery colour is caused by tiny, papery scales which protect the young leaf from the drying effect of salt water. The plant, which survives in the tough conditions of salt-marshes, has sprawling stems and elliptical, untoothed leaves. The male flower is easily distinguished from the female, which has styles projecting from enclosing bracts – creating the effect of a tiny, horned animal's head.

Bracts of female flower are three-lobed

Female flower has styles projecting from bracts

Flowers in leafless spikes

Leaves elliptical

i

Sea-purslane

Atriplex portulacoides

To 1000cm

J	F	M	A	M	J
J	A	S	O	N	D

Salt-marshes, especially on banks of dykes and pools; absent from most of Scotland.

Male flower has five sepals

ANNUAL SEABLITE

This plant is a true halophyte, or 'salt lover'. When growing on the seashore, the plant may be covered by the tide twice a day. Its leaves are stalkless and fleshy, flat on top and rounded at the back. The stems and leaves are often tinged purplish, turning bright red in autumn. The plant is a member of the goosefoot family, which includes several plants with edible leaves; 'blite' is an Old English word from the Latin for spinach.

Flower with five sepals

Fleshy narrow leaves

Red-tinted stems

Tiny flowers grow at junction of leaf and stem

Annual seablite

Suaeda maritima

7.5-30cm

J F M A M J
J A S O N D

Seashores and salt-marshes on most coasts.

IVY

The clinging ivy is one of Britain's few climbers to reach any great size – up to 30m with support. Its stems have many fibrous, adhesive roots which enable it to clamber vigorously over walls, rocks and trees. The familiar lobed leaves borne on the non-flowering stems are dark green and shiny, often marbled with pale markings; they may be purplish in winter. Leaves on the flowering stems are usually without lobes. In autumn, flowers are produced. They have plentiful nectar and are very attractive to insects. The fruit is a black berry.

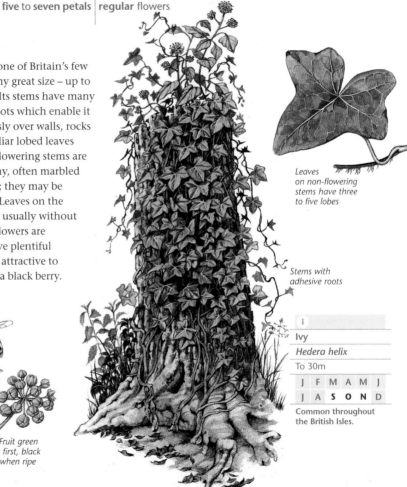

Leaves on non-flowering stems have three to five lobes

Stems with adhesive roots

Wasp pollinates globe-shaped flower cluster

Fruit green at first, black when ripe

i					

Ivy

Hedera helix

To 30m

J	F	M	A	M	J
J	A	S	O	N	D

Common throughout the British Isles.

NAVELWORT

This plant gets its name from the navel-like dimple in the centre of the fleshy leaf; its alternative name of pennywort refers to the leaf's coin-like shape. The stalk joins the leaf beneath the central dimple. Above the leaves, drooping, bell-like greenish-cream flowers grow abundantly on tall stalks. Navelwort is a familiar sight in parts of western Britain and in Ireland, growing between stones on high roadside banks. It is also found in rock crevices and on cliffs. Its size depends on the location.

Long straight stalks

i
Navelwort
Umbilicus rupestris
10-40cm

| J | F | M | A | M | J |
| J | A | S | O | N | D |

Mostly in western Britain and Ireland.

Dimpled round leaves

Flowers bell-shaped and drooping

CURLED DOCK

In places where nettles thrive, nature often provides docks as well – for 'medicine'. Country walkers still use dock leaves to neutralise nettle stings. Curled dock is an upright plant with slender flower spikes; its leaves have curled, wavy edges and grow to 30cm. Its inner sepals are untoothed and there are up to three swellings on the fruit, whereas the fruit of the aptly named broad-leaved dock usually has one swelling; its leaf has wavy but uncurled edges. The plant grows to 100cm.

Slender, leafy flower spikes

Greenish bisexual flower

Broader, flatter leaf

Leaves lance-shaped, with curled and wavy edges

Broad-leaved dock
Rumex obtusifolius

ⓘ

Curled dock

Rumex crispus

50-100cm

| J | F | M | A | M | J |
| J | A | S | O | N | D |

Grassland, waste ground, roadsides and coastal shingle; common throughout the British Isles.

CLUSTERED DOCK

Also known as sharp dock, this species favours wet grassy places. It has spreading branches and a stem that is inclined to zigzag. Its leaves are narrow and roughly oblong; the flowers grow in whorls forming a leafy spike. Clustered dock has fruit with three prominent oval swellings. Wood dock is similar to clustered dock but has more upright branches, and usually only one rounded swelling on the fruit.

Greenish flower with petal-like sepals

Three oval swellings on fruit

Flowers in whorls

Leaves narrow

Clustered dock

Rumex conglomeratus

To 60cm

J F M A M J
J A S O N D

Wet grassland especially beside ponds and rivers throughout the British Isles; rarer in Scotland.

Branches make narrow angle with stem

Usually just one round swelling on fruit

Bracts only at base of flower spikes

Wood dock
Rumex sanguineus

PELLITORY-OF-THE-WALL

This non-stinging relative of the nettle brings a cheerful red colouring to walls and rocks, where it flourishes in cracks and crevices. The hairy stems are reddish and the flowers, initially green, turn red in fruit. Flowers grow in clusters of three or more at the base of the leaf-stalks, with the female flowers towards the centre surrounded by male or bisexual flowers.

Reddish hairy stems

Flowers in clusters at base of leaf-stalk

Hairy leaves stalked and untoothed

i
Pellitory-of-the-wall
Parietaria judaica
To 40cm

J	F	M	A	M	J
J	**A**	**S**	**O**	**N**	D

Locally common in England, Wales and Ireland; rare in Scotland.

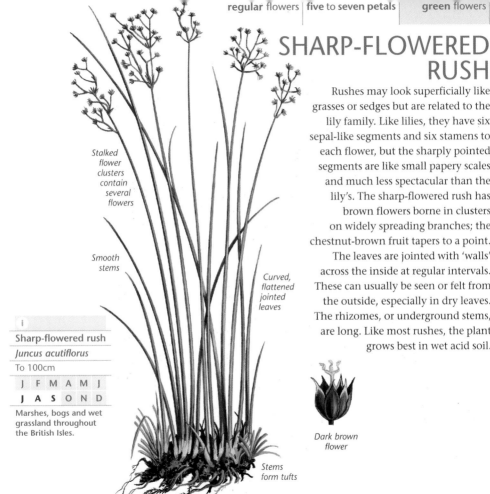

SHARP-FLOWERED RUSH

Rushes may look superficially like grasses or sedges but are related to the lily family. Like lilies, they have six sepal-like segments and six stamens to each flower, but the sharply pointed segments are like small papery scales and much less spectacular than the lily's. The sharp-flowered rush has brown flowers borne in clusters on widely spreading branches; the chestnut-brown fruit tapers to a point. The leaves are jointed with 'walls' across the inside at regular intervals. These can usually be seen or felt from the outside, especially in dry leaves. The rhizomes, or underground stems, are long. Like most rushes, the plant grows best in wet acid soil.

Stalked flower clusters contain several flowers

Smooth stems

Curved, flattened jointed leaves

Sharp-flowered rush

Juncus acutiflorus

To 100cm

| J | F | M | A | M | J |
| J | A | S | O | N | D |

Marshes, bogs and wet grassland throughout the British Isles.

Dark brown flower

Stems form tufts

SOFT-RUSH

Despite its name, this is a stiff, upright plant, with cylindrical glossy, bright green leaves bearing a close resemblance to the leafless stems, which form dense tufts. The loose, rounded flower-head grows on one side of the smooth or very finely ridged stem, some way from the top. The fruit is blunt.

Compact rush differs in its flower-heads. On the soft-rush these have stalks and branches and usually grow loosely; on the compact rush, however, they form dense domes on the stem's side. The stems are distinctly ridged and not glossy.

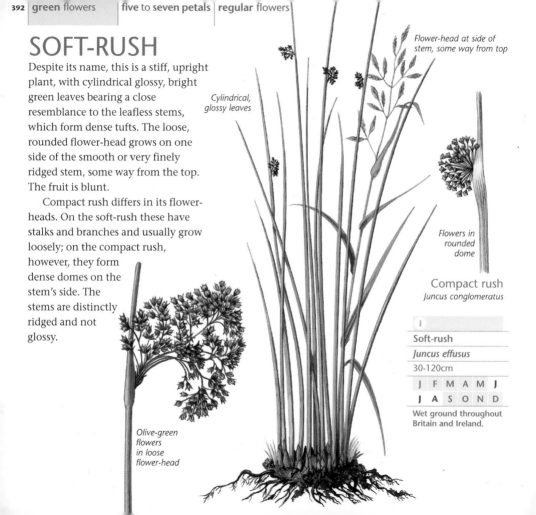

Flower-head at side of stem, some way from top

Cylindrical, glossy leaves

Flowers in rounded dome

Compact rush
Juncus conglomeratus

i

Soft-rush

Juncus effusus

30-120cm

J	F	M	A	M	J
J	A	S	O	N	D

Wet ground throughout Britain and Ireland.

Olive-green flowers in loose flower-head

TOAD RUSH

A rush that looks more like a grass, toad rush has thread-like, branching stems and narrow leaves. Its greenish flowers are solitary, and each has two leaf-like bracts below. Like most rushes, toad rush is wind-pollinated, and numerous seeds are packed in each dark brown oval capsule. Bulbous rush, also grass-like and similar in size to toad rush, is very variable. It grows on wet ground, often completely submerged. The flowers are frequently replaced by tiny green plantlets.

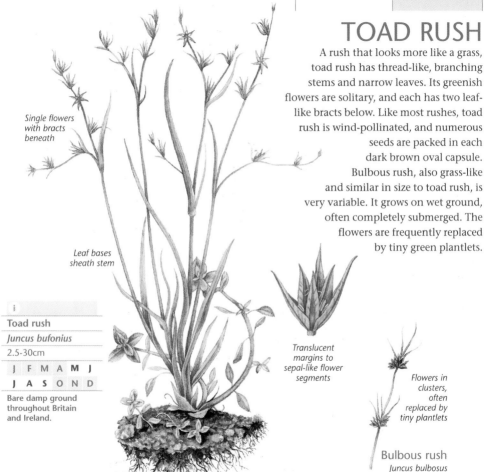

Single flowers with bracts beneath

Leaf bases sheath stem

Toad rush

Juncus bufonius

2.5-30cm

| J | F | M | A | M | J |
| J | A | S | O | N | D |

Bare damp ground throughout Britain and Ireland.

Translucent margins to sepal-like flower segments

Flowers in clusters, often replaced by tiny plantlets

Bulbous rush
Juncus bulbosus

FIELD WOOD-RUSH

An alternative name for field wood-rush is Good Friday grass, as it is usually in flower at Easter. It is also sometimes called sweep's brush, because of the crowded appearance of its flower-heads. Its leaves have soft hairs, while those of true rushes are hairless. The small, chestnut-brown flowers have conspicuous yellow anthers.

Great wood-rush grows to 80cm, with dense tufts of bright green, glossy and somewhat hairy leaves. The flower clusters are on widely spreading branches. It grows on peaty soil in woods and on shady streamsides.

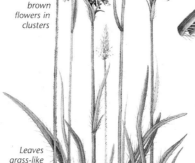

Chestnut-brown flowers in clusters

Leaf fringed with hairs

Large yellow anthers

Leaves grass-like

Leaves and stems form loose tufts

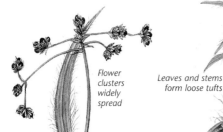

Flower clusters widely spread

Great wood-rush
Luzula sylvatica

i

Field wood-rush

Luzula campestris

To 15cm

J	F	**M**	**A**	**M**	J
J	**A**	S	O	N	D

Short grasslands throughout Britain and Ireland.

BLACK BRYONY

This climbing perennial is the only British member of the yam family – a group of mostly tropical plants with edible tubers. Black bryony's tubers, however, are poisonous. The plant has tiny yellowish-green flowers and red poisonous berries; it gets its name from the colour of its fleshy underground tubers. The stem is slender, unbranched and hairless; the glossy, heart-shaped leaves are on long stalks. Female and male flowers are on different plants, the female flowers on a short spike and the male flowers forming long, upright spikes. Pollination is by insects.

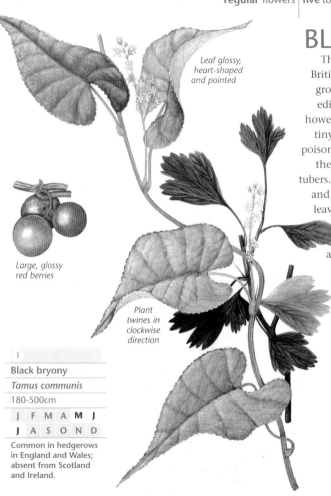

Leaf glossy, heart-shaped and pointed

Large, glossy red berries

Plant twines in clockwise direction

Female flowers on short spike

i

Black bryony

Tamus communis

180-500cm

| J | F | M | A | **M** | **J** |

| **J** | A | S | O | N | D |

Common in hedgerows in England and Wales; absent from Scotland and Ireland.

WHITE BRYONY

This climber is unrelated to black bryony, but shares with it the distinction of being an 'odd one out', being the only British representative of the tropical gourd family, and so closely related to marrow, melon, pumpkin and cucumber. It climbs by means of tendrils. Greenish-cream male and female flowers are borne on separate plants, the male flowers in long-stalked clusters and the female clusters almost stalkless. The white roots at one time were sold by fairground charlatans as the reputedly magical Mediterranean plant mandrake. All parts of white bryony are poisonous.

Clusters of female flowers

Small berries turn red when ripe

Leaf has five lobes

Male flowers in long-stalked clusters

Female flowers stalkless

Tendrils unbranched and spirally coiled

White bryony		
Bryonia dioica		
To 400cm		

| J | F | M | A | M | J |
| J | A | S | O | N | D |

Hedgerows in England, usually on lime-rich soils; rarer in Wales and absent from Scotland and Ireland.

Petal-like sepals

Flower bell-shaped, purple-edged

Many stamens

Many-flowered clusters

STINKING HELLEBORE

The smell of this rare woodland plant is, as its name implies, unpleasant, especially when the stem or leaves are crushed. However, it serves its purpose by attracting bees and other insects to the nectar. The plant has clusters of lime-green, bell-shaped flowers, tipped with purple. The dark, evergreen leaves have many narrow toothed leaflets. Green hellebore is a smaller plant of similar habitats, growing to 40cm, with flatter green flowers and broader leaflets on lower leaves. All parts of both species are poisonous.

Toothed evergreen leaflets

Few-flowered clusters

No purple edge on flowers

Petal-like sepals open flat

Stinking hellebore

Helleborus foetidus

To 80cm

| J | F | M | A | M | J |
| J | A | S | O | N | D |

Rare. Scattered in woods on chalk and limestone in southern England and Wales.

Green hellebore
Helleborus viridis

ROCK SAMPHIRE

In Shakespeare's time rock samphire was a popular vegetable, its leaves pickled in vinegar. It has thick, fleshy leaves which conserve moisture, with narrow, untoothed segments, and a solid stem. The umbrella-like heads of flowers are pale yellowish-green, with both upper and lower bracts. The oval fruit has thick ridges, and each half contains a single seed. When crushed, the leaves give off a smell often described as being like furniture polish. Rock samphire usually grows on cliffs and rocks by the sea, but occasionally on shingle beaches.

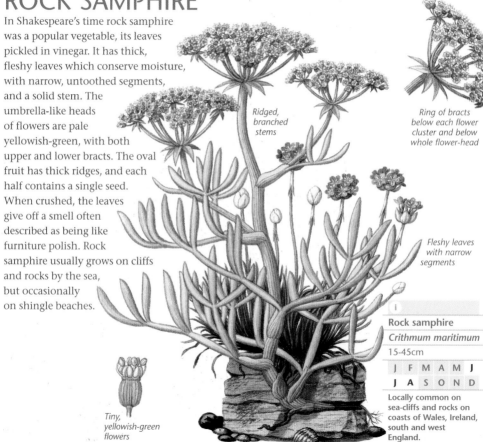

Ridged, branched stems

Ring of bracts below each flower cluster and below whole flower-head

Fleshy leaves with narrow segments

Tiny, yellowish-green flowers

Rock samphire

Crithmum maritimum

15-45cm

J	F	M	A	M	**J**
J	**A**	S	O	N	D

Locally common on sea-cliffs and rocks on coasts of Wales, Ireland, south and west England.

HOP

Since the Middle Ages when beer was drunk even for breakfast, hops have been used to preserve and flavour it. The hop is a native of woods in southern England, but its use in brewing originated on the Continent, and it only began to be cultivated on a large scale in Britain from the end of the 16th century. Many of the hops now growing wild have escaped from cultivation. The stems wind themselves in a clockwise direction up trees, shrubs or telegraph poles. The female flowers grow in a cone-like catkin, with overlapping green scales hiding the tiny flowers, while the male flowers, borne on separate plants, are in much branched, many-flowered loose clusters.

Male flower has five stamens

Female flower-heads in little-branched clusters

Twisting stems

Pairs of toothed, lobed leaves

Scales papery when fruit ripe

i
Hop
Humulus lupulus
To 8m

J	F	M	A	M	J
J	A	S	O	N	D

Widespread in hedges and scrub; native in southern Britain, naturalised elsewhere.

MOSCHATEL

This pretty little plant hardly deserves its generic name *Adoxa*, which means 'without glory'. There is much about moschatel that is fascinating – not least its other name, 'town-hall clock'. This refers to the neat arrangement of five yellowish-green flowers together – four facing outwards at right angles and one upwards. The plant owes the name moschatel to its faint musk-like scent, which is stronger at dusk and in dampness. Each flowering stem has one pair of leaves some distance below the flower-head. The plants usually spread by sending up shoots from their rootstock. Moschatel is the only member of its family.

Fruits hang down

Leaves have three lobed leaflets

Cube-shaped flower-head

Long leaf-stalks

Five petals in side flowers

Four petals in top flower

Moschatel

Adoxa moschatellina

5-15cm

J	F	M	**A**	**M**	J
J	**A**	S	**O**	**N**	D

Widespread in woods and hedgebanks throughout Britain but absent from far north; very rare in Ireland.

No tendril at tip of leaf

Smooth, curving pods

Straggling zigzag stems

WILD LIQUORICE

Growing in tall grass, often in scrubby places, this plant – also called milk-vetch – can easily be overlooked because its greenish-cream flowers blend with the colour of its foliage. The leaves are made up of 7 to 15 leaflets, with no tendrils at the leaf tips. Its straggling stems bend when they give rise to a leaf, and the result is a zigzag appearance. The name milk-vetch comes from an old claim that goats eating it would yield more milk. It is not the plant used medicinally or for making sweets.

ⓘ

Wild liquorice

Astragalus glycyphyllos

60-100cm

| J | F | M | A | M | J |
| J | A | S | O | N | D |

Rough, grassy places and scrub, mostly on chalk and limestone; rarer in Wales and Scotland and absent from Ireland.

Many flowers in flower-head

COMMON TWAYBLADE

The green flowers of this orchid often pass unnoticed in grassland, the distinctive spreading pair of large oval leaves ('tway blades') towards the base of the stem perhaps being the most noticeable feature of the plant. The flowers have a long, hanging, forked lip, with a groove in the middle frilled with nectar. Insects follow this nectar trail to the top, where they touch the modified stamens and the sticky pollen masses attach themselves to the insect's head, to be deposited on the next flower it visits. The remaining flower segments form a hood at the top of the flower.

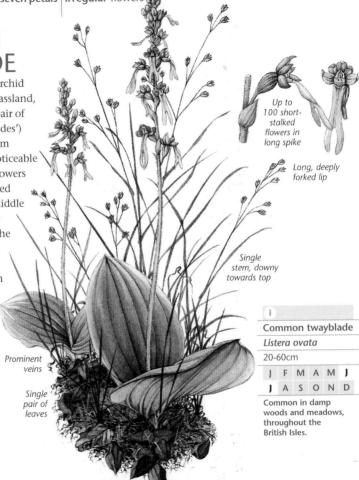

Up to 100 short-stalked flowers in long spike

Long, deeply forked lip

Single stem, downy towards top

Prominent veins

Single pair of leaves

Common twayblade

Listera ovata

20-60cm

| J | F | M | A | M | J |
| J | A | S | O | N | D |

Common in damp woods and meadows, throughout the British Isles.

BIRD'S-NEST ORCHID

The appearance of its densely matted roots inspired this plant's name. It lives in darkest woodland, usually beech woods, and depends for its survival on a fungus which surrounds its roots, absorbing nutrients from rotting leaves and passing them on to the plant. Bird's-nest orchid is honey-coloured, lacking any green colouring. Its flowers have a honey fragrance.

Single stem, hairy on top half

No leaves

Brown, papery scales on stem

i
Bird's-nest orchid
Neottia nidus-avis
20–50cm

J	F	M	A	M	J
J	A	S	O	N	D

Widespread, but local and decreasing, in shaded woodland throughout Britain and Ireland.

Flower with long two-lobed lip

MUGWORT

Almost any piece of waste ground
in lowland areas is likely to produce
plants of mugwort. This very common
member of the daisy family is a tall
sturdy plant with upright purple-red
stems which are much-branched. The
leaves are deeply divided, dark green
and hairless on the upper surface,
white-felted beneath, and faintly
aromatic. Each flower-head is made
up of tiny reddish-brown disc florets,
the outer ones female, the inner
ones bisexual, surrounded by woolly
bracts. The flower-heads are arranged
in long clusters on side branches.

*Flower-heads
bunched near
ends of
branches*

*Stem
reddish
and grooved*

*Leaves dark
green above,
whitish below*

i

Mugwort

Artemisia vulgaris

60-150cm

J	F	M	A	M	J
J	A	S	O	N	D

Roadsides, waste
places and hedgerows,
throughout the British
Isles but less common
in Scotland and Ireland.

PINEAPPLE WEED

This very common weed has clusters of yellowish-green flower-heads looking like tiny pineapples. It is, in fact, as exotic as its appearance suggests, since it is a native of north-east Asia, introduced to Britain in 1871. The plant is strongly pineapple-scented. The disc florets are surrounded by a ring of green bracts which have white edges.

Domed flower-head, with white-edged bracts

Leaves much divided

Plant hairless

Stems with many branches

Long, narrow segments at end of leaf

i

Pineapple weed

Matricaria discoidea

5-35cm

| J | F | M | A | **M** | **J** |
| **J** | **A** | **S** | **O** | N | D |

Bare and waste places, especially on much-trodden ground, throughout Britain.

MARSH CUDWEED

This delicate, silvery plant grows not in marshes but in rutted tracks, muddy puddles and damp, acid arable land. The dense clusters of small, yellow-brown disc florets are almost hidden by the brown bracts and the clusters of flower-heads are surrounded by the topmost leaves. An infusion of the leaves is sometimes used as a gargle.

Flower-heads in clusters surrounded by leaves

Leaves greyish-green and hairy above; densely hairy below

Dense flower-head, with brownish bracts

Grey, hairy stem branched

Female florets (left) surround larger bisexual florets (right)

i

Marsh cudweed

Gnaphalium uliginosum

4-25cm

J	F	M	A	M	J
J	**A**	S	O	N	D

Common in damp bare places, often on acid soils, throughout Britain and Ireland.

INDEX

ACKNOWLEDGMENTS

The artworks in this book were created by the following artists and are copyright of Reader's Digest. Where more than one artist contributed to a page the positions of the illustrations are indicated by letters:

t (top), b (bottom), c (centre), l (left) and r (right).

These artworks were previously published in *Reader's Digest Guide to Britain's Wildlife, Plants & Flowers* and *Nature Lover's Library: Field Guide to the Wild Flowers of Britain*.

ARTWORKS

Colin Emberson: 4-5; 12bl; 19, 60-61, 99, 101, 105-106, 125, 127-132, 135, 150-151, 155, 173, 194, 197, 199, 204-205, 242, 262, 274-275, 295-297, 324, 328-329, 331, 336-338, 352-353, 364, 375, 379, 386, 388-390, 402.

Line Mailhé: 6l, 14cr, 65, 83-84, 97-98, 170, 181, 195200, 235-236,264, 283, 347, 351, 355,395

Helen Senior: 6r, 100, 172, 207, 233-234, 279-282, 284-285, 339, 358

Wendy Bramall: 6-7r, 12br, 14br, 14bc, 24-26, 29-30, 32-33, 40, 46-48, 51-52, 74, 94, 96, 110, 112-113, 115, 202-203, 244, 356, 360,362, 380-384, 405

Barbara Walker: 8-9, 92, 95, 160-161, 256, 263, 330, 334-335, 365, 367

Helen Cowcher: 10, 23, 37, 39, 118-120, 142, 182, 232, 237, 252, 266, 269-272, 299, 311, 346, 385

Delyth Jones: 11tc, 277-278

Stuart Lafford: 11tr, 14 tr, 14br, 41, 68-72, 175, 134, 152-154, 171, 213-216, 220, 248, 258-259, 286, 302, 312, 315, 317-318, 320, 341-342, 350, 372, 376, 393-394

Brenda Katté: 11b, 14bl, 20-22, 38, 90, 111, 121-122, 136-137, 157, 188, 217-219, 239-241, 247, 249, 253, 257, 265, 276, 292, 304-310, 343, 354, 368, 403

Victoria Goaman: 12tl, tc, bc; tr, 16, 42-45, 62, 67, 107-108, 117, 143, 166-167, 169, 183, 319, 363

Shirley Hooper: 13tl, 27-28, 31, 49, 85, 87, 89, 102-104, 124, 156, 176-178, 180, 243, 267, 291, 314, 348-349

Rosemary Wise: 13bl, 175, 268

Frankie Coventry: 13tc, 76, 79, 91, 223, 300, 373

Leonora Box: 13bc, 17, 50, 59, 66, 93, 116, 148, 158, 162-163, 174, 179, 190-191, 196, 208, 221-222, 260-261, 273, 313, 322-323, 340, 370-371, 374, 401

John Rignall: 13tr, 34, 36, 53, 63, 80-82, 86, 88,123, 149, 211, 224-225, 228-230, 301, 321, 344, 398

Josiane Campan: 13br, 15, 164, 226-227, 255, 325, 333

Roger Hughes: 18, 64, 139, 245, 251, 293, 303, 316, 332

Paul Wrigley: 35, 54-58, 144-147, 168, 361, 387, 396

Guy Michel: 73, 114, 138, 140-141, 189, 250, 326-327, 359, 366, 377-378, 399, 404

Marie-Claude Guyetand: 77, 345

Sarah Fox-Davies: 78, 109, 159, 186-187, 210, 231, 254, 294, 298, 369, 406

Norman Lacey: 126, 133

Stephanie Harrison: 165, 397

Philippe Couté: 184, 206, 209,391-392, 400

Maurice Espérance: 185, 357

Derek Rodgers: 192-193

Marie-Claire Nivoix: 198, 201, 212, 246, 289-290

Marjory Saynor: 238, 287-288

PHOTOGRAPHS

Front cover: © www.osf.uk.com/Ifa-Bilderteam Gmbh
Back cover: © Nature Picture Library/Ross Hoddinott
2-3: © www.osf.uk.com/Ifa-Bilderteam Gmbh

Wild Britain: Wild Flowers is based on material in
*Reader's Digest Guide to Britain's Wildlife, Plants
& Flowers* and *Nature Lover's Library: Field Guide
to the Wild Flowers of Britain*, both published by
The Reader's Digest Association Limited, London.

First Edition Copyright © 2007
The Reader's Digest Association Limited,
11 Westferry Circus, Canary Wharf,
London E14 4HE
www.readersdigest.co.uk

Origination by Colour Systems Limited, London
Printed in China

We are committed to both the quality of our
products and the service we provide to our
customers. We value your comments, so please
feel free to contact us on **08705 113366**, or via
our website at **www.readersdigest.co.uk**

If you have any comments about the content of our
books, email us at **gbeditorial@readersdigest.co.uk**

EDITOR Caroline Boucher
ART EDITOR Austin Taylor
SUB-EDITOR Helen Spence
EDITORIAL CONSULTANT
Helen Pellant
PROOFREADER Barry Gage
INDEXER Marie Lorimer

Reader's Digest General Books
EDITORIAL DIRECTOR Julian Browne
ART DIRECTOR Anne-Marie Bulat
MANAGING EDITOR Alastair Holmes
HEAD OF BOOK DEVELOPMENT
Sarah Bloxham
PICTURE RESOURCE MANAGER
Sarah Stewart-Richardson
PRE-PRESS ACCOUNT MANAGER
Penelope Grose
SENIOR PRODUCTION CONTROLLER
Deborah Trott
PRODUCT PRODUCTION MANAGER
Claudette Bramble

Book code 400-318 UP0000-1
ISBN 978 0 276 44213 1
Oracle code 250010896S.00.24